THE ENGLISH OCCUPATION
OF TOURNAI
1513-1519

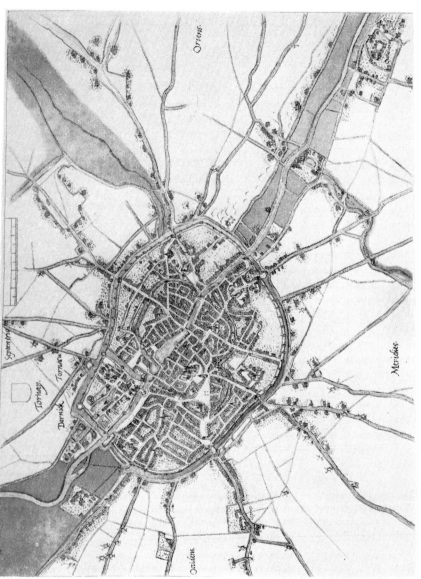

Plan of Tournai by Jacob van Deventer (*circa* 1560)
(*By courtesy of the Trustees of the British Museum*)

THE
ENGLISH
OCCUPATION
OF TOURNAI
1513-1519

BY

C. G. CRUICKSHANK

CLARENDON PRESS · OXFORD

1971

Oxford University Press, Ely House, London W.1

GLASGOW   NEW YORK   TORONTO   MELBOURNE   WELLINGTON
CAPE TOWN   SALISBURY   IBADAN   NAIROBI   DAR ES SALAAM   LUSAKA   ADDIS ABABA
BOMBAY   CALCUTTA   MADRAS   KARACHI   LAHORE   DACCA
KUALA LUMPUR   SINGAPORE   HONG KONG   TOKYO

PRINTED IN GREAT BRITAIN
BY WILLIAM CLOWES AND SONS, LIMITED
LONDON, BECCLES AND COLCHESTER

PREFACE

THIS book is an expansion of Chapter XII in *Army Royal*[1] which deals briefly with the English occupation of Tournai, after studying in greater detail the invasion of France by Henry VIII in 1513 that led to the surrender and occupation of the city. It became apparent while *Army Royal* was being written that to do full justice to the occupation would make an unbalanced book, since it was intended to deal primarily with the organization and administration of the early sixteenth-century English army as illustrated by an actual campaign.

It is strange that there has been no full-scale study of the occupation of Tournai until the present time. It is as a rule dismissed in a few lines in the general histories of the period, if indeed it is mentioned at all. Even Continental historians have not paid much attention to it. An important exception is Adolphe Hocquet, who was archivist of Tournai at the beginning of the present century. He printed a number of documents from the city's records and prefaced them with a scholarly essay on the occupation. The value of this collection was enhanced when the originals were destroyed by enemy action in 1940.

Some of the documents printed by Hocquet and others in the Tournai archives bearing on the occupation were transcribed for the proposed new edition of Rymer's *Foedera* in the nineteenth century. The new edition was not proceeded with, but the transcripts are now in the Public Record Office in London and supplement Hocquet's collection. The great bulk of the raw material for the present work, however, is contained in the manuscript collections of the British Museum, principally the Cottonian; and in the State Papers, Exchequer, and Chancery records in the Public Record Office.

Many of the documents cited exist in more than one form; and, for the convenience of readers who may wish to pursue in greater depth a particular aspect of the subject, all the places where a document may be found are as a rule mentioned in the footnotes.

[1] *Army Royal: Henry VIII's Invasion of France, 1513* (Clarendon Press, 1969).

I have modernized the spelling of quotations from contemporary English documents, but not French. I plead in defence of this inconsistency that English, not French, is my native language.

I must record my gratitude for help from Professor S. T. Bindoff, of Queen Mary College, London; Mr. Philip Grierson, Reader in Medieval Numismatics at Cambridge; Miss Marion Archibald, of the Department of Coins and Medals, British Museum; Mr. Howard Colvin, of St. John's College, Oxford; Dr. Jeremy Goring, of Goldsmiths' College, London; Dr. Prys Morgan, University College of Swansea; and Dr. Gabriel Wymans, Conservateur des Archives de l'État at Mons and Tournai.

For the third time in five years I thank many unseen hands in the Clarendon Press, in particular for the speed and efficiency with which this volume was produced.

C. G. C.

CONTENTS

LIST OF ILLUSTRATIONS

ABBREVIATIONS

MANUSCRIPT SOURCES

British Museum:

Add. MS.	Additional Manuscript.
Cal.	Cotton Manuscript, Caligula.
Cleo.	Cotton Manuscript, Cleopatra.
Galba	Cotton Manuscript, Galba.
Harl. MS.	Harleian Manuscript.
La. MS.	Lansdowne Manuscript.
St. MS.	Stowe Manuscript.
Vesp.	Cotton Manuscript, Vespasian.
Vit.	Cotton Manuscript, Vitellius.

Public Record Office:

C 76	Chancery Enrolments: French Roll.
C 82	Chancery Warrants for the Great Seal, Series II.
E 30	Exchequer (Treasury of the Receipt) Diplomatic Documents.
E 36	Exchequer (Treasury of the Receipt) Miscellaneous Books.
E 101	Exchequer, Various Accounts, King's Remembrancer.
E 159	Exchequer Memoranda Rolls, King's Remembrancer.
PRO 31/8	Record Commission Transcripts, Series II.
PRO 31/9	Rome Archives (Transcripts), Series I.
SC 7	Special Collections: Papal Bulls, John—Henry VIII.
SP 1	State Papers, Domestic and Foreign, Henry VIII.

Other Collection:

Vat. Arch.	Vatican Archives.

PRINTED SOURCES

(*a*) SOURCE COLLECTIONS

Arch.	*Archaeologia; or miscellaneous tracts relating to antiquity* (London, 1770 ff.).
Ellis	Sir Henry Ellis, *Original letters illustrative of English history* (London, 1824; 1827; 1846).
Giust.	Sebastian Giustiniani, *Four years at the court of Henry VIII: Selection of despatches written by Sebastian Giustiniani to the Signory of Venice,* trans. R. Brown (2 vols., London, 1854).

Hocquet (a) A. Hocquet, *Tournai et l'occupation anglaise* (Tournai, 1900).

Le Glay A. J. G. le Glay, *Négociations diplomatiques entre la France et l'Autriche durant les trentes premières années du xvi siècle* (2 vols., Paris, 1845).

LP *Letters and papers, foreign and domestic, of the reign of Henry VIII* (London, 1862–1910; 1920; 1929–32).

MC *Calendar of state papers, Milan (1385–1618)* (London, 1912).

Ordonnances *Recueil des ordonnances des Pays-Bas*, IIᵉ série: *1506–1700*, vol. i (Bruxelles, 1893).

Rymer Thomas Rymer, *Foedera, etc.*, vol. xiii (London, 1712).

Strype John Strype, *Ecclesiastical memorials*, vol. i, pt. 2 (Oxford, 1822).

VC *Calendar of state papers, Venetian (1202–1603)* (London, 1864–98).

(b) CHRONICLES

du Bellay *Mémoires de messire Martin du Bellay, seigneur de Langey: Mémoires particuliers relatifs à l'histoire de France*, xvii (London and Paris, 1786).

Fleuranges *Mémoires mis en escript par Robert de la Marck, seigneur de Fleuranges et de Sedan et Maréchal de France dit le jeune advantureux: Mémoires particuliers relatifs à l'histoire de France*, xvi (London and Paris, 1786).

Hall Edward Hall, *The union of the two noble and illustre famelies of Lancastre and Yorke* (London, 1548). References are to edition of 1809.

Macquereau Robert Macquereau, *Chronicque de la maison de Bourgoigne* (Paris, 1838).

(c) LATER WORKS

Army Royal C. G. Cruickshank, *Army Royal: Henry VIII's invasion of France, 1513* (Oxford, 1969).

Aubert Félix Aubert, *Histoire du Parlement de Paris* (Paris, 1894).

Chotin A. G. Chotin, *Histoire de Tournai et du Tournésis* (vol. ii, Tournai, 1840).

Cousin Jean Cousin, *Histoire de Tournay: ou quatre livres des chroniques, annales ou demonstrations du Christianisme de l'evesché de Tournay* (Douai, 1619).

Craig Sir John Craig, *A History of the London mint, from A.D. 287 to 1948* (Cambridge, 1953).

Elizabeth's Army C. G. Cruickshank, *Elizabeth's Army*, 2nd edn. (Oxford, 1966).

Hocquet (b) A. Hocquet, *Tournai et le Tournaisis au xvi siècle au point de vue politique et social* (Tournai, 1906).

Hoverlant	Hoverlant de Beauwelaere, *Essai chronologique pour servir à l'histoire de Tournay* (105 vols., Tournai, Lille, Courtrai, 1805–34).
Jopken	E. Jopken, *La peste de 1514 à Tournay* (Tournai, 1892).
Rapin	Paul de Rapin-Thoyras, *Histoire d'Angleterre* (La Haye 1724–36).
Scarisbrick	J. J. Scarisbrick, *Henry VIII* (London, 1968).

I · THE FIRST WEEKS

Henry VIII made his ceremonial entry into Tournai on Sunday 25 September 1513, ten days after his troops first invested the city.

The siege had been shamefully one-sided. The youthful Henry—he celebrated his twenty-second birthday two days before he left England—had come to France in search of honour and glory. The capture of Tournai, although it was not part of the original plan, was to be the climax of a brilliant campaign, at least as he saw it, in which he had routed the flower of French chivalry at the Battle of the Spurs. But there were no professional soldiers in Tournai; the city walls with their ninety-nine towers looked strong enough, but they could not stand up to the English siege guns, the best that Europe could provide; the cannon mounted on the walls were antiquated, and probably more dangerous to the amateurs who manned them than to the besieging force; and such hand weapons as the citizens found in their armouries were hardly likely to deter the English troops when eventually they poured through the breaches to administer the *coup de grâce* to the city and load themselves with plunder.

The Tournaisiens were under no illusions about their fate if the city fell. The dire threats spelled out in the summons to surrender, proclaimed in Henry's name by Thomas Benolt, Clarenceux King of Arms, must still have been fresh in their minds. The most high, most powerful, and Most Christian[1] King of France and England had demanded that they should open their gates to him within ten days, promising that if they did so their lives would be spared and their goods and chattels untouched. If they resisted and the city had to be taken by force they would all be put to fire and the sword and their property confiscated.[2] This announcement was formal in the sense that under the lingering rules of chivalry the siege could not honour-

---

[1] Henry had assumed the full title of the King of France.
[2] A model for the summons of Tournai is in La. MS. 818, f. 7 b.

ably begin without it;[1] but it also had the practical significance
that if the troops were forced to fight their way into the city it
made legitimate in the eyes of both God and man the slaughter
of the inhabitants and the plunder of their property. The Tournaisiens had fair warning of their fate if they were foolhardy
enough to risk putting up an unsuccessful resistance.

The anonymous citizen who left a detailed account of the
siege and the capitulation says that most of the English host
were eager for the assault, being under the mistaken impression
that there were enough riches in the city to give them all
affluence for the rest of their days.[2] The leading burgesses were
satisfied that the city must inevitably fall, and they had therefore earlier tried to negotiate a financial settlement with Henry;
but he had no interest in a hollow victory and refused to do
business with them. He was aided and abetted by the common
people in the city, who had more spirit than the wealthier
classes, were better Frenchmen, and had much less to lose. They
insisted on making a fight of it, but it was not long before they
too had to admit that resistance was futile. It had become clear
that the French army was in no position to raise the siege.

On 21 September, while the besiegers' guns thundered and
their cannon-balls crashed relentlessly against the crumbling
walls and into the deserted streets, the thirty-six *collèges des
bannières* met in an atmosphere of terror and crisis to consider
what to do. During the night Lord Lisle, the high marshal, had
launched against the western wall a small force which had
gained a foothold in the towers of the Lille Gate without too
much difficulty. Most of the citizens saw that it was now only a
matter of time before this success was repeated elsewhere. The
chronicler Hall tells us that 'they which at the last council cried
"War! War!" now cried "Peace! Peace!"' [3]

A handful of citizens still argued in favour of resistance, but
the turning-point in the discussion came when one delegate
stood up and said: 'Sirs, if the town be assaulted once again

---

[1] This belief was still current in the second half of the sixteenth century. See
Elizabeth's Army, p. 200.

[2] Hocquet (a), v, pp. 89–90: 'la plus grande partie dudit oost estoit fort affecté
à donner l'assault pour avoir le pillaige et tous les biens de ladicte ville que on
extimoit en beaucoup plus grand nombre que à la vérité n'estoient, et par ce
moyen esperoient tant trouver de biens que à tousjours ilz en seroient riches.'

[3] Hall, p. 565.

with a great number, surely it will be taken. You saw the experience at the last assault'—the attack on the Lille Gate— 'and then consider if it be taken by force, who is there that can say he is sure of his life? But by entreaty[1] the King of England is merciful that we may fortune to save both life and goods'.[2] This led to a unanimous recommendation to the four councils, the supreme governing body, that they should take whatever steps were deemed necessary to save the city from utter destruction. The councils accepted the recommendation and immediately appointed a committee to meet Henry and his ally the Emperor Maximilian to admit defeat and save what they could from the wreck.[3]

The committee went at ten o'clock in the morning to the St. Fontaine Gate and were met by Clarenceux King of Arms and a herald from the Emperor. They were escorted to the village of Maire, a short distance from the city in the direction of Lille, where the *Bailli* of Tournai had at one time held his court,[4] and were quickly joined in the former court-house by the English delegation. Henry had appointed a powerful team to represent him. It consisted of Richard Fox, Bishop of Winchester, Lord Lisle, second-in-command of the invading army, Thomas Wolsey, who had been responsible for most of the preparatory work of the invasion, although he was as yet no more than King's almoner, Sir Edward Poynings, Sir Robert Wingfield, and the Master of the Rolls, John Young. The most notable of the city's representatives was Jean le Sellier, one of the *prévôts*, who was to play a big part in the affairs of Tournai during the first years of the occupation.

Hall, whose version of these events is for the most part accurate, rather allows his imagination to run away with him in describing the meeting of the beaten Tournaisiens and the English higher command. He could hardly do otherwise, for a truthful account would reveal the hero of his Chronicle as no more than a bully who sat down and waited for a great commercial city, its fortifications hastily patched up by women and children,[5] and defended by workmen and clerks, to drop into his hand like an overripe plum. Hall makes the Tournaisiens

[1] i.e. by negotiation. [2] Hall, p. 565.
[3] Hocquet (a), xvi; *LP* i, 2294(2). [4] Hocquet (b), p. 23 n.
[5] Hocquet (a), xii; *LP* i, 2294(2).

kneel humbly before Henry, after which Jean le Sellier says:

Right high and mighty prince, although the city of Tournai is strong, well-walled, well replenished with people, victuals, artillery, yea, and the people in fear and dread of nothing, yet we know that against your great puissance it cannot continue long . . . wherefore we, knowing by report your honour, your wisdom, your justice and noble heart, are content to become your subjects and vassals so that we may have and enjoy our old laws, customs, liberties and franchises under you as we have before this done under other princes.[1]

In short, an impregnable fortress defended by men of steel has graciously elected to surrender to a paragon among sovereigns. Nothing could be further from the truth.

The Tournaisiens in fact adopted a more realistic position. They frankly admitted that they had been anxious to surrender much sooner, but had been forced to wait for the hot-headed common people to come to their senses—which they had done only that morning. They were tireless debaters, however, and now that they were freed from the immediate pressures of the siege (although their fellow townsmen continued to be bombarded) they spent the greater part of the day trying to argue themselves out of their difficult situation. In particular, they revived a suggestion that they should be allowed to surrender to Maximilian rather than to Henry. But they were not arguing from strength, whatever Hall may say. They well knew that the bombardment could be cruelly intensified at a moment's notice, and that the final assault would follow swiftly thereafter.[2]

Late in the day, after they had prevailed on the besiegers to silence their cannon, they threw their hand in. They would surrender to the English King. The two delegations adjourned to the royal presence and the final speeches were made. Henry wound up the proceedings by saying: 'Sirs, he that asketh mercy of us shall not be denied', and commanding the two sides to sit down together to draft formal documents embodying the conditions of surrender.[3] Henry's German mercenaries, and also

---

[1] Hall, p. 565.   [2] Hocquet (a), v, p. 88; *LP* i, 2294(2).

[3] Hall, p. 565. A paper dated 11 September 1513, which lists rewards paid to the household of Margaret of Savoy 'at the King's first being at Lille' totalling £487. 5s. 4d., includes an item of 10 marks to 'the audiensarie [audiencer: a Chancery officer] for the making of the treaty of Tournai'. If the date is correct it

those from the Low Countries, were incensed at the outcome. They had been counting on an assault followed by pillage, and had even equipped themselves with sacks to carry the booty and hired a fleet of small boats on the river Scheldt, which flowed through the city, to take it away. The records suggest that the English troops took this misfortune more philosophically, perhaps because it would have been difficult for them to get their plunder home.[1]

The main heads of the agreement had been hammered out during the day, but as it was too late to commit them to paper that evening the Tournaisiens were escorted back to the city. Early next morning they reported to a meeting of the four councils what had transpired in their discussions with the besiegers; and they were no doubt much relieved to find that it was unanimously considered that they had made the best bargain possible. The assembled company praised God for allowing them to escape so lightly from such dire extremity. They authorized the delegation to return to the English headquarters in the afternoon, taking with them the *procureur général* Éloi de la Rue to watch their interests in the drafting of the treaty, which was to be in the form of letters patent from Henry reciting the conditions to be imposed,[2] and a document from the city formally accepting them.[3]

The preamble to the former describes how Henry has invaded France to restore English rule there. Having captured Thérouanne, he came on to Tournai, where he gave the citizens every opportunity to acknowledge him as their sovereign before his armies laid siege to the city; but in spite of his 'just and reasonable overtures' they closed the gates and made it clear that they intended to defy him, their lawful ruler. This left him no alternative but to plant his artillery round the city and to take all other measures necessary to reduce it. Whereupon the citizens,

---

suggests that the English higher command believed that Tournai must fall even before the siege began; and in fact Henry was in Lille on 11 September. The date of the paper cannot be right, however, as it also includes one or two payments which could have been made only after the city had fallen, for example, £3. 6s. 8d. to 'the keeper of the house [in Tournai] where the King stood when the citizens made their fidelity' (St. MS. 146, f. 96.)

[1] Chotin, p. 92.
[2] PRO 31/8/144, ff. 268–269 b; Hocquet (a), xvii; *LP* i, 2294(1).
[3] PRO 31/8/137, f. 227; *LP* i, 2294(2).

recognizing that they were in the wrong, and also because they were well aware of the great danger in which they stood, humbly begged that he should show himself merciful and receive them again as his subjects.

There is then provision for the transfer of Tournai's allegiance to England; and the document concludes by setting out the price which the citizens will pay for their error of judgment in resisting the English army. First, a lump sum of 50,000 écus d'or,[1] which may be paid in silver plate bearing the hallmark of Tournai or one of the cities in the Low Countries,[2] and 4,000 livres tournois[3] for ten years. Second, the annual payment of 6,000 livres customarily made to the French Crown will be transferred to England. Finally, Henry and his heirs and successors will enjoy all rents and other forms of income that Louis and his predecessors have been eligible to receive from the city and its appurtenances in the last hundred years.[4]

The conditions of surrender were accepted on Friday 23 September by the representatives of the municipality and four of the city's spiritual leaders—Charles de Créquy, Dean of the cathedral church of Notre Dame, the Abbots of St. Martin's and St. Nicholas des Prés, and the vicar general of the Bishop elect of Tournai. (The Bishop elect was not in the city at this time nor would he have been welcome. His father was one of the leading men in Louis XII's government.) The ceremony took place in the magnificent cloth of gold tent that Henry used on important occasions and which had been erected by his pavilioners on high ground outside the village of Orcq, a short distance from Tournai.[5] The tent, 'huge and very rich, with a golden lion on top and bearing in Roman lettering the inscription *Dieu et mon droit*', much impressed the Tournaisiens, as indeed it had done all who saw it during the campaign. It was clearly visible from the battlements and while the surrender was taking place its side walls were drawn back to let as many people as possible see what was going on.[6]

---

[1] The *écu d'or* was worth about 4s. 0d.

[2] 'en vaisselle d'argent portant les poinchons de Tournai ou des villes dudit Seigneur Archeduc'.

[3] The *livre tournois* (a unit of account) was worth about 2s. 2d.

[4] PRO 31/8/144, f. 268 b: 'deniers, cens, rentes, demaine, subsides, et autres droictures prouffitz et esmolumens'; *LP* i, 2294(1).

[5] Hocquet (a), v, p. 91; *LP* i, 2294(2).   [6] Macquereau, p. 47.

Henry came from the Château de la Marlière where he had been lodging—it seems that he did not make use of his ingenious portable timber house during the siege[1]—accompanied by many of his courtiers splendidly dressed. As his new subjects approached his presence they 'thrice did him reverence to the best of their knowledge and ability'. In a humble address their spokesman Michel Allegambe said that they had come to do homage 'to the noble, powerful, and undoubted King of France and England, Lord of Ireland and Aquitaine', to make him lord and master of their city, and to beg for mercy. Then the keys of the town, hung on green and white ribbons—Henry's colours— were presented to him and handed on to Lord Lisle, who was to be responsible for installing the garrison. Henry made a brief speech, assuring the assembled company that he would be 'good master and lord' to them and that he would see to it that the promises he had given to keep the town safe from its enemies would be faithfully kept.[2]

The document in which the Tournaisiens finally transferred their allegiance—their response to Henry's letters patent—is couched in suitably obsequious terms. It has pleased the most exalted, most excellent, and most powerful prince, the Most Christian Henry, King of France and England, their undoubted sovereign lord, to listen to their humble prayer, and in his mercy to accept their submission, subject to certain matters set out in his letters patent, the text of which is then quoted verbatim. The original of this document was lost in 1940, when virtually all the contemporary archives in Tournai were destroyed by enemy action; but a copy survives in the French national archives.[3] There is whole-hearted acknowledgement that the city accepts without reservation every condition laid down by the English. Further, in the event of their breaking the agreement they bind themselves to submit 'à la voulenté de nostre dit souverain', and to accept all censures that may be directed against them by the Holy See in consequence of their breaking the treaty; and they waive any protection which the laws or customs of Tournai may appear to afford them.

---

[1] For a description of Henry's wooden house see *Army Royal*, pp. 43–4.

[2] Hocquet (a), v, p. 91; Macquereau, p. 48; *LP* i, 2294(2).

[3] Trésor des Chartes: Supplément J 922. A transcript of this document is in PRO 31/8/137, ff. 227–230 b.

The Tournaisiens were now English, at least so far as legal processes could make them so; and the stage was set for the King to make his ceremonial entry into the captured city, and enjoy the climax of his three-months' adventure in Europe.

The several independent accounts of Henry's entry into his new possession support each other well.[1] The occupying troops —4,000 infantry, including archers, pikemen, halberdiers and hand gunners, and 1,000 cavalry—were led in by the high marshal, Lord Lisle, supported by Lord Abergavenny and Lord Willoughby, at four o'clock in the afternoon of Friday 23 September. This gave the men a chance to establish themselves before Henry ventured into the city, and to ensure as far as possible that it would be safe for him to show himself before the people.

They marched in companies, probably forty or fifty of them, each led by its standard-bearer and captain, with trumpeters and buglers interspersed in the long column.[2] We cannot determine how many companies there were, since there was no uniformity in the size of the unit at this time, although it was beginning to settle down at round about a hundred strong. After the men had been drawn up in the market-place, Garter King of Arms ordered a herald to set a flag with the red cross and royal arms of England 'high on the belfry' and another on 'the town house'. A second herald hoisted banners of St. George at all the city gates. It was then proclaimed to the crowds of spectators that they had nothing to fear and that they would be well treated by their conquerors.[3]

Detachments of troops were told off to carry out a house-to-house search 'for fear of treason'; and at nightfall a strong guard was posted on the ramparts, despite the presence of the main body of the English army outside the town, which afforded all

---

[1] They include an eyewitness account of the whole of the siege and the first days of the occupation, formerly preserved in the archives of Tournai and printed as Preuve v in Hocquet (a); an extract from the Tournai archives printed in *Arch.* xxvii, pp. 258–60; a brief description in La. MS. 818, f. 8; Dr. John Taylor's Diary, in Cleo. C V, ff. 64 et seq.; Macquereau; and Chotin, based on another destroyed Tournai manuscript. Taylor's Diary is transcribed and translated in R. E. Brock's unpublished M.A. thesis 'The career of John Tayler, Master of the Rolls' (London, 1950).

[2] Hocquet (a), v, p. 92; *LP* i, 2294(2).

[3] La. MS. 818, f. 8; Chotin, p. 93.

the protection needed from attack from without. The potential danger from within was greater. Groups of sentries were therefore stationed at all the main cross-roads in the city to nip in the bud any attempt that might be made under the cover of darkness against the occupying force.[1]

On Wednesday 5 October the municipal authorities were formally notified that Henry intended to exercise his right under the treaty to occupy the town permanently. The four councils were summoned to be told that Sir Edward Poynings, who would be invested with the full authority of the King, had been ordered to stay behind with a force of 5,000.[2] This corresponds to the number initially installed in the city, but it is not clear if they were the same men, nor, indeed, how the permanent garrison was selected. Presumably volunteers were called for. When the army left England four months earlier, the rank and file must have regarded the enterprise as no more than an opportunity to 'do a mischief' to the French, and perhaps enrich themselves by capturing a prisoner worth a ransom or by winning booty with a good market value; and they must have assumed that if they survived they would be back in the bosom of their families before winter set in.

Whatever the method of selection there was no difficulty in finding the numbers needed. It may be that those who were left behind were made aware of the King's intention to return to France with a new army in the spring of the following year, and given the hope that they might join it while others took their place in Tournai; or it may have been understood that the garrison troops would be replaced at regular intervals. Some of them, however, saw their whole career in Tournai, for they married and started families; and it came as a great shock to these men when the city was handed back to the French five and a half years later and they found themselves homeless.

Henry had announced his intention of entering the city at ten o'clock on the morning of Sunday 25 September, which left little time for preparations. The streets were still littered with cannon-balls and broken masonry, and the normal garbage disposal arrangements had of course been suspended during the siege.[3] The citizens feared that they might not be able to do

---

[1] Hall, p. 565.   [2] Hocquet (a), xxi; *LP* i, 2336.
[3] *Arch.* p. 259; *LP* i, 2302.

justice to the occasion and they set to with a will. They may
have been helped by earlier preparations for their annual
religious procession, which should have taken place on Wednesday 14 September, but had been put off because of the siege.
(Many who had come in from the surrounding district to take
part in the procession had been trapped in the town when the
siege began.) One of the features of the triumphal route was a
series of tableaux that may have been designed for the religious
festival, and which the thrifty Tournaisiens did not want to
waste.[1]

The municipal leaders, accompanied by the *greffiers, pro-
cureurs*, and other officials, went on horseback to meet the royal
party half-way between Tournai and Orcq, and escorted them
back to the St. Fontaine Gate, where the formal procession was
drawn up. It was led off by members of the religious community, carrying among other relics a fragment of the true
Cross, and a group of civic dignitaries with flaming 'staff
torches'. They were followed by the principal English courtiers,
dressed no less splendidly than the King himself, walking in
single file so that each might show off his finery without being
overshadowed by his neighbour.

Then came Henry on a magnificently-barded grey courser,
the bard being hung with myriads of tiny golden bells. On
either side of him walked three senior burgesses supporting a
canopy of red and blue velvet embroidered with fleurs-de-lis
and leopards. As usual the King cut a splendid figure. He wore
a robe of cloth of gold with a rich golden collar studded with
pearls and precious stones, and a hat with a huge yellow plume.
The collar alone was reckoned to be worth 'un petit pays'. It is
recorded that as he set off for the centre of the city the crowds
watching the spectacle managed to raise a few shouts of 'Vive
le roi!'; but judging by the lukewarm reception he received
later on, and the hostility which the Tournaisiens showed to the
English throughout the occupation, there was probably little
real enthusiasm for their new sovereign. It might have been
different if they had been paying homage to the Emperor,
whom they regarded as the lesser of two evils.

His sword-bearer rode immediately in front of Henry;

---

[1] Hocquet (a), v, p. 92; *LP* i, 2294(2).

immediately behind came thirteen pages 'bare-headed and richly accoutred', their horses barded with cloth of gold covered with gold and silver bells. The pages themselves wore cloth of gold and blue velvet, and their tunics were embroidered with fleurs-de-lis and little golden crowns. Close on their heels followed the King's war charger, wearing full armour and led by a member of the household; and the henchmen carrying the King's weapons. Henry and his entourage were completely surrounded by the yeomen of the guard—all 600 of them—to afford the maximum protection against any attempt on his life, although it would have been easy enough for a loyal Tournaisien to pick him off with a shot from a bow or a hand-gun. The yeomen, like everyone else, were dressed in their finest—tunics of Henry's colours of green and white, with cuffs and collars of cloth of gold, and a red cross on the front and back.[1]

The procession made its way from the St. Fontaine Gate to the Rue St. Jacques, one of the main thoroughfares, past the Ferrain Gate which had been the main gate of medieval Tournai,[2] across the market-place and finally along the Rue Notre Dame to the cathedral. The houses on the processional route were gaily decorated with tapestries and bunting; and from the upper windows the occupants watched the proceedings, which were enlivened by the music of the King's minstrels and the pealing of bells in all the parish churches. At the cathedral there was a low mass (the chronicler says that there was no time for a high mass), and when it was over Henry called up fifty men who had distinguished themselves in the campaign which had just ended, and honoured them with knighthood.[3] This was, of course, the sovereign's prerogative, although it could be exercised also by his commander-in-chief on active service. A fortnight earlier the Earl of Surrey had knighted forty men after defeating the Scots at Flodden. At the end of the sixteenth century Elizabeth I became very jealous of her generals' use of the prerogative. She commanded them to dub only those who had given outstanding proof of their bravery in the field and who had ample private means.[4]

[1] Hocquet (a), v, p. 92; Chotin, p. 93; *LP* i, 2294(2).   [2] Chotin, p. 94.
[3] Their names are listed in Harl. MS. 6,069, f. 112; *LP* i, 2301.
[4] *Elizabeth's Army*, pp. 46–7. See also H. H. Leonard's unpublished Ph.D. thesis 'Knights and knighthood in Tudor England' (London, 1970).

The investiture over, Henry proceeded to the house of Canon
Simon Huland for his midday meal. In the afternoon he rested.
When he reappeared he rode to the market-place where the
people had been assembled. He mounted a platform in full view
of the crowd and swore that he would faithfully abide by the
terms of the agreement he had made with the city.[1] Then a
herald read a proclamation 'in the name of the most excellent
King of France and of England', first in French and then in
English. Unfortunately the text of the proclamation does not
survive, but the gist was that no person, of what degree soever
he might be, should take anything from the inhabitants without
payment, on pain of death. According to the account in the
Lansdowne manuscripts this delighted the citizens, who cried
'Vive le roi!' so loud 'that ye might have heard them half an
English mile out of the town'.[2] Edward Hall, however, tells
us that during the proclamation, which was to the effect that
no man should grieve the citizens, the Tournaisiens 'scarce
looked up, nor showed once to him any amiable countenance,
which was much marked', in spite of the King's manifest
eagerness to ingratiate himself with his new subjects; and as
soon as 'the cry' was over Henry made haste to leave the city
and return to the more congenial atmosphere of the English
camp.[3]

It may be that as Henry and his councillors made their way
back to headquarters they began to realize for the first time the
magnitude of the task which they had suddenly undertaken.
The precedent of Calais was not very encouraging. Although
that city was a mere twenty miles from English soil and less than
a hundred miles from the seat of government in Westminster, it
did raise substantial problems from time to time, in spite of the
fact that it had been an English possession for the better part of
two centuries. How much more difficult, then, to administer a
larger city many miles further away, admittedly in the middle
of a friendly country, but constantly threatened by France, the
strongest power in Europe? How long would it be before the
French King, stung by the humiliation he had suffered at the
hands of the upstart Henry, directed all his energies towards the

---

[1] Hocquet (a), v, p. 93; *LP* i, 2294(2).   [2] La. MS. 818, f. 8.
[3] Hall, p. 566.

recovery of this, one of the fairest jewels in his crown? Above all, what chance had the English garrison of controlling the large element in Tournai that was passionately loyal to France? On the showing of Henry's first day in the city the prospects looked pretty bleak.

However, the task had now to be faced, if Henry was not to make himself the laughing-stock of Europe; and in Thomas Wolsey the King had a brilliant administrator who could at least start off the new government in the right direction. There is virtually no direct evidence of Wolsey's hand busily at work during the three weeks Henry and his councillors remained at Tournai, but it seems inevitable in the light of his later career that the drive came from Wolsey. No doubt proposals were debated by the council of war and discussed with the representatives of the city, but it is likely that Henry himself, who spent a good deal of the time in social activities, left all plans to his Almoner. He had no great love for the business of state, although he was capable of transacting it with drive and efficiency when he could not escape it; and while Margaret of Savoy and her ladies were there to be entertained with feasting and dancing he was almost certainly content to leave most of the hard work and thought to Wolsey.

A good deal was accomplished in a very short space of time. The most urgent business was the appointment of a Governor and council to run the city in conjunction with the existing municipal government; and this matter at least Henry must have dealt with himself, no doubt after seeking the advice of the council of war. Sir Edward Poynings was an admirable choice for Governor, not only because he was a man of wide experience, but because he was old enough to be absent from Court without the constant worry that his career would thereby be prejudiced.

Henry took one other important decision, surely without advice, for it is difficult to believe that the council of war could have been collectively so stupid. When he first entered the city he exercised his prerogative of clemency, in a grandiose gesture, by ordering the release from prison of all criminals and restoring their citizenship to all who were banished from Tournai and the Tournaisis. This was doubtless part of his plan to ingratiate himself with the people and establish the image of a generous and benevolent monarch; but the citizens understandably thought that he had gone too far.

He sought to retrieve the position in letters patent issued on 1 October. The preamble recites that at his joyous first entry into Tournai he had restored their citizenship to all who were at that time banished, whether for one, three, or seven years, and under whatever financial penalty; and that the municipal authorities had now petitioned him to remove from the amnesty a long list of offences. The document concludes by declaring very firmly that it is not Henry's intention to extend his 'grace, pardon, or remission' now or in the future to those who have committed crimes, nor to take any step that might be prejudicial to the laws and customs of Tournai.[1]

This was not enough for the municipal authorities, however. Five days later Henry had to repeat his retraction in a more elaborate form. This second document also refers to his first entry, when a number of men who had been banished either from Tournai or from the whole of France had appeared before him and begged forgiveness for their crimes. The King, preferring mercy to justice, had listened with sympathy to their pleas and had pardoned them, agreeing that all their property that had not been disposed of after confiscation should be restored. But, as in the earlier letters patent, serious crimes are to be excepted, although 'murder' becomes '*murdre precogité*' and is distinguished from 'homicide', which is to be forgiven.

The *Bailli* of Tournai (now Sir Edward Poynings), his deputy, and the officers and citizens are commanded to see to it that those who have been pardoned are accepted back into the community and treated reasonably. Further, those who cannot receive their pardons in the due form (perhaps because of their inability to take up residence within a given period) are to have their petition enrolled in the court register in which their conviction and banishment were entered, on the strength of the counter-signature of Jean Meautis, the King's French secretary —as if each had personally received the King's letters patent.[2]

It was important in the early days of the occupation—particularly so long as Henry remained in the neighbourhood of Tournai—to ensure that the citizens had no chance of striking

[1] PRO 31/8/144, f. 225; *LP* i, 2331.
[2] PRO 31/8/144, ff. 227–227 b; *LP* i, 2338(1).

back. The strong patriotism of the lower classes, who had
wanted to continue the defence of the city long after the senior
burgesses were prepared to throw their hand in, might easily
have led to sporadic attempts against the garrison troops; and
although they would have had little hope of success against the
overwhelming strength and superior equipment of the English
forces, they could have undermined the confidence of the
English council in the wisdom of their decision to hold Tournai
indefinitely. The inhabitants had been required to take an oath
of loyalty to Henry and their houses had been searched as a
precautionary measure; but it was not until 30 September that
the order went out that all those who had received arms from
the city's arsenals on the eve of the siege should return them
forthwith, on pain of confiscation of their property. The order
was issued by the four councils, no doubt after discussion with
the Governor, and specifies the following weapons: harque-
buses, cross-bows, pikes, leaden maces, bows and arrows, bills,
helmets, trenching-spades, 'et autres instruments de guerre
appartenant à ceste ville'.[1]

A second precautionary measure was the return to safe
custody of the *bannières*, which were to the craft guilds what their
standards were to companies in the army. Each of the thirty-six
guilds had its banner, to which all the members owed their
loyalty, and which they were expected to defend to the last drop
of their blood. So long as the banners were in the hands of the
people there was a real danger that they might be used as
rallying-points against the occupying troops. While Henry was
still in Tournai the deans were ordered to return them, ostensibly because they bore the arms of Louis XII of France; but
they ignored the order.[2] In December 1513 Sir Edward Poynings
had to send his representative to a meeting of the four councils
to remind them that the banners should have been handed in.
He asked that this should now be done as a matter of urgency,
to avoid the great dangers and inconveniences that might ensue
if they remained any longer in the possession of the guilds. The
councils were assured that this would not prejudice any of their
rights and privileges.[3]

Henry went to extraordinary lengths to reassure his new

---

[1] Hocquet (a), xix; *LP* i, 2318(2).   [2] Hocquet (a), xx; *LP* i, 2336.
[3] Hocquet (a), xxviii; *LP* i, 2520.

subjects about their rights and privileges. They were vitally important, for the city's position as a great emporium depended largely on them; and the citizens were well aware of it. They seem to have quickly sensed that Henry, having achieved his ambition to make a name for himself in Europe, was quite prepared to take a soft line with them. They were not to be exploited as a colonial territory, but rather to be included on equal terms within the King's dominions; and indeed this was logical since one of the ostensible objectives of Henry's military intervention in Europe had been the recovery of England's French possessions, and not the enslavement of a foreign country. Moreover, if he seriously contemplated winning the allegiance of other parts of France in the years to come, it would be easier if he had established a reputation for clemency. Had it been necessary to take Tournai by assault the position might have been very different; but the citizens saved themselves by surrendering in the nick of time, and they made it quite clear that they expected that in return for their co-operation the commercial life of the city would be allowed to carry on exactly as before.

Henry's original agreement with the citizens safeguarded their privileges, and it was strengthened by further letters patent.[1] Much the same ground was covered on other occasions. For example, when a group of Henry's councillors told the municipal authorities that he was going to leave a garrison, they referred again to his great desire that all the city's former rights should be unimpaired, and even added that if the authorities wanted any new franchises they had only to say so. The councillors would do their best to see that they were granted.[2]

Again, some hair-splitting minds among the city fathers fancied they saw danger in the article in the treaty allowing citizens who refused to swear fealty to Henry to remove their goods and chattels from the city and take up residence in territory not hostile to Henry.[3] Might not this be interpreted as meaning that citizens who had expressed their loyalty to the new regime did *not* have the right to move with their belongings to other friendly territories? The argument may seem far-fetched, but it was taken seriously by the English authorities,

[1] See below, p. 38.　　　　[2] Hocquet (a), xxi; *LP* i, 2336.
[3] PRO 31/8/144, ff. 268–269 b; *LP* i, 2294(1).

who solemnly drafted further letters patent. There had been no intention to subtract anything from the city's ancient liberties and franchises; but to make it crystal clear that those who took the oath of loyalty would not be at a disadvantage as compared with those who did not, it was proclaimed that the citizens who had taken the oath were free to leave the city and take up their residence elsewhere. They could transfer as much of their property as they wanted to, as they had always been free to do, so long as they did not move into a hostile country.[1]

Although the treaty ranged widely, it missed one important point. What was the position of merchants absent from the city at the time of the capitulation, who could not return to take the oath of loyalty within the prescribed period? This difficulty manifested itself only after Henry had left Tournai, when the wives and friends of a number of absent merchants suddenly realized that they could not get back before the forty days expired. They were away at Paris, Rouen, Lyon, and other distant places, and although none of these was more than forty days' journey from Tournai, by the time they became aware of the terms of the treaty most of the forty days had gone. In any case, they were away on normal business trips, and it was unreasonable to expect them to leave their business unfinished and perhaps incur heavy losses. A petition was therefore sent post-haste after Henry. It caught him at Calais, where he was waiting for a ship to carry him back to England.

He was naturally sympathetic. His general line with the Tournaisiens had been conciliatory, and he was not going to be difficult with petitioners who had a good case. The absent merchants were told that the time limit was extended, so far as they were concerned, to the feast of Notre Dame Chandeleur (Candlemas) which fell on 2 February. In the meantime they were free to carry on whatever business they were engaged in, and then to return to Tournai to take the oath in proper form. All judicial officers, citizens, captains, and soldiers were commanded to see that the merchants, who were individually named in the letters patent, were properly treated when eventually they did come home.[2]

---

[1] PRO 31/8/144, f. 229; Hocquet (a), xxiii; *LP* i, 2338(2).
[2] Hocquet (a), xxvi; *LP* i, 2336.

Henry was content to leave the groundwork of the occupation to Wolsey and his colleagues, but during his three-week stay in Tournai he took a deep personal interest in the organization of social events, which were more to his taste than deliberations in the council chamber. He had to return the good cheer he had received at the hands of Margaret of Savoy in Lille before the capitulation; and above all he had to celebrate the end of a successful campaign by holding a tournament, in which he could demonstrate to his new subjects his horsemanship and skill with the lance. On 27 September the Milanese ambassador reported to the Duke of Milan that the King and his people had decided to hold a fine jousting, and that they were asking the townspeople for the things required to make some show of rejoicing for their victories.[1]

An invitation was sent to Margaret to join Henry in Tournai. She was staying with Maximilian at the Château d'Antoing, and it seems inevitable that the Emperor was included in the invitation; but when Margaret arrived in the city during the evening of Monday 26 September, only a day after the King had formally entered the town, she came alone. The King and 'all his nobles in a fine company' met her carriage outside the gates. They escorted her and her ladies, who were mounted on white horses, to the Bishop's palace, which was vacant, as the French Bishop elect had never taken up residence. There she entertained Henry to supper. Later the citizens presented her with a costly tapestry called 'The city of women'—perhaps in gratitude for her efforts to plead the city's cause before Henry and Maximilian finally committed themselves to attack.[2]

Maximilian's behaviour at this time caused some comment among the people of Tournai. On Tuesday 27 September he visited the city from Antoing 'without any announcement or triumph', accompanied by a bodyguard of men-of-arms on horseback. He came in through the Marvis Gate and made straight for Margaret's lodging, where he spent some time in conversation with her. Then he and his company left as swiftly as they had come. According to Robert Macquereau, the burgess of Valenciennes who recorded these events, Henry was furious that the Emperor had not warned him of his visit, as he

---

[1] *MC* 664.
[2] Hocquet (a), v, p. 94; *LP* i, 2294(2); Chotin, p. 95; Macquereau, p. 50.

would have liked to put on a great banquet in his honour; and this seems quite likely. Maximilian returned the following day, and this time did at least deign to meet Henry, although he refused to dismount. The King pressed him to stay to dinner, but he was adamant in his refusal. He had come simply to say goodbye. As he was about to ride off Henry seized the bridle of his horse, and would not let go until at least the Emperor had drunk a stirrup-cup. This done, Maximilian bade him farewell and left the city 'le plus tost qu'il peult'.[1] The Tournai chronicler's version differs slightly from Macquereau's. Henry met Maximilian at one gate, rode across the city with him, and said goodbye at another gate;[2] but, whatever happened, the Emperor wanted to make himself scarce, and people found it surprising.

There are several possible explanations of the Emperor's anxiety to shake the dust of Tournai from his feet. It may simply be that he was an old man who disliked feasting and dancing as much as the youthful Henry enjoyed them—at fifty-four he was more than twice Henry's age. When Margaret had entertained the King at Lille two or three weeks earlier, and they danced until dawn, Henry in his shirt sleeves and his stockinged feet, Maximilian went off to bed immediately after supper.[3] Again, he had been long away from his council chamber, and pressing business may have called him back. Thirdly, and this was the explanation that some contemporaries preferred, he may have taken himself off in a fit of pique because his plan to inveigle Henry into capturing Tournai for him misfired when the English King decided to occupy the city. In fact, the Emperor must have had enough sense to realize that the English occupation was a godsend, although it was perhaps unfortunate from the point of view of his own prestige. It neutralized an important French city at no cost to him. The truth probably is that he saw that he had got as much out of the campaign as he could reasonably hope for, and that there was no longer any need for him to consort with an arrogant young man whom he despised.

Henry may have deprecated the sudden departure of his ally, which threatened to detract from the splendour of the

[1] Macquereau, p. 50. [2] Hocquet (a), v, p. 94; LP i, 2294(2).
[3] MC 654.

festive occasions he was planning, but at least it left him in sole command of the stage. As the days passed and there was no sign of any hostile demonstration by the citizens, he became more willing to rub shoulders with them, and left the safety of the camp at Orcq for rather less secure quarters in the city. He explored every part of it and also made trips to the outlying parts of the *bailliage* and to the castle of Mortagne, which he awarded to Antoine de Ligne, Count of Faulconberg, for services rendered in the campaign that had just ended[1] and was to prove a bone of contention at the end of the occupation. Some of the time he devoted to riding, at which he excelled, and to playing tennis—royal tennis—in the Roc St. Nicaise, a street near the Lille Gate, which was fitted up with galleries specially for the purpose; and he also spent a good deal of time disporting himself with Margaret and the ladies of her Court.[2]

The almost furtive departure of Maximilian was compensated for by the arrival of his grandson, Henry's nephew, which provided the occasion for yet another splendid 'triumph'. Robert Macquereau has left a graphic description of their meeting, in which Henry features just as prominently as the Prince, although the latter was Macquereau's true hero. While the two were still a long way apart, they leaped from their horses and ran towards each other, doffing their hats and bowing low several times. They embraced, and exchanged the most cordial of greetings.[3] Henry, according to the chronicler, was so touched by the Prince's deferential attitude towards him that he wept for joy. At last they remounted 'en grant gloire'. One and all cried 'Vive la Bourgogne! Vive l'Angleterre!' and the trumpets sounded so melodiously that it was a wonder to hear them.[4] Henry later wrote to the Pope saying that he was much delighted by Charles's conversation;[5] and Dr. John Taylor noted in his Diary that he was a boy of great promise.[6]

The procession was led back by the city fathers and digni-

[1] Macquereau, p. 56.

[2] Hocquet (a), v, p. 95; *LP* i, 2294(2): 'Soy esbattant avecq les dames en ladicte court épiscoppale à dansser et passer le temps'.

[3] Macquereau, p. 53: 'Se entre-accollerent, disant de belles parolles à tieste nue. Longuement tindrent les mains l'ung à l'aultre.'

[4] Ibid.: 'Les clarions des deux princes jouoyent melodieusement a monter les deulx princes à chevaulx. C'estoit merveille de les oyr.'

[5] Add. MS. 15,387, f. 4; *LP* i, 2355.   [6] Cleo. C V, f. 64; *LP* i, 2391.

taries from Malines, Brussels, Ghent, and Bruges, walking three by three. Then came some noblemen of the Low Countries with their retainers; twenty Spaniards, all in black, on an embassy to Margaret; ten of Charles's trumpeters, whose joyous fanfares were answered by ten of Henry's; a group of Englishmen, among whom the Duke of Buckingham, in green velvet embroidered in gold, was outstanding. He might have been a Paris or a Hector of Troy—high praise from a chronicler whose objective was to glorify the House of Burgundy.[1] The Englishmen were followed by all the heralds riding together, and the members of the Order of the Golden Fleece.

Henry, with Charles on his left hand, came next. The trappings of the King's horse were decorated with golden apples and pears and little bells; and on its hindquarters, set in a huge silver rose, a bigger bell jangled. Henry wore the inevitable cloth of gold tunic, red hose with golden stripes like the rays of the sun, a hat with scarlet plumes, and the Golden Fleece with which the King of Castile had honoured him when he was in England eight years earlier.[2] Charles was in red velvet, with a round cape 'in the new style' trimmed with gold and a scarlet bonnet. Behind the royal pair came thirteen of the King's pages, the captain of the guard with 800 English yeomen, marching in fours in perfect order, and fifty of the Prince's archers armed from head to foot. The yeomen of the guard carried halberds ornamented on the blade with the Tudor rose.[3]

Henry was an expert horseman and loved showing off his skill. He could not resist putting his mount through its paces, much to the Prince's chagrin, for his pony was firmly led by a groom, and he was given no chance of showing that he was just as good a horseman as his uncle. When Henry had had his fill of leaping and prancing he took up his position again beside Charles and the procession moved off in the direction of Tournai.[4]

It was evening when they reached the town. The streets were hung with tapestry, for which Tournai was famous, illuminated

---

[1] Macquereau, pp. 52–3.   [2] Ibid. p. 11.
[3] Ibid. p. 54.
[4] Ibid.: 'le cheval du roi triumphoit chà et là, en saultant d'uncosté et d'aultre.'

by torches kindled outside the burgesses' houses. When the King and Prince rode across the Pont-à-Pont into the heart of the city the shouts of 'Vive la Bourgogne! Vive l'Angleterre!' rang out again, so deafeningly that nothing else could be heard. The King escorted Charles through the cheering populace to the lodgings that had been prepared for him in the Abbey of St. Martin, and after appropriate courtesies, took his leave.[1]

The tournament, the main event during Henry's sojourn in Tournai, was held the following day. The best place for it was the market-place adjoining the Cathedral and the lofty bell-tower, both of which had stood there for centuries. It was surrounded by public buildings and dwelling-houses which were readymade grandstands; but horses could not gallop safely on its paving-stones. Nothing was too much trouble, however, when a joust was in prospect. Henry commanded that the paving-stones should be ripped up to provide a surface of beaten earth for the tilt-yard. The cloth of gold marquee, which was always brought out on special occasions—it had last been used at Orcq for the surrender ceremony—was erected beside the bell-tower to serve as 'armoury and relief'. As usual it was the object of universal admiration. 'Je croy que en la crétienté n'en y a pas une plus belle' says Robert Macquereau. 'C'estoit triumphe de le veoir'.[2] Sir Edward Guildford, who had been knighted by Henry for his services in the campaign, was in charge of the preparations and was authorized by the King to spend £125 'for costs of making the tilts and jousting places, scaffolds, and other necessaries against our royal jousts made at Tournai, as for provision of stuff, spears, and other necessaries'.[3]

The lists were not the only innovation in the market-place. It became, in the words of Chotin, a vast hostelry. Booths sprang up everywhere, and round the square there were drawn up carts laden with Rhine wine and beer from England and the Low Countries, which were sold tax-free in honour of the occasion. Many people jumped at the chance of making some money out of the thousands of thirsty English soldiers who had suddenly arrived in their midst, and turned their homes into

---

[1] Macquereau, p. 54.   [2] Ibid.
[3] St. MS. 146, f. 101; *LP* i, 2359.

public houses. Others set up stalls in the nearby Rue Puits l'Eau and on the Pont-à-Pont, and so great was the demand that there was no time to bottle beer or wine. Everything was sold straight from the cask.[1] Enterprising householders also erected stands for spectators in front of their houses, for the use of which they made a charge.[2]

After mass Prince Charles joined Margaret for midday dinner. Then in the middle of the afternoon he made his way from the Bishop's palace to the market-place, accompanied by noblemen of his Court, and followed by his aunt in a litter and her ladies-in-waiting on white hackneys. The royal party took up their positions in houses specially prepared for them. Margaret was allocated the house next door to the Halle du Guet,[3] in which it had been considered necessary to enlarge some of the rooms by knocking down a partition wall; and the other principal spectators were allotted windows according to their degree. Charles watched the proceedings with a dignity which the onlookers thought remarkable in one so young.[4] If any of the chroniclers reckoned that he was simply bored they did not venture to commit their thoughts to paper.

Three heralds, two English and the Herald of the Golden Fleece, were deputed to keep the score. One of the Englishmen brought the contestants' names to the judges' stand half-way down the lists opposite the Cloth Hall. The other, using the traditional complicated notation, recorded the number of courses run, and on the instructions of the four judges, the lances broken on body (or helmet, which counted more), the attaints (fair blows which failed to shatter the lance), and so on.[5] The heralds were paid 100 marks for their services.[6] Henry had nominated two of the judges—the Duke of Buckingham, and someone who is identified by Macquereau as the 'gouverneur de la ville de Londre'; and Prince Charles had nominated the other two—the Seigneur de Ravenstein, and Maximilian's high chamberlain, the Seigneur de Berghes.[7] The judges had an unenviable task, for Henry was accustomed to being declared

---

[1] Chotin, pp. 96–7.   [2] Macquereau, p. 56.
[3] Ibid. p. 55.   [4] Hocquet (a), v; *LP* i, 2294(2).
[5] See Sydney Anglo, Archives of the English Tournament: Score Cheques and Lists, *Journal of the Society of Archivists*, vol. ii, pp. 153–62, 1961.
[6] Add. MS. 6,133, f. 9; *LP* i, 2347.   [7] Macquereau, p. 56.

the winner when he jousted, and he was no doubt more anxious than usual to succeed on this occasion.

The King waited until the principal spectators were in their places before he emerged from the tent of cloth of gold, to a fanfare of trumpets. He was magnificently armed, and his helmet carried a great white plume and a scarf—the chronicler tells us that the latter was for the sake of some damsel or other. He entered the lists at the bell-tower end, and his first opponent, the young de Walhain, son of the Seigneur de Berghes, took up his position at the other end. He too was richly accoutred and was led in by a throng of supporters—squires, trumpeters from his retinue, two dozen lackeys, and an unspecified number of kinsmen. According to Macquereau the lists were seventy yards[1] long and the wall which separated the jousters was over seven feet high. This left little more than the head and shoulders of the contestant exposed to his adversary as they charged against each other, and it may have been a precaution in the interests of the King's safety.[2] There is no doubt that the wall was unusually high. The Milanese ambassador records that some of the competitors ran without their shields (implying that they were taking unnecessary risks); but he adds that 'the lists were very high' (implying that they would see very little of each other, and that shields were almost unnecessary).[3]

Henry, seeing through his visor that his opponent was ready, took his lance. He saluted Margaret, then de Walhain, and the signal to attack was given. Lances couched, challenger and answerer spurred their chargers into a ponderous gallop. As they met half-way down the lists their lances struck home and splinters flew in all directions. Henry had upheld the honour of England, at least in the first course. The heavens now opened, but the programme went on without interruption, although the muddy surface of the market-place became very treacherous. There were five more courses to be run in the first contest, and in four of them de Walhain broke his lance 'vaillamment et bien honnestement' on the King's breast-plate. It is not recorded how Henry fared, but he had to admit defeat, no doubt to his great mortification. Meanwhile the rain continued. The Milanese ambassador reported to the Duke of Milan that the tournament was 'honoured by a constant downpour, by no

---

[1] 'Destres'.   [2] Macquereau, p. 51.   [3] *MC* 669.

means slight';[1] but there was no question of cancelling it. Too much effort had gone into the occasion for it to be washed out by a mere rainstorm.

Henry, having lost the first match, remained mounted until the second answerer appeared—Arriere, a Spanish captain. After a single course against him in which both riders broke their lances Henry retired to the cloth of gold tent and left it to Lord Lisle to take on Arriere, which he did with conspicuous lack of success. The Spaniard shattered his lance without difficulty on the high marshal, but the unfortunate Lisle had a clean miss and was immediately replaced by Henry, who this time was able to hold his own. So the afternoon wore on, Henry and Lisle taking it in turn to meet seven of the leading nobility of the Low Countries and Spain, and an eighth man who wanted to remain anonymous for the occasion. 'Mais tousjours, en ce faisant, pluvoit merveilleusement.'[2]

At last all who had answered the Englishmen's challenge had had their chance against them; and while Henry took off his helmet and rode round the lists saluting the spectators 'in most honourable fashion' the judges completed their difficult task. According to the Milanese ambassador the King seemed 'fresher after this awful exertion than before'. There is an interesting disagreement as to who actually won the tournament. Robert Macquereau records that de Walhain won first prize and that Arriere was runner-up; but then he was writing for readers in the Low Countries.[3] Dr. John Taylor claims in his Diary that the King exceeded all others 'as much in agility and in breaking spears, as in nobleness of stature', but does not go so far as to make him the winner.[4] The Milanese ambassador, writing home on the evening of the jousts, says that he has not yet heard what the prize is, but that Henry 'had the honour of having done best, and without flattery we all say that he has done excellently and broken many lances'.[5] Perhaps the most revealing assessment comes from Edward Hall, who would surely not have failed to award Henry the prize had he in fact been declared winner. He tells us simply that many spears were broken and many a good buffet given, and that de Walhain

---

[1] *MC* 669.
[2] Macquereau, p. 56.
[3] Ibid.
[4] Cleo. C V, f. 64; *LP* i, 2391.
[5] *MC* 669.

'did right well'.[1] Perhaps we are justified in concluding that the doctrine that the King could do no wrong applied just as much in the tilt-yard as elsewhere. If the King was victor he must be given full credit; if he was not, he had still done well enough to outshine all others.

That evening there was 'a sumptuous banquet of a hundred dishes' followed by dancing far into the night. It was the usual splendid affair, attended by Margaret and her ladies, the Prince, and those of the English nobles who were still with Henry.[2] The account books of Richard Gibson, the yeoman tailor, show that no expense was spared to make the occasion memorable. 'Stuff' was specially bought and made up into garments—white satin and yellow damask, for example, for the minstrels' outfits.[3] Elaborate disguises were provided for the twelve maskers, one of whom was the King. It may even be that the unknown poet with a keen eye to the main chance, but rather less poetic vision, who composed a set of verses lauding Henry and the English higher command (and received forty shillings for his pains),[4] was allowed a few moments to say his piece.[5] When the banquet and the mummery were over, 'the garments of the mask were cast off among the ladies take who could take' according to the custom.[6] Gibson, a good civil servant who liked to keep his accounts straight, notes regretfully that he could not remember the names of the people who managed to get hold of the costly garments.[7]

Now that the tournament was over there was nothing to keep Henry in Tournai. Winter was fast approaching and the campaigning season was nearing its end. The King wrote to Leo X that he had intended to pursue the French army but he des-

---

[1] Hall, p. 566. [2] Ibid.
[3] SP 1/7, f. 74; *LP* i, 2562. [4] St. MS. 146, f. 104; *LP* i, 2375.
[5] La. MS. 818, f. 7 b. The first verse runs:

> Que ne vous rendrez
> > Povres Theourneoys
> Trop vous abusrez
> > Tenantz pour les Francoys
> Car voycy les Angloys
> > Qui vous ont fait la guerre
> Pour et au nom du prienx
> > Henry Roy d'Angleterre.

[6] Hall, p. 566. [7] SP 1/7, f. 74; *LP* i, 2562.

paired of catching up with it. In any case he had to go home for a meeting of Parliament, and to consider his relations with Scotland after the rout of the Scots army at Flodden. He had made up his mind, however, to return to France next year to build on the foundation laid in the campaign of 1513.[1]

On Thursday 13 October the four councils were summoned to be told that the King was leaving that day.[2] The city fathers escorted him some way along the road to Lille, and when they bade him farewell showed themselves 'true and loving subjects', at least in the view of one eyewitness. Henry for his part expressed the hope that the Almighty would have them in His safe-keeping.[3] His party was accompanied by Margaret and her Court; and once again he could not resist the temptation to show off in front of the ladies. He rode a fine bay horse on which 'he performed marvels before Madame and her damsels'.[4]

That day and the next he held two more investitures, in which about seventy men were knighted.[5] Then he ordered the greater part of the army to head for the coast. (Some companies had already left for home via the inland waterways while the King was still in Tournai.[6]) Lord Lisle and Lord Herbert started off at the head of separate contingents, but on hearing that there were detachments of the French army in the neighbourhood joined forces for greater protection. Macquereau says that they were attacked on the march, but that the two leaders were 'soubtilz en telz afferes' and routed the enemy with heavy casualties. Only half a dozen Englishmen were lost.[7] Fleuranges simply says that Henry, seeing that the French were not prepared to give battle, departed with his whole army.[8] That there is no English record of an engagement does not mean that there was none. When the army was commanded by the sovereign in person there was no need to send home frequent dispatches.[9]

There was, however, still one important thing to be done

---

[1] Add. MS. 15,387, f. 4; *LP* i, 2355.
[2] Hocquet (a), xxiv; *LP* i, 2358.
[3] Macquereau, p. 57.   [4] *MC* 671.
[5] Harl. MS. 5177; *LP* i, Ap. 26.   [6] *MC* 669.
[7] Macquereau, p. 57. The Milanese ambassador reported from Ghent on 15 October that 7,000 French troops were making for Boulogne 'to take the King of England if they can' (*MC* 672).
[8] Fleuranges, p. 152.   [9] See *Army Royal*, p. 8.

before the King himself went home. He and his advisers had wondered about leaving part of the army to winter in France, so that next year's campaign might get off to an early start. Their thinking on this subject is revealed in the dispatches of the Milanese ambassador. On 18 September, nearly a week before Tournai capitulated, he said that he had it on good authority that, while Henry intended to remain in France as long as possible, he might be forced to return to England to raise more money or to finish off the war with the Scots. In that event the King would leave 8,000 to 10,000 infantry and 6,000 cavalry with Maximilian 'to keep things going during the winter'.[1] A week later he was less certain about Henry's intentions. He still thought the King would go home for money, but could not be sure. He would be more definite about the King's movements in two weeks' time. In the same dispatch he said that the marriage between Henry's sister Mary and the Prince of Castile, which had been rumoured, would shortly be confirmed.[2] Two days later he reported that Henry's plans were now quite clear. As soon as the jousts were over he would go home to make arrangements to continue the war; and he would return to France in the spring.[3]

The position changed, of course, when Tournai was captured. The council of war recognized that they must do something to support an isolated garrison far from England. Sooner or later the French would assemble a force powerful enough to besiege the city. They could pick their moment, and when they did there would be little hope of recruiting men in England in time to be of any use. It had taken something like six months to organize the invasion of 1513, and even if that time was cut by half Tournai would be French again long before an English expeditionary force could cross the Channel. Nor could the Calais garrison help. It had fewer than 1,000 men, and to withdraw them would be tantamount to presenting Louis with Calais and the Pale—a much more serious disaster than the loss of Tournai.

The solution was to persuade Maximilian to accept some responsibility for the defence of the city, and this was the main purpose of Henry's second visit to Lille. The Emperor had been sulking, however, ever since his ungracious departure from

[1] MC 657.   [2] MC 662.   [3] MC 664.

Tournai, and although it was understood that he would come to Lille to give his blessing to the arrangements provisionally made for the winter, and to say farewell to his ally, he never turned up. Fleuranges says that he was angry at his failure to persuade Henry to hand over Tournai to Charles—and goodness knows, it was sitting there waiting for him, right in the middle of his territory![1] Margaret feared that if the Emperor did not return, Henry's proposal to finance a substantial military force during the winter would be withdrawn. She twice wrote to him begging him to 'hasten his coming', telling him that Wolsey and the Bishop of Winchester had asked that he should either come to Lille or appoint commissioners to act for him. If he did neither they would 'repute all that had passed between him and the King void'. She added that if he persisted in his refusal it could mean the ruin of her realm.[2]

Maximilian *did* persist and Margaret had to carry on the negotiation of the treaty herself. She was a very able woman, however, and the agreement was successfully concluded on 15 October.[3] In it Henry refers to the commitment he had undertaken in the previous year to invade France, and puts on record the fact that he has done all that was required of him— he has routed the French army, captured and destroyed Thérouanne, and captured and occupied Tournai. Now, however, 'for certain urgent causes and reasons, and especially because it is inappropriate to wage war in winter, and it is necessary to lead off the troops from camp to their winter quarters', it is agreed that he may return to England whenever it suits him, taking with him the whole of his army, except for the sufficient garrison that he has left in Tournai. It is further agreed that for the safe-keeping of the territories of the Prince

---

[1] Fleuranges, p. 153: 'et certes elle luy estoit bien séante, et au milieu de ces pays.'

[2] *LP* i, 2367, 2369. The Milanese ambassador also was annoyed by Maximilian's behaviour. He had been instructed to discuss certain matters with him and was assured by Margaret that he would put in an appearance at any moment. But he did not, and da Laude asked permission to go to him. Margaret refused, on the pretext that the ambassador might lose his way. She was sure that the Emperor would come soon. When da Laude tried to discuss his business with her, she put him off, on the ground that she was too busy dealing with Henry; and in fact the ambassador was not allowed to go to the Emperor until after Henry had left Lille (*MC* 671; *LP* i, 2372).

[3] Galba B III, f. 90; Rymer, pp. 379–81; *LP* i, 2366.

of Castile and for the support of Tournai 'Serenissima Domina Margareta' will keep 4,000 cavalry and 6,000 infantry under arms in the towns of Artois, Hainaut, and the neighbouring territories. These troops are not to be reserved for defensive operations. In spite of the difficulty of waging war in winter they will do what they can to carry the attack to the French forces.

Henry agrees to pay a total of 200,000 gold crowns for this service—30,000 a month from November to April, and 20,000 in May. To ensure that he gets value for money, payment is to be authorized by four commissioners of musters, two appointed by Henry and two by Maximilian, after they have satisfied themselves that the agreed numbers are actually in service. This is intended to be a holding arrangement, aimed at at least containing the French, and protecting Tournai, until Henry or his lieutenant returns, some time before 1 June 1514, with a new army to carry on the conquest of France where he left off in September 1513.

By far the greater part of the treaty is devoted to these military provisions. Towards the end a single paragraph deals with the marriage of Prince Charles and Mary which is to take place in Calais before 15 May 1514. Had the marriage ever taken place it would have had important consequences for sixteenth-century Europe; but it seems unlikely that Maximilian took it seriously. He probably considered that it would be easier to extract another 200,000 crowns from Henry, who had financed virtually the whole of the 1513 expedition single-handed, if he dangled the best match in Europe before the King's sister. In the event the marriage never came off. Moreover, there is little sign that the 10,000 men contracted for ever provided the services expected of them. In reporting on the terms of the agreement the Milanese ambassador says that many considered Henry would have been better advised to take two hundred leading Tournaisiens to England 'as security for their French magnates'; that he had not done so was due to his great kindness and his hope that the city would willingly accept him as their sovereign lord.[1]

On Henry's last night in Lille he took part in what Dr. John Taylor describes in his Diary as a new kind of tournament. It is

[1] MC 671.

difficult to envisage just what this was, but it seems that the contests took place on 'a wide, oblong dais, raised many steps above the ground and covered with hewn stones like black marble'. The contestants were fully armed, and their horses were shod with cord or felt instead of iron, so that they would not slip or make too much noise on the polished surface. Taylor says that after the lances had been broken the fights continued with very sharp swords.[1]

Henry left Lille on 17 October, after distributing nearly another £500 in 'rewards' to the officers and servants of Margaret's household.[2] He spent three nights on the journey to Calais, the first in the Benedictine monastery at Ypres, but when he reached the coast there was no ship ready for him, and he did not sail until 21 October.[3] Part of the time was devoted to handing out more rewards—nearly £3,000 worth, mostly to captains from the Low Countries who had served in the expedition.[4] As soon as he reached Dover he rode post-haste to Richmond, where Catherine was; and in the words of Edward Hall there 'was such a loving meeting that every creature rejoiced'.[5]

The campaign of 1513 was finally over; but the battle to integrate Tournai with the realm of England was only just beginning.

[1] Cleo. C V, f. 64; *LP* i, 2391. [2] St. MS. 146, f. 104; *LP* i, 2375.
[3] Cleo. C V, f. 64; *LP* i, 2391. [4] St. MS. 146, f. 105; *LP* i, 2383.
[5] Hall, p. 567.

II · MUNICIPAL GOVERNMENT

TWO immediate tasks faced Sir Edward Poynings and 'the King's council' over which he presided.[1] First, they had to work out a *modus vivendi* with the municipal authorities. This was simple, at least in theory. It meant no more than transferring to the new Governor the functions which the French *Bailli* had exercised in relation to the local courts and city councils, and ensuring that their officials accepted his authority—which had the backing of 5,000 trained troops.

Second, those processes of government which had hitherto been carried on between the city and the Council in Paris through the agency of the royal *Bailli*—which had been abruptly terminated by the occupation—had either to be managed by the Governor in Tournai or grafted on to the machinery of government in London. This meant for some purposes substituting the authority of the King's Council for the various branches of the Council in Paris. It was, however, more difficult to communicate with London than with Paris, because of the greater distance and the uncertainties of the Channel crossing. It would inevitably be a slow process to establish the new lines of authority and difficult to keep them working smoothly.

If we are to understand the problems that had to be solved by the Council in England and the Governor in Tournai, it is necessary to examine briefly the peculiar status of Tournai within the French kingdom and the complex municipal government machinery.

Tournai had a long history of siege, capture, pillage, and destruction before Henry took it in 1513. Towards the end of the Roman occupation, when it ranked as the seventh city of the second Belgian province, it was twice attacked by the

[1] Although the English council in Tournai was 'the King's council', I have referred to it in general as 'the Governor's council', to avoid confusion with 'the King's Council' or 'Council' in England.

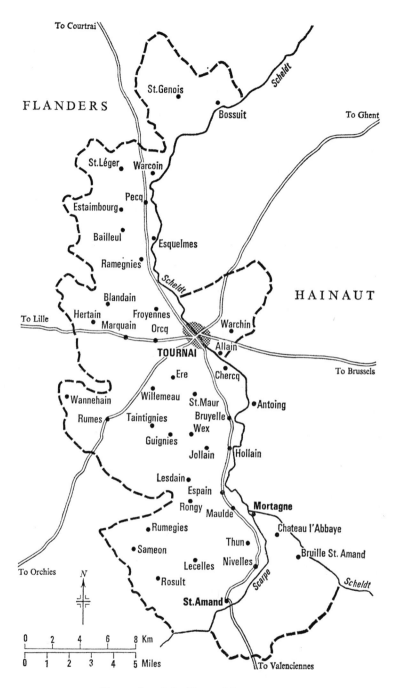

Tournai and the Tournaisis, 1513–19

barbarians. During the next seven centuries it suffered seven major upheavals; and although it was to remain French from the twelfth century until it fell to Henry VIII its troubles were by no means over. It was, for example, sacked by the Count of Flanders in 1213, and unsuccessfully besieged by Edward III of England in 1347 during the campaign in which he captured Calais.[1]

When Philip Augustus annexed Tournai in 1187 it became 'a French island lost in the middle of a dangerous sea';[2] and the relationship of the city with its neighbours changed. Tournai was more than forty miles from the nearest point in metropolitan France, completely surrounded by territories which in 1513 owed their loyalty to the young Prince of Castile. It may seem strange that a tiny fragment of France should survive in a hostile environment; and that it did shows how in the early sixteenth century the frontiers of a country were the walls of its fortified cities rather than its geographical boundaries. The hundred square miles of the Pale of Calais are clearly defined on contemporary maps; but the true frontiers of the Pale in time of war were the walls of Calais and those of the satellite Fort Risban, Fort Nieulay, Hammes Castle, and the town of Guines. The territory between was a no-man's-land in which anyone might travel freely, so long as he was prepared to defend himself should the need arise.

It was not until the race between the improvement of artillery and the improvement of fortifications began to be won by the former that frontiers began to correspond to the lines drawn on maps. Thus, in spite of its isolation, Tournai was little more vulnerable to enemy attack than the other fortified cities of France.

It was, of course, necessary that the fortified towns, the sum total of which was the early sixteenth-century defensive unit, should be kept strong. This was all the more important in the case of Tournai because of its nearness to the potential enemy; and it was recognized by the French Crown, which gave the Tournaisiens special encouragement to keep their defences efficient. Louis XII authorized a levy on sales of the city's principal manufactures, which was devoted to maintaining the

---

[1] Hoverlant, vol. 12, pp. 105, 109, 260, 271.
[2] Hocquet (b), p. 12.

fortifications. He also excused the citizens from the military service they owed to the central authority in return for their ancient charters, so that they might concentrate on their own defence.[1]

The status of the city changed fundamentally in 1478, when, under a treaty with Marie and Maximilian, the citizens undertook to dispense with a professional garrison in return for the right to resume peaceful trading with Burgundy. The proposition that a country's frontiers were the walls of its fortified cities held good only so long as the walls were defended by professional soldiers; and by denying the Tournaisiens a permanent trained garrison Marie and Maximilian made the city much more vulnerable, although it was to be thirty-five years before the fruits of their labours were harvested—by Henry, as it turned out.

These events affected the problems of government that faced Sir Edward Poynings and his advisers. To the extent that Tournai had become self-governing and had been allowed to deal direct with foreign countries almost as an independent city-state, it was the easier for Poynings and his colleagues to fit themselves into the machinery of government. Had there been close administrative ties with the central government in Paris, the substitution of the English Crown for the French would have given rise to difficulties. It would have been necessary to ascertain what powers were exercised from Paris, and to provide for them to be exercised either by the Governor in Tournai, or by the Council in London. It seems unlikely that there would have been anything like a systematic attempt to study the problems. They would have been coped with as they arose, which would have meant delay and dissatisfaction while solutions were being provided.

The new Governor thus found a city that for geographical and historical reasons was relatively independent of the French Crown. He also found well-established municipal institutions which could be allowed to run on without modification. Indeed, the various governing bodies were so complex and interdependent that even a small change in one of them would probably

[1] Hocquet (b), p. 15.

have upset the balance and thrown the whole machinery of municipal government out of gear. The institutions had either to be accepted as they stood, or completely replaced; and although the intention was to integrate Tournai with Henry's other dominions, it was not considered necessary to remodel the municipal councils as part of the process of integration.

Their complexity is illustrated by the form of address used in royal decrees. They were directed to 'noz chers et bien amez les prevostz, jurez, eschevins, esgardeurs, doyens, soubz-doiens des mestiers et toute la communaulté de nostre ville et cité de Tournay', who made up four separate councils. Thirty *éwardeurs* were elected by property holders to form a council which elected two other councils on 20 February each year. These were the senior council, of two *prévôts* and eighteen *jurés*, which played the leading part in the management of the city's affairs —the *grand prévôt* was in effect the lord mayor; and the council of two *maïeurs* and twelve *échevins* who carried out the functions of notaries or justices of the peace, and were concerned with proving wills, drawing up deeds of sale, the scrutiny of wardship accounts, and so on.

The fourth council was comparatively recent, at least in terms of Tournai's long history. It was set up in 1424 when the lower classes demanded a greater share in the government of their town. Each of the thirty-six *bannières* or guilds elected a dean and sub-dean, and these seventy-two officers sat together as a council primarily to deal with guild affairs. They did, however, join with the other councils when major decisions had to be taken. A subject was debated in each council, and then the four (known as the *Magistrat* or *Loi*) met and voted by council. If there was no agreement after three votes, the proposition was put to a meeting of all the citizens, when a two-thirds majority was necessary.

The councils were represented collectively by the *Chefs de la Loi*, comprising the two *prévôts*, the two *maïeurs* of the *échevins*, the two *maïeurs* of the *éwardeurs*, and the grand dean and grand sub-dean of the *bannières*.[1]

The system was less democratic than it seems. The *éwardeurs* were elected by parishes, and, since the wealthier parishes had proportionately more representatives than the poorer, the

---

[1] Hocquet (b), p. 60n.

primary electoral college had a strong upper-class bias; and this was reflected in the two councils which it chose. The council of deans was intended to correct this imbalance, but every Tournaisien of substance belonged to a craft guild and the burgesses were often able to secure the election of a puppet to the deanship. They could thus temper the line taken by the *bannières* and keep the control of the city's destinies very much in their own hands.[1]

The independence of the city and its well-seasoned institutions simplified Poynings' tasks in the early days of his governorship. A third important factor was the treaty made between Henry and the Tournaisiens before the King left for England, which was in the nature of a miniature written constitution for the new regime. It revealed to the citizens exactly where they would stand under English rule, and it freed the Governor and his council from having to legislate on a number of major issues in the early days of the occupation, before they had time to get the feel of things.

The first article of the treaty provides for the substitution of Henry for Louis as the rightful King of Tournai. Both the spirituality and the temporality are required to submit to him letters 'made and passed in good and ample form' renouncing for themselves and their heirs and successors Louis, the *soi-disant* King of France. All relationships with the French Crown are to be broken, and in particular the servants of the French Crown, the principal of whom was the *Bailli*, the head of the judicial system in Tournai and its *bailliage*, are no longer to be recognized. Instead, the citizens must accept Henry as their natural sovereign lord, and take an oath of loyalty to him as often as he or his deputy shall require. Whenever the King so commands, the good people of Tournai will admit members of his household into the city to prepare his lodging, and ensure that they have everything they need; and they will welcome the King himself with all the honour and ceremonial due to their sovereign from loyal subjects.

The position of the individual citizen is then dealt with. It is open to any man to refuse to take the oath of loyalty to his new sovereign; but if he does so he must leave the city within twenty

[1] Hocquet (b) provides a detailed study of the *Magistrat* (pp. 54 ff.).

days after Henry's entry, on pain of banishment and the confiscation of his property. During the period of twenty days' grace those who are not prepared to accept Henry may arrange to carry from the city all their goods and chattels, and go wherever they like without let or hindrance; and they may continue to enjoy any income arising from property they own in Tournai, so long as they do not take up residence in territory hostile to Henry, which in practice meant France. Citizens who are at present away on business are given forty days to return and take the oath of loyalty; but if they do not want to remain in Tournai under English rule, they too must leave within twenty days after their return. Those who intend to remain will have to provide a certificate sealed with the *scel aux causes* of the city, confirming that they are in fact citizens; but newcomers will be welcome, provided that they are prepared to take the oath normally required of new residents.

The citizens could hardly have had more generous treatment, but it was not enough. They demanded a more detailed statement of their position; and in this they revealed the businesslike persistence that characterized their negotiations with the English representatives before and during the siege, and which they showed throughout the occupation. They were always prepared to argue to the last ditch—indeed, it seems to have been a matter of honour that they should argue long after the need for argument had gone, either because they had won their point, as in the present case, or because it had become clear that they would never win.

They were rewarded a week after the main agreement had been concluded by further letters patent from Henry. These recited how the citizens had drawn his attention to the fact that his predecessors, the kings of France, had accorded *their* predecessors 'pluiseurs beaulx privillèges, droictz, usaiges, franchises et libertéz' which they have enjoyed until the present time; and now that they have taken the oath of loyalty they beg Henry to be equally generous. He, being well aware that they are loyal and anxious to serve him well, agrees that they should continue to enjoy their privileges, and commands the *Bailli* of Tournai and all other officers to see that this is done without let or hindrance.[1]

---

[1] PRO 31/8/144, f. 223; Hocquet (a), xvii; *LP* ii, 2318; *Ordonnances*, p. 273.

It was to be expected, given (1) the geographical position of Tournai, completely surrounded by the Low Countries, (2) the rôle that the Emperor Maximilian had taken as Henry's ally in the invasion of France, and (3) the historic association between the city and its immediate neighbours, that the surrender document should pay some attention to its future relationship with the imperial territories. If any Tournaisiens have been guilty of criminal words or deeds against the Emperor, Henry, or their allies, they are forgiven, and the penalties they have incurred are waived. Tournai is bound not to sustain or receive the enemies of the Archduke Charles, or those who have been banished from his dominions for treason, conspiracy, or other offences against the state; and if any such enter the city they must be handed over. Those who are engaged in trade and commerce, however, may freely visit the territories of the Emperor and Charles for the purpose of their business.

Henry's decision to leave a garrison in Tournai raised a special problem. The treaty of 1478 between the city and Maximilian gave the Tournaisiens the right to trade freely with his subjects, so long as they took no part in war against him and so long as they received no garrison within their walls. It is therefore stipulated that the presence of an English garrison will not affect the city's position under the treaty with Maximilian, and that property owned by the citizens in the Low Countries will not be at risk. This is to be confirmed in letters patent of the Emperor, acting on behalf of his grandson Charles, who is not yet of age.[1] The letters patent were issued on 8 October, signed by both Maximilian and Charles.[2] It was also desirable to reassure the citizens about the behaviour of the English garrison, and in the agreement with the city Henry makes it clear that, although he reserves the right to put as many soldiers into Tournai as he pleases, they will all be men of good character.[3] This was an important point in France, where

---

[1] Hocquet (a), i. The relevant section of the treaty runs as follows: The citizens 'ne feront, souffriront, procuront ou feront faire, directement ou indirectement par quelque voye ou manière, que ce soit, par leurs manans ou subjectz ou aultres estans en ladicte ville et povoir de Tournesis, guerre à nous, noz pays et subjectz, ne aussy recepvront ou soustiendront en leurdicte ville garnison de gens d'armes soubz umbre de la garde de la ville ne aultrement'.

[2] *Ordonnances*, p. 276.

[3] 'Gens de honneste estat, vie, et converssacion'.

soldiers were as a rule hated and feared by their fellow-countrymen.

When Henry first entered Tournai the citizens took an oath of loyalty which was probably quite simple. According to one account it was administered by Wolsey to the assembled population.[1] There survives in the State Papers, however, the draft of a more elaborate document, designed to ensure the obedience of Henry's new subjects and to strengthen the hand of the new Governor. The citizens are to swear loyalty to the King as often as may be deemed necessary. They are to accept him as their supreme overlord, to promise to maintain due obedience for ever, to defend the city against enemy attack, to obey all statutes, laws, and ordinances made by the King for their good government, and to report to him or his lieutenant anything that might be to his hurt or prejudice. The citizens are to bind themselves to appear before a judge and two notaries to make public admission that they will faithfully observe the terms of the oath, to ask that they should be excommunicated if they break their undertaking, and to promise not to seek absolution, or even to accept absolution freely offered, until they have made satisfaction to the King. It is not certain, however, that this undertaking, which bound the citizens body and soul to the King, was ever required of them.[2]

Finally, provision is made for the large numbers who had flocked into the city before the siege began, and who posed problems of administration. They may freely return to their former occupations in Tournaisis, Mortagne, and St. Amand. It is also made clear that the annual elections to the *Magistrat* will continue to be held in the usual way, and on the due date.

Sir Edward Poynings was well qualified to be the first Governor of English Tournai. As a young man he had been responsible for inspecting the defences of Calais and therefore was familiar with conditions in an outpost in a foreign country. In 1492 he had commanded a force sent to help Maximilian to put down a revolt of his subjects in the Low Countries. Two years later he was appointed Lord Deputy of Ireland at a time when a strong hand was needed there. During his time in Ireland he was faced by problems which had something in

[1] Hall, p. 565.   [2] SP 1/230, ff. 65–67b; *LP* i, 2319.

common with those which were to arise in Tournai; and he used his influence to make the administration of the country more dependent on the central government in Westminster, partly through 'Poynings' Law'. At the beginning of Henry VIII's reign he was ambassador in the Low Countries and was sent to recruit mercenaries there on the eve of the 1513 expedition. He served in the expedition in command of 500 men, one of the biggest single contingents in the King's ward. Thus the whole of his career fitted him for his new post. The only thing against him was his age. At fifty-four he was too old for the job, and moreover he did not enjoy the best of health during his term of office.

His formal commission does not survive, although it is referred to by Sir Richard Jerningham in 1517.[1] The appointment was made by Henry while he was still in Tournai, and perhaps no copy of the commission found its way back to London. The main surviving instrument recognizing his appointment is an Act of Parliament[2] which recites that his absence from England is 'to the common weal of the same realm profitable', and provides that all legal proceedings shall be 'utterly void and of none effect' so long as he holds the post of Governor of Tournai. Poynings served until February 1515. He may have found the strain of office too great, for early in that year he asked to be relieved of his charge, ostensibly so that he might make a pilgrimage to Rome. Henry agreed, and first proposed to replace him with Sir Robert Wingfield, then ambassador to the Emperor. He told Maximilian that Wingfield would make an admirable Governor, particularly because of his knowledge of French and his friendship with Margaret of Savoy and Charles.[3]

The proposal to appoint Wingfield fell through, however, and the choice fell on William Blount, fourth Lord Mountjoy, who must have been selected at very short notice. At round about forty (the exact date of his birth is not known) he was a younger man than Poynings, but he was not entirely without experience, having been for some years lieutenant of Hammes Castle in the Pale of Calais. He had also shared in the task of providing transports for the 1513 expedition, although he him-

---

[1] Cal. E I, f. 130; *LP* ii, 2902.   [2] 5 Henry VIII, c. 18.
[3] SP 1/10, f. 38; *LP* ii, 83.

self did not accompany it. He was the Queen's Chamberlain, and along with others of the Queen's servants was exempted from overseas service on this occasion to avoid depleting her household too much. He had studied under Erasmus in Paris and remained his firm friend in later years.

He received separate letters patent authorizing him to act as Governor[1] and *Bailli*[2] on 20 January 1515. The latter is almost exclusively concerned with his judicial functions, while the former mainly defines his duties and powers as commander of the garrison troops. The King, recognizing his 'prudence, honesty, industry, fidelity, integrity, ability and great experience', commits to him the full control over the inhabitants of Tournai and the Tournaisis, to whom he is to administer the oath of loyalty. He may raise forces for the defence of the city, examine and decide both civil and military causes among the soldiers, punish their crimes, if necessary by death, pardon offences, and issue safe-conducts. His commission as Governor does, however, provide for some non-military functions. He is to appoint a master of the mint (he was at this time himself Master of the Mint in London), and he may dismiss and replace unsatisfactory officials.

His term of office was not happy, nor was he much of a success. He claimed that he was heavily out of pocket, but could not cut down his expenses without damage 'to the King's honour and my poor honesty'.[3] He had been required to leave England at short notice at a time when his business affairs were in a mess, and he begged to be allowed to come home to put them in order. He would be able to tell the King and the Council 'of divers things concerning this city better far than I can do by writing'; and Sir Richard Whethill could act as Governor during his absence.[4] All this was of no avail. Leave of absence was not granted. However, the Governor kept up the attack. He told Henry that to do him service meant spending at least as much as he would do in England, and probably a good deal more.[5] There were, of course, compensations—he was able

---

[1] C 76/196, pt. 2, m. 6; Rymer, pp. 472–3; Hocquet (a), xl; *LP* ii, 41.
[2] C 76/194, m. 6; Rymer, pp. 387–8; *LP* i, 2617(22). (This document is dated 20 January 1514 in the French Roll of that year, but this must be a mistake.)
[3] SP 1/13, f. 39; *LP* ii, 1622.   [4] SP 1/13, f. 133; *LP* ii, 1860.
[5] Cal. E I, f. 103; *LP* ii, 1894.

to play host to his dear friend Erasmus[1]—but it needed steady encouragement from London to keep him in the post.[2] In September 1516 he reminded Wolsey that Henry had agreed that he should come home at Michaelmas or Hallowe'en. He was anxious to avail himself of this licence and asked who had been chosen to replace him. To forestall some of the arguments against his leaving he painted a rosy picture of the state of affairs in the city. The new citadel was well advanced, and so long as the watch kept on their toes there would be no real danger from enemy attack. It was vital that he should be in England before Hallowe'en; and if there was anything he could do for Wolsey he had simply to name it and it would be done.[3]

His unconcealed anxiety to return to England earned him the King's displeasure. On 22 November he received an immediate dispatch from his opposite number in Calais saying that Henry believed that he had either left Tournai or was on the point of leaving. A special messenger had therefore been sent to intercept him if he had already left, and to require him to return to his post forthwith 'all excuses laid apart'. Mountjoy was naturally much upset by the King's attitude, which he considered to be quite unjustified. He wrote to Wolsey: 'My lord, I assure you no greater grief can come to my heart than for to have any part of the King's displeasure; and thereto to be accounted so light, having so great a charge, so to leave it without knowing of the King's pleasure to whom I should commit it. And if I had been of that mind it had been pity that ever I should have seen England.'[4]

Mountjoy was still Governor at the beginning of 1517 and a note of despair began to creep into his letters. He begged Wolsey to ask the King to discharge him, or at least to allow him to come home on leave. He said once again that he had left his business affairs in the hands of friends who were handling them badly. In the long run he would become impoverished and therefore less well able to serve the King. Moreover, when he thought that Henry had approved his return he had sent all his household effects back to England. He was now living most uncomfortably and life was even more miserable than before.[5]

[1] LP ii, App. 24.   [2] SP 1/13, f. 157; LP ii, App. 25.
[3] SP 1/14, f. 19; LP ii, 2365.   [4] SP 1/14, ff. 106–7; LP ii, 2578.
[5] SP 1/14, ff. 211–12; LP ii, 2820.

This final plea seems to have been accepted, and early in 1517 he was replaced, not by Sir Richard Whethill, who had been his own suggestion, but by Sir Richard Jerningham. On 22 January he left Tournai, accompanied by his wife, who had loyally remained with him for the whole of his unhappy tour of duty.[1]

Jerningham had been captain of the guard at the beginning of the occupation. He was one of the large number of men who distinguished themselves in the 1513 campaign and were knighted by Henry in Tournai Cathedral when the King made his triumphal entry into the city. In April 1516 he was promoted to the important post of treasurer,[2] and having made a success of that was the obvious person to succeed Mountjoy. He was appointed by letter, which he considered to be inadequate, for he asked Wolsey to procure for him 'as large a commission' as his two predecessors had.[3] Nothing happened, however, and two months later he reminded Wolsey that he had written several times 'for to have commission and authority as well for the town as for the *bailliage* and as yet hath had none answer thereof'. It was being said in the town, the garrison, and the *bailliage* that as he had no formal commission he had no power; and this would certainly cause the people 'to give less regard unto such things as I shall do in the King's behalf'.[4] It is uncertain if he ever got his commissions, but on the whole he seems to have carried out his duties as Governor admirably, in particular when he was landed with the difficult job of evacuating the garrison and handing the town back to the French at the beginning of 1519.

At about the same time as Jerningham was made Governor, Dr. Richard Sampson, who had been fighting hard to get Wolsey accepted as Bishop of Tournai,[5] was appointed the King's 'procurator, attorney and representative'. He was given very great powers in this capacity, some of which may seem to impinge on those of the Governor (for example, 'to demand the reform of our state'); but it seems likely that Sampson's position was strengthened, not to enable him to compete with the Governor, or even to support him, but simply to facilitate his

[1] Cal. E I, f. 125; *LP* ii, 2825.   [2] SP 1/13, f. 120; *LP* ii, 1798.
[3] Cal. E I, f. 130; *LP* ii, 2902.   [4] SP 1/15, f. 77; *LP* ii, 3100.
[5] See Ch. VI below.

spiritual campaign against the French Bishop elect, who stood between Wolsey and the revenues of the see of Tournai.[1]

The Governor, the representative of the English Crown, was of course supreme. His commission left no doubt about that. The council of Englishmen over which he presided was the King's council. He was the commander-in-chief of the armed forces, that is the English garrison and the troops from the Low Countries who supplemented it, although for most purposes the marshal was the effective head of the forces. In his capacity of *Bailli* he was the apex of the judicial system, subject to appeals to the Court of Chancery. The day-to-day management of civic affairs, however, was mainly left to the four councils, although the Governor occasionally intervened on major questions. In 1516, for example, when it was feared that the city might be in for a siege, he ordered the councils to buy wheat, to be held as a reserve stock, which was done quickly, and, for once, without argument.[2]

The separation of the management of civic affairs from the other functions of government was one of the factors that militated against the integration of the city with the rest of Henry's dominions. The four councils carried on their business as they had always done, and they did their best to resist intervention by the Governor. They did not regard him as their ultimate authority, to whom difficult decisions had to be referred, but rather as the representative of a foreign power, with whom the decisions they had already taken had to be negotiated. The separate existence of the garrison had much the same effect. So long as the Grand'Place was thronged with foreign soldiers, the Tournaisiens, who for a generation had been responsible for their own defence, were constantly reminded that this was no longer so. It was virtually impossible for them to regard themselves as Henry's loyal subjects when their loyalty was guaranteed by a large force for which they were ineligible.

Although municipal government remained in the hands of the four councils, there had to be some contact with the Governor's council, if only for the sake of appearances. When the first municipal elections after the surrender of the city were

---

[1] C 76/197, m. 6; Rymer, p. 579; *LP* ii, 2770.
[2] Hocquet (a), xliii.

held in February 1514, the city fathers asked that the Governor and his colleagues should be present when the electors (the *éwardeurs*) were chosen (a process which took four hours). They were also invited to be present when the members of the councils themselves were elected. The chosen men were duly presented to the Governor and sworn in before him in the customary fashion. In Poynings' opinion 'they were all ancient men, and by all likelihood of good condition'. This was too optimistic, for in spite of many protestations of loyalty to the new regime the councils remained at heart 'good French'. The only important exception was Jean le Sellier, who was *prévôt* at this time. In his dispatch about the elections the Governor said that le Sellier deserved Henry's special favour, and asked Wolsey 'to hold your hand that the King may be good lord and consider the provost of this town for in my faith he hath well endeavoured him in every thing that I could desire him on the King's behalf sith the King's departing'.[1]

The council set up to advise the Governor was on the same lines as the council of Calais, and may have been modelled on it. The principal members were the marshal, who was the Governor's deputy; the treasurer or comptroller, who probably ranked equal with the marshal, except when the Governor was absent, when the marshal took precedence; and the porter, who kept the keys of the city and was generally responsible for security. The first marshal was Sir Anthony Oughtred, who had been in the King's ward in the 1513 expedition. He returned to England to take up the governorship of Berwick at the beginning of 1515,[2] and was briefly replaced by Sir Sampson Norton, who survived in office only a few days before he was chased out by the enraged soldiers.[3] He was replaced in turn by Sir Richard Whethill, one of the 'King's spears' in Calais, who had also served in the King's ward, but returned to his post in Calais at the end of the campaign. He was a simple, stolid, straightforward man—few of his contemporaries reveal their character in their letters with such engaging clarity—and he remained marshal until the end of the occupation.

The key post of treasurer was first occupied by Sir Robert Dymock, who had been in charge of the finances of the rear

---

[1] SP 1/7, f. 94; *LP* i, 2657.   [2] *LP* ii, 549.   [3] See Ch. III below.

ward in the 1513 expedition. He was followed at the beginning of 1515 by Sir Edward Bensted, treasurer-at-war in the north of England in 1512. Sir Richard Jerningham took over from Bensted in April 1516, and continued to act as treasurer for the remainder of the occupation, even after he became Governor. The porter for the greater part of the occupation was Sir John Tremayle, also a 'King's spear' in Calais, who had been knighted by Henry before he left Lille.[1]

The council members ran the risk of becoming forgotten men, and at one time or another all seem to have been worried that their absence from Court would count against them. One of the first things that Mountjoy did on arriving at Tournai was to send Lancaster Herald to England with a dispatch that included a long list of people to whom he was to be remembered. This was not simply a friendly greeting: it was an attempt to keep his name before influential men at home.[2] Their absence also made it difficult for the councillors to control their financial affairs. In March 1516 Mountjoy had to appeal to Wolsey 'to move the King for mine annuity in the Exchequer, which is resumed.[3] For my lord I assure you beside my daily business and attendance here I am at greater charge more than I may well away with. And less I may not do for the King's honour and my poor honesty.'[4] He repeated his plea two months later, this time on the ground that it would be a great discomfort to his friends, and presumably in particular the members of the council, to learn that he had lost any office or fee because of his service in Tournai; and the better to enlist Wolsey's sympathy he offered to do him any service within his power.[5] In another letter to the King about the same time he said 'divers of your garrison here call upon me for saving of their offices and annuities resumed at this late parliament,' and he stressed in particular that his own annuity should be continued.[6]

In 1515 Sir Richard Jerningham told Richard Sampson that if any man in England wanted his position in Tournai 'I pray God send it him' provided always that his replacement was worthy to serve the King.[7] Later he found himself in difficulty

[1] Harl. MS. 5177, f. 102; *LP* i, App. 26.
[2] SP 1/10, f. 51; *LP* ii, App. 3.   [3] i.e. withdrawn.
[4] SP 1/13, f. 39; *LP* ii, 1622.   [5] SP 1/13, f. 157; *LP* ii, App. 25.
[6] Cal. E I, f. 99; *LP* ii, 1855.   [7] SP 1/11, f. 144; *LP* ii, 1112.

as one of the Squires of the Body. He could not carry out his duties, since he was in Tournai, and Henry therefore proposed to replace him. Jerningham pointed out that he had paid 200 marks for the office and asked to be allowed to come to England to fill it, 'if the necessity be such that the room must needs be furnished'. He would rather be in London serving the King than in Tournai with wages of 1,000 marks a year.[1] Some time later he turned down a suggestion by Wolsey that he should visit England in the interests of his promotion, on the ground that the city was threatened by the French and his presence there was necessary.[2]

Sir Richard Whethill pleaded with Wolsey to ensure that his annuity of forty marks should not be stopped, and offered to do something in return for this service. 'If there be any thing you would have bought or bespoken in these parts for you according to your pleasure to the sum of twenty pounds, if it please you to send me your mind I shall buy or bespeak it, and send it unto your grace; and also shall be ready in any other thing or things that it shall please your grace to command me.'[3]

Whethill seems to have been particularly unfortunate. He had property in the Pale of Calais, where he lived before he moved to Tournai, and at the beginning of 1516 he told Wolsey that he and all the other King's tenants in the Guines area were in financial difficulty. He reckoned that the last year had cost him £100. His sub-tenants 'had lost all their beasts, besides other great losses, so that they were fain to borrow money to buy beasts to plough the land'. This meant that they were unable to pay any rent to Whethill; and when he pressed them for payment they said they would rather give up their farms—which would have meant an even greater loss to him.[4] It was hardly surprising, therefore, that Whethill should have been seriously worried about the danger of losing his annuity.

No Tournaisien was appointed a member of the council, in spite of the theory that the city had become part of the realm of England. Jean le Sellier worked very closely with the Governor and his colleagues, and enjoyed a great measure of their trust, and if it had been decided to add a Tournaisien to the council he would almost certainly have been chosen. Shortly after the

---

[1] SP 1/15, f. 77; *LP* ii, 3100. [2] SP 1/16, f. 147; *LP* ii, 3958.
[3] SP 1/12, f. 117; *LP* ii, 1437. [4] SP 1/12, f. 117; *LP* ii, 1437.

Earl of Worcester arrived in the city in 1515, he told Henry that, while le Sellier was 'undoubtedly your true and faithful subject, as far as we can perceive and understand', he had not made him privy to 'the secrecy of our charges'. Le Sellier was convinced that the garrison could not safely be reduced (no doubt he was at least partly thinking of his personal safety), and Worcester thought that if he discovered the purpose of his mission, which was to explore the possibility of running down the garrison, he would either go straight to the King to protest or leave Tournai for some other city. Worcester proposed that le Sellier should be 'put in some authority'; but this did not mean that he should become a council member.[1] Had the occupation lasted indefinitely, some Tournaisien must have been appointed to the council; but five years was too short for the necessary mutual trust to develop.[2]

Nevertheless, although no Tournaisien ever became a member of the King's council in the city, at least on one occasion there were Tournaisien members of Parliament in Westminster. The first indication that it had been decided to extend parliamentary representation to the conquered city is in a letter from Henry to the citizens written from Windsor on 18 November, shortly after his return to England. He is worried about the fact that many people are leaving Tournai despite his assurances that they will be well treated under English rule; and in particular he is upset by a rumour that he means to hand the city over to some other prince. They will learn that this is quite without foundation from the deputies whom they are to send over to represent them in the next Parliament, which will begin after Christmas.[3] It is clear from this letter that the decision to invite representatives from Tournai had been taken some time earlier, and the chances are that Henry issued the invitation while he was still in Tournai and still believed that it would be possible to integrate the city with the rest of his dominions. The four councils were given the job of choosing the representatives

---

[1] Cal. E I, f. 60 b; *LP* ii, 820.

[2] Some royal offices, however, went to local people. Allard Bentinck, steward of Margaret of Savoy's household, was appointed receiver at her request (SP 1/14, ff. 159–60; *LP* ii, 2686). The keepership of the seal royal went to a Tournaisien; and the '*tabellions* and notaries royal' were also Tournaisiens (Cal. D VI, f. 98 b; *LP* i, 2767 (2)).

[3] Hocquet (a), xxvii; *LP* i, 2450.

and found it difficult. No conclusion was reached at a meeting on 20 December, and the discussion had to be resumed the following day.[1]

Deputies were eventually selected, however, and they turned up at the session of Parliament which ran from 23 January to 4 March. It is recorded on 26 February 1514 that the representatives of Tournai attending the Parliament at Westminster have drawn attention to problems in the administration of justice in the city consequent on the substitution of the English Crown for the French, and that provision has been made for their solution.[2] While the session was in progress a number of other matters were settled—the establishment of a tribunal of five judges in Tournai,[3] provisions about trading with England,[4] the restoration of the arrangement whereby the city was entitled to requisition one-sixth of the grain entering by the river Scheldt (to be used as a stockpile),[5] and the cancellation of certain payments due to people resident in territories hostile to England.[6] The session also passed 'An act concerning ministration of justice in the city of Tournai',[7] on which the city's representatives must have had a good deal to say while they were in London.

We are indebted to Dr. Richard Sampson, Wolsey's vicar general at Tournai, for the name of one of the city's members—Jean le Sellier, the principal collaborator. This is an interesting choice, and the fact that it took the four councils two days to make it suggests that it may also have been difficult, and possibly even one that was influenced by the Governor. There is no record of the name of the other member—there were at least two. The words used by Sampson, who says that le Sellier 'was in England at the Parliament, for Tournai', seem to suggest that the representatives from Tournai were regarded as ordinary members of Parliament.[8]

It does not appear that representatives from Tournai attended any further sessions, perhaps because Henry's dream of

---

[1] Hocquet (a), xxviii; *LP* i, 2520.
[2] PRO 31/8/144, f. 239; Hocquet (a), xxix; *LP* i, 2676(2).
[3] PRO 31/8/144, f. 237; Hocquet (a), xxx; *LP* i, 2676(1).
[4] PRO 31/8/144, f. 243; Hocquet (a), xxxii; *LP* i, 2728.
[5] Hocquet (a), xxxi; *LP* i, 2676(3).
[6] PRO 31/8/144, f. 245; Hocquet (a), xxxiii; *LP* i, 2735.
[7] 5 Henry VIII, c. 1.   [8] Galba D V, f. 366.

integrating the city with England quickly faded. Had the municipal authorities given the Governor their whole-hearted co-operation, and been prepared to work against the interests of France, the seed of parliamentary representation might have germinated and flourished; but in the event it was probably written off as a hopeless failure. Indeed, it may have been seen to be potentially dangerous. So long as the Tournaisiens were for all practical purposes French, and hostile to the English regime, it might seem to be the height of folly to welcome them into the bosom of Parliament.[1]

In spite of the fact that the Governor's commission was wide-ranging it was not unusual for relatively unimportant matters to be decided in England by the King, or in the King's name. Further, the Governor's position was sometimes undermined by the reversal of sensible decisions which had been arrived at after due debate in his council. On one occasion Henry appointed a certain Hacheman to be keeper of the seal of the *bailliage*. Mountjoy remonstrated and pointed out that Poynings had given this post to 'a learned man of this town' who was well equipped for it and was still in office. Henry's man was a yeoman of the guard who had 'neither learning nor great language', the latter a serious deficiency in a bilingual community. To be fair to both parties the Governor decided to ask them to bring their grants 'into the court', where it would be determined which had the better title. He assumed that Henry would agree with this procedure.[2]

The encouragement which the government in England gave to direct discussion between the civic authorities and the King and Council also weakened the authority of the Governor. He often had no idea where he stood, and the citizens, realizing that they had the ear of the King and his immediate advisers, felt that their own position was much strengthened. This was particularly true in the early years of the occupation while

---

[1] These paragraphs are based on my note 'Parliamentary representation of Tournai', *EHR* lxxxiii, pp. 775–6. A letter from Mountjoy to the King in May 1516 says 'for setting up of the parliament here [it is] a thing very necessary, and that folks call for . . .'. It seems likely, however, that he had in mind the *Cour de Parlement*, and not an extension of the English Parliament (Cal. E I, f. 99 b; *LP* ii, 1855).

[2] Cal. D VI, f. 305; *LP* ii, 701.

Henry still had some benevolent feelings towards his new subjects.

The extent to which the Governor was required to depend on instructions from England was probably the greatest single weakness in the administration of Tournai during the occupation. There was a strong case for giving him a good deal of autonomy, if only because of the difficulty of communication. This is a recurrent theme. There were frequent complaints about serious and damaging delay in replying to correspondence. The problem was not confined to Tournai. The English ambassadors Knight, Wingfield, and Spinelly, writing from Malines in April 1514, claimed that their mission was hampered by poor communications and asked that the posts should be doubled.[1] Nor was it simply a question of distance and the vagaries of wind and weather. The natural hazards of the Channel crossing were supplemented by the activities of pirates. Sir Thomas Lovell, writing from Calais in 1514, explained that his letters for London had been delayed because the ship carrying them had been chased back into Calais Roads by French and Scottish pirates.[2]

Letters between London and Tournai took on the average about ten days;[3] and if the Council spent another ten days in arriving at a decision it meant that the Governor might have to wait a month to get a reply on any question of policy. In practice, however, it took the Council—or Wolsey himself—a good deal longer to consider most matters put to them. In April 1515 Mountjoy told Wolsey that he had twice asked 'to be advertised of the King's pleasure of divers other causes concerning my charge, and yet I have none answer'.[4] Shortly afterwards the Earl of Worcester complained that he was awaiting replies to his last four letters, and added rather desperately 'I am in good hope to have (a reply) of this with the help of God!'[5] Two months later he said that he and his fellows thought it a very long time since they had received instructions from the King or Wolsey.[6] In the following year things were no better.

---

[1] SP 1/7, f. 153; *LP* i, 2782.   [2] SP 1/8, f. 159; *LP* i, 3087.

[3] e.g. SP 1/11, ff. 67, 77; 1/15, f. 38. The time taken could, however, be as little as five days (Cal. E I, f. 61; *LP* ii, 820); and on at least one occasion three days (SP 1/13, f. 227; *LP* ii, 2097).

[4] SP 1/10, f. 150; *LP* ii, 326.   [5] SP 1/11, f. 66; *LP* ii, 857.

[6] Cal. D VI, f. 279 b; *LP* ii, 1197.

Mountjoy said that 'as in other causes which I wrote for by Richmond[1] and since, for the citadel making, and other things, as yet I hear no word. I trust I shall do shortly.'[2] It was not only matters of state that were handled dilatorily. Sir Richard Jerningham wrote to Henry in 1515 saying that he had sent him four letters in the last six weeks, 'but of the same letters, to the writing hereof, I have had none answer'. He added that he was impatiently awaiting an answer to a letter telling the King that he had found some good tilting horses, 'but I will not meddle with them till I may know your pleasure'.[3] Wolsey's man, Richard Hansard, the under-marshal, fared no better. He told his master 'the especial cause of my writing to you at this time is letting your lordship to wit I have written divers letters to you of the which I never heard word again.'[4] When Jerningham became Governor the trouble persisted. He besought Wolsey 'in the most humble wise that I can that I may hear more often from your Grace of such things as I write . . . for lack of the same hath been great discomfort to me and all the council here'. This was all the more disappointing as Wolsey had promised that he would mend his ways when they had last met in London.[5]

At first the council in Tournai seems to have left the administration of the garrison, or at least the discussion of policy with Westminster, very much to the Governor. This may have been due to Poynings' long experience and strength of character. After his resignation, however, the picture changes. Dispatches are as a rule written in the name of the council as a whole, and are signed by several—sometimes all—of the leading members. An occasional dispatch dictated by the Governor is signed by other members of the council, suggesting that it was desirable to carry the whole council on matters of policy. Towards the end of the occupation we find that William Pawne, who was in charge of the King's works, and even the under-marshal Richard Hansard, frequently add their signatures. They were both intimately concerned with the affairs of the garrison. Richard Sampson, however, also took part in the deliberations of the council when he was in Tournai, although he had no

[1] i.e. Richmond Herald.   [2] SP 1/13, f. 39; *LP* ii, 1622.
[3] SP 1/10, f. 58; *LP* ii, 166.   [4] SP 1/8, f. 145; *LP* i, 3058.
[5] SP 1/15, f. 73 b; *LP* ii, 3098.

responsibilities for the garrison; but as Wolsey's vicar general, and later as the King's procurator, he had a special position, although it seems that he was appointed to the council on the Governor's own authority.[1]

It is surprising how many minor matters were dealt with by the King, although probably most of the time it was no more than a question of signing at the top of a document approved by Wolsey. For example, the King formally authorized Sir Richard Jerningham to pay 'unto our trusty and well-beloved John Russell one of our spears' £6. 13s. 4d. for the construction of a tilt-yard in Tournai[2]—surely something that could have been left to the Governor. There are many examples of transactions which do not seem important enough to necessitate the King's signature.

Sometimes an appointment would be made by the King for a special purpose. In November 1515 the council in Tournai were informed that Christopher Mores had been appointed 'to do unto us service as well within this our realm as elsewhere'. The Governor was ordered to ensure that Mores, who was a gunner quartermaster, should be allowed to come and go freely with all his bag and baggage, so long as he found a replacement to cover his absences from his post. It is not clear what special service was expected of Mores, or why he should be given such freedom of movement, but he was probably a spy. Whatever the nature of his special task it cannot have been good for discipline for a gunner quartermaster to carry a licence signed by the King to come and go as he saw fit, and to be responsible to the King rather than to the Governor in Tournai.[3]

There were, of course, some matters clearly within the royal prerogative which could not be determined by the Governor. The King alone could decide how lands forfeited within Tournai and the Tournaisis were to be disposed of. It was through Henry's 'especial and abundant grace' that the attainted property of Jean d'Étables and Jean de Malines was allocated to the three Knyvett brothers.[4] When Jacques de Moye, seigneur of Chin in the Tournaisis, had his estate confiscated for refusing to take the oath of loyalty and for joining forces with the French, it was Henry who awarded it to John

[1] SP 1/10, f. 51; *LP* ii, App. 3.   [2] C 82/434 $\frac{8}{18}$; *LP* ii, 1907.
[3] C 82/426 $\frac{7}{237}$; *LP* ii, 1210.   [4] PRO 31/8/144, f. 255; *LP* ii, 554.

Joiner, Richmond Herald, in recognition of his long and faithful service.[1] Again it was the King who gave John Russell land in Tournai forfeited by the Dame de Vendôme.[2] On the other hand there were some offices which the Governor claimed to be in his gift, one of which was the receivership of the city.[3]

The Earl of Worcester was sent on an embassy to Tournai in the middle of 1515, and remained in the city for several months. The purpose of his mission was to negotiate a radical change in the relationship between the Governor and his council and the civic authorities. This was clearly something that the Governor could not have handled on his own, partly because he did not have the time, and partly because he was too close to the problems which had to be examined to take a balanced view of them. Worcester's mission was not another example of unwise interference in the administration of the city, but a sensible intervention with the laudable objective of reducing the cost to the English exchequer of holding Tournai. Mountjoy, Sampson, Jerningham, Bensted, and Whethill were also named as ambassadors in Worcester's commission, which meant not only that he had the benefit of their advice but also that their status in the eyes of the Tournaisiens was not impaired by the arrival in their midst of Henry's special representative.[4]

It was not long before Worcester became disenchanted with Tournai. He had been there only a week or two when he told Wolsey that he had written to the King beseeching him to be 'so good and gracious lord' as to allow him to return home. 'For I see no matter here to do but my lord's lieutenant here and a doctor [i.e. of laws] with him may do as well or better than I. . . .' He assured Wolsey that if he saw the slightest chance of doing the King 'honour or acceptable service' it would be to his great joy and comfort, regardless of the pain and cost that he should suffer; but as it was he saw no hope of serving the King.[5] Shortly afterwards, however, he came to accept that there was a job to be done, 'for here is a multitude which undiscreetly do order themselves, whereof we be sorry; but to the appeasing and reforming thereof to our power we will endeavour ourselves';[6]

[1] C 76/197, m. 13; *LP* ii, 1570.   [2] C 76/198, m. 6; *LP* ii, 2982.
[3] Cal. E I, f. 144; *LP* ii, 3099.   [4] C 76/197, m. 22; *LP* ii, 980.
[5] SP 1/11, f. 66; *LP* ii, 857.   [6] SP 1/11, f. 86; *LP* ii, 917.

and in fact it was many months before he was allowed to escape
from Tournai. When he did, his original assessment proved
right. He had achieved virtually nothing.[1]

Under the surrender treaty the citizens agreed to transfer to
Henry the annual payment of 6,000 *livres tournois* which they
were accustomed to make to France, to pay him an additional
4,000 *livres* a year for ten years, and to pay a lump sum of
50,000 gold crowns. They could hardly have settled for less
when Henry's 'twelve apostles' and a multitude of other siege
guns were trained on their walls, but when they tried to make
the first payment they ran into difficulty. The new annual
tribute—only £430—was easy enough. It was regularly paid
for the first fourteen quarters, and thereafter was diverted, with
the agreement of the English authorities, to compensate householders whose property had been demolished to make way for
the new citadel.[2] But the 50,000 crowns, which was due
immediately after the surrender, was troublesome, as it was
equivalent to about £10,000.[3]

Tournai had been going through a difficult period, and the
municipal coffers were empty—which the citizens who signed
the surrender agreement must have known. A few years earlier,
in spite of the fact that it was to all outward appearances prosperous, the city had faced bankruptcy. The civic authorities had
two main sources of revenue: straightforward taxation, for
example on the principal manufactures; and the sale of annuities, the annual payments on which were made out of revenue
from ordinary taxes. The sale of annuities was a very tempting
device, for it enabled the municipality to raise substantial sums
at short notice, and to leave it to their successors in office to
find the money to meet the annual payments to the annuitants.
For this reason it was subject to a very close scrutiny by the
central government, and it was necessary to get the King's
express authority before this method of financing was adopted.

A few years before Henry took over the city a royal commission had been sent by Louis XII to examine its finances,

---

[1] See Chs. III and IV below.
[2] Cal. D VI, ff. 96–7; Rymer, pp. 377–8; *LP* ii, 4449.
[3] In fact the sum paid was exactly £10,000 (E 36/256, p. 383; *LP* ii, 1512).

and had found that although the position was serious, it was showing some sign of improvement. The annual deficit on account of annuities had been reduced from 17,000 francs to 4,000; and the arrears had fallen from 70,000 francs to 20,000. This was considered good enough to justify the raising of further sums through annuities, but Louis made it clear that the money raised must be devoted to paying off earlier annuities, and to nothing else.[1] In 1513, however, the coffers were empty again.

The ink on the surrender treaty was scarcely dry before the citizens were claiming that they could not find even part of the sums due; and they sought the King's permission to raise the money by selling annuities. Henry, no doubt anxious to see some financial return for the enormously costly campaign that had entrapped him in Tournai, readily agreed. It might not be sound financial policy to squeeze the last crown out of the burgesses, and to mortage the future prosperity of the city, but these were secondary considerations. The King commanded the municipal authorities to sell annuities in the accustomed way at the best price they could get; and he authorized them to provide for the resultant annual payments by imposing new taxes on imports into Tournai of such foodstuffs and merchandise as they deemed appropriate, and in the best form and manner that they could devise. The citizens were also granted permission to impose taxes to defray the great expense to which they had been put on the occasion of the King's 'joyous entry' into the city.[2] Even so, it took some little time to raise the 50,000 crowns, and Henry tried to ease the financial position of the citizens (at the same time striking a small economic blow at the French) by absolving them from paying annuities due to people resident in hostile territory.[3] It was not until June 1514, however, that Michel Joseph and Michel Cambry, acting as agents for the city, paid over the 50,000 crowns to the treasurer, Sir Robert Dymock, partly in cash and partly in silver plate, as they were allowed to do under the treaty.[4]

The maladministration which had ruined the city's finances in the first decade of the century, and which was unfavourably

[1] *Ordonnances*, pp. 152–3.   [2] PRO 31/8/144, f. 249; *LP* i, 2303.
[3] C 82/402 $\frac{5}{464}$; Hocquet (a), xxxiii; *Ordonnances*, pp. 288–9; *LP* i, 2735.
[4] PRO 31/8/144, f. 251; Hocquet (a), xxiv; *LP* i, 2984.

commented on in 1510 by Louis XII's commissioners,[1] persisted during the occupation; but, since the civic authorities were left in charge of the ordinary administration of the city, there was little that the Governor and his council could do beyond observing what went on and reporting the facts to Westminster. The citizens regularly pleaded poverty when they were asked to make an increased contribution to administration or defence, which the English found exasperating. In January 1517 the Governor was consulted by the King about a long memorandum which the city had submitted to him; and in commenting on it Mountjoy took the opportunity of venting a good deal of spleen about the financial performance of the civic authorities.

He claimed indignantly that the 'poverty and indigence' of the town resulted not from its capture by Henry nor even from its payments to the Duke of Burgundy under its treaty with him —at least *that* wound had been healed long ago—but simply from the shameful corruption of the leading men of the city. There had been great competition for positions of authority in the municipal government, and rival factions had bribed the common people to support their candidates. From time to time the offenders had been prosecuted, some of them being executed and others banished (perhaps Mountjoy had in mind Nicolas de St. Genois),[2] but 'as yet unto this present they have not lost all their course accustomed'. In particular, they were on the weakest possible ground in complaining about the 6,000 *livres tournois* which they paid Henry. This was no novelty, but a well-established payment.[3]

Mountjoy then goes on to refer to the 'grace and grant obtained by them to sell life rents upon the said town' to raise the money to pay the 50,000 crowns. The money had been raised all right, but no proper arrangements had been made to pay the annuities to which people were entitled. The civic authorities had paid to some 'a little and a little by small portions' out of the new taxes which they had been allowed to impose, in particular a levy on 'the great mills for the brewers'. The implication was that, once the capital sum had been raised

---

[1] They considered that the city had come near to bankruptcy, 'tant par les guerres comme aussi par les mauvais gouvernemens d'aulcuns de ladite ville' (*Ordonnances*, p. 152).
[2] See below, p. 62.   [3] SP 1/14, ff. 238–238 b; *LP* ii, 2858.

and paid over to Henry, a good deal of the money to pay the annuitants had found its way into the pockets of the municipal authorities. Apart from this, their financial position had been considerably improved, first by the departure of large numbers who had refused to remain in Tournai under English rule, and had thereby forfeited their annuities; and second by heavy mortality due to the plague. So many people having life rents on the town had died that the civic treasury was reckoned to have had a windfall of 3,000 francs a year through 'dead rents' —which must mean 'dead rents' over and above the normal actuarial expectations of the day. It was significant that the town's 'principal farmers and receivers' were even more prosperous than they had been before the capitulation.[1]

The truth of the matter, according to Mountjoy, was that, although the 50,000 crowns were duly raised, and the appropriate 'letters of rent' (i.e. annuities) prepared and signed on behalf of the city, the letters were 'revoked, cancelled, annulled, or burned'. This happened even to annuities bought by the richest citizens, who had spared no effort that they might 'come through corruption to have their said letters sealed'. Nevertheless, a number of letters were issued in favour of members of a delegation from the four councils 'to defray their voyage oversea' before they left for London. The annual value of these annuities was over £120. The implication of Mountjoy's summing-up is that there was one law for the civic authorities, and another for everyone else; and he urged that there should be a 'visitation' to investigate the city's finances.[2]

Every military occupation breeds its collaborators. Indeed, this may be one of society's defence mechanisms. The collaborator provides a focal point for opportunists willing to burn their boats and throw their lot in with the new regime. More important, he encourages those loyal to the old regime to cling more strongly to their loyalty. He is a necessary evil, paradoxically hated by his less opportunist fellows, although perhaps he deserves their gratitude for strengthening their resolution.

Jean le Sellier was Tournai's principal collaborator during the occupation. He was one of the *prévôts* at the time of the surrender and seems to have had no hesitation in siding with the

<hr />

[1] SP 1/14, ff. 239–239 b; *LP* ii, 2858. [2] SP 1/14, f. 241 b; *LP* ii, 2858.

conquerors right from the start. He took the gamble that all collaborators take, but he had the satisfaction of knowing that the English were grateful for his help and were prepared to stand by him in time of need. When the reduction of the size of the garrison was being examined in 1515, and the Earl of Worcester sought instructions from the King about helping the foreign troops who would lose their jobs, he also dealt with le Sellier's position, pointing out that he would be in great danger when he no longer had the complete protection of the occupying forces.[1] In fact, le Sellier had his due reward when he was made a Gentleman Usher of the Chamber; and in 1516, 'in consideration of the good service to us heretofore done . . . and that hereafter he intendeth to do', Henry awarded him a pension of £20 a year.[2]

In January 1516, when le Sellier carried a dispatch from Tournai to England, Richard Sampson sang his praises to Wolsey, saying that he was anxious to serve Wolsey at all times and was, indeed, the only helpful person in the whole of Tournai and the Tournaisis. Everyone else was convinced that the city would shortly return to France, and little desired 'to do service or pleasure either to the King's highness, your Grace, or any other nobleman of England. What mind they shall have for the time to come, God knoweth!' Every Tournaisien knew that le Sellier was faithful to Henry, and there was nothing more odious to them than to see him in the street. Sampson thought it right that Wolsey should know of his 'good both mind and deeds', so that he would treat him well when he came to England.[3]

Sir Richard Jerningham echoed Sampson's assessment when he later sent le Sellier to Wolsey to 'commune with him of the secrets of Tournai and Tournaisis, as well of the spirituality as of the temporality'. What he had to say would be of great value and Wolsey need have no hesitation in trusting him, 'for hitherto I have always found him the best Englishman that is born within Tournai, wherefore he is not a little hated among the Tournaisiens'.[4] Early in 1517, when le Sellier was going on another trip to England, Mountjoy was full of praise for him. He said he was 'a faithful and diligent servant to the King, and

---

[1] SP 1/11, f. 77; *LP* ii, 891. [2] C 82/435 -⁸⁄₅₇-; *LP* ii, 2091.
[3] SP 1/12, f. 84; *LP* ii, 1411. [4] SP 1/12, f. 150; *LP* ii, 1499.

informeth me in many causes for the King's honour and profit, full like a true man'.[1] The Tournaisien did his best to be all things to all men. He expressed profound regret when Poynings resigned; but this did not deter him from expressing equally profound satisfaction at the appointment of Mountjoy, whom he had met in England. At the same time he said that Allard Bentinck, Margaret of Savoy's steward, who had been made receiver of the annual tribute which the city paid Henry, was useless; and hinted that he himself would do the job much better.[2]

Although le Sellier was cordially detested by the great majority of his fellow-citizens, not many of them were prepared to risk their lives in an attempt to overthrow the English forces in the city. Only one such attempt was made during the occupation; and little is known about it except that it failed.[3] Indeed, it was doomed to failure from the outset, because of the foresight of Sir Edward Poynings. The ringleaders were Jean d'Étables (who had made his way through the besiegers' lines in 1513 to try to persuade Louis XII to raise the siege) and Jean de Malines. That the Governor's council had ample warning of the conspiracy was due to the help of the second main collaborator, who was not hated by his fellow-citizens simply because they were satisfied that his loyalty was above suspicion.

Poynings had realized that even if he was able to keep a firm grip on the city there remained the danger that the citizens who had refused to take the oath of loyalty to Henry, and who had gone to Paris, might seek to organize an assault with the support of the French government. He and his men might then find themselves caught between two fires, for it was unlikely that the Tournaisiens inside the city would remain passive if their friends were outside the walls with a substantial body of French troops. An intelligence report records that in April 1515 (after Poynings had handed over to Mountjoy) the people of Tournai were complaining that they were being treated like dogs by the English, and suggests that they were likely to avenge

---

[1] SP 1/14, ff. 211–12; *LP* ii, 2820.   [2] Cal. D VI, f. 315; *LP* ii, 150.
[3] As soon as he arrived in Tournai Mountjoy expressed alarm to Henry about the large quantity of armour and weapons in the hands of the citizens, some of which they had bought from English soldiers who had been discharged (Cal. E I, f. 44 b; *LP* ii, 148).

themselves by some trick if they were not carefully watched.[1]
Poynings was a man of great resource, however. Not only did he
watch the citizens carefully but he contrived to plant an agent
at the French Court to keep him informed about the intentions
of the citizens who had fled to Paris.

He selected Nicolas de St. Genois, 'a man of good substance',
as he explained to Henry, 'who hath great authority and rule in
this your city'. This de St. Genois was admirably qualified for
the job. At one time or another he had held most of the municipal offices—*juré, éwardeur, second prévôt*, and *grand prévôt*. He was
a man of action, for in 1501, during his term of office as *grand
prévôt*, he captured the town of St. Amand from the Burgundians. He was also a convicted criminal, having been sentenced
to perpetual banishment for embezzling 40,000 florins from the
city treasury. He must have had a plausible tongue, for in 1513
he was back in Tournai, again enjoying the full support of the
citizens. Poynings summed him up quickly. He arranged that
he should be banished for a second time, on a trumped-up
charge 'whereof the Frenchmen have the more confidence in
him', and that he should find his way to the French Court, full
of assumed hatred for the English. He was welcomed by the
French, who discussed with him their plans for the recovery of
Tournai. The Governor, in reporting these facts to Henry,
ventured to add: 'under correction, I think it expedient both in
war and in peace that your Grace have such one in the French
King's Court.'[2]

Poynings' scheme paid off, and several times during the first
half of 1514 he had reports from Paris which he sent on to the
King. By far the most important came in June. It is in French,
addressed to 'Colart' (the code name for Poynings), and in
addition to reporting matters of current interest says that 'a plot
to surprise Tournai' had been taken up by the father of the
Bishop elect of Tournai (the vice-president of the *Cour de Parlement*), and discussed by him with the Bishop of Paris and 'other
governors of France'. The plan was to send companies of
infantry and cavalry to the city, where the infantry would try to
gain access by means of boats secretly assembled on the river
Scheldt (which flowed through the middle of Tournai), while
the cavalry made a diversionary attack on another part of the

---

[1] Vit. B II, f. 155; *LP* ii, 399.   [2] SP 1/8, ff. 139, 140; *LP* i, 3025, 3026.

town. De St. Genois was himself asked to show the plan to Louis, who suggested that it should be deferred until August.[1] It seems likely that the plan crystallized during the next month and that Poynings was kept fully informed, for in September he suddenly arrested a number of men in Tournai, presumably when their guilt was fully established but before they had been able to make a move against the garrison. He wrote at the same time to Margaret of Savoy, telling her about the attempt to recapture the city, and claiming that the conspirators had intended to use Tournai as a base against Hainaut 'and other countries belonging to the Archduke'. Some of the ringleaders were supposed to be at Lille and Mons, and he asked Margaret to see that they were arrested.[2] Poynings must surely have reported to Henry the failure of the attempted coup, if only to demonstrate the value of his agent in Paris, but no copy of his dispatch survives. Indeed, the next reference to the conspiracy comes six months after Mountjoy had replaced Poynings as Governor. Mountjoy said in a letter to the King that before his predecessor had left he had handed him the confessions of certain prisoners, who had been detained ever since the rebellion organized by Jean d'Étables and Jean de Malines, in which the details of the conspiracy were fully recorded. This was known to the conspirators, and those still in France 'durst not return hither by no means as long as Sir Edward Poynings was here'.

After the change of Governor, however, one of them, a brewer called Arnold Beaufitz, decided to take a chance and return to Tournai, 'thinking as we suppose, that your lieutenant now had no knowledge neither of his person nor of his conspiracy'. He was promptly seized and thrown into prison, where he was 'examined divers and sundry times'. He revealed the names of many more fellow-conspirators who were still in the town, some of whom were also arrested; but Mountjoy concluded that 'if all the other should be taken which be accused we think a great rumour [i.e. disturbance] should follow, and no good, seeing that it is a matter past and the chief doers thereof be fled.[3]'

The only course was to banish the principal offenders (it was

[1] Cal. E I, f. 26; *LP* i, 3004.   [2] Le Glay, i, p. 585; *LP* i, 3258.
[3] Cal. E I, ff. 62–3; *LP* ii, 824.

too dangerous to sentence them to death) and pardon the rest; but Mountjoy promised that he would not extend the King's pardon until he was satisfied that the offenders would 'conform in such causes as they had to be treated with in Wolsey's behalf' —a circumlocution which meant that he would blackmail influential citizens into supporting Wolsey's claim to the bishopric of Tournai in return for their freedom.[1]

The Governor's advice was accepted and the pardon was signed by the King on 1 October 1515. It rehearses how the offenders had taken the oath of loyalty to their new sovereign along with all the other inhabitants, and how they subsequently broke their oath by meeting secretly with the King's enemies and plotting against his noble person. They departed from the city to carry out their plans, and appealed to others of the inhabitants to join them in their conspiracy. With God's help (in the circumstances credit could hardly be given to Sir Edward Poynings), the plot has been discovered and the guilty have been duly prosecuted and sentenced. Some have been banished from the King's dominions and their property confiscated. Others have been thrown into prison, where, unless they are spared by the King's grace and mercy, they may end their days in misery. Henry, however, wishing to be merciful rather than to insist that justice should be done, and in the hope that the people of Tournai will henceforth prove to be good and faithful subjects, has decided to remit all bodily and pecuniary penalties incurred by the conspirators; and he has imposed perpetual silence on his Governor and all future Governors with regard to their recent offences. He commands his *Bailli* to allow those concerned to take advantage of his gracious clemency, to set at liberty all who have been imprisoned, and to restore all confiscated property.

There remained one problem. How could they let it be known to the French that de St. Genois, who was still in Paris, was supposed to be guilty, without actually subjecting him to the penalties which the principal conspirators suffered? If he was not clearly treated as an offender, the French would become suspicious, and his position would be very vulnerable. Therefore, for the benfit of the French authorities, he was formally excluded from the King's pardon, along with Jean de Malines

---

[1] Cal. E I, f. 64 b; *LP* ii, 825.

and Jean d'Étables. It was no doubt hoped that the details of the pardon, which must have been widely publicized in Tournai and the neighbouring towns, would reach Paris, and there be regarded as a further guarantee of de St. Genois's loyalty to the French cause.[1]

His loyalty to the English cause was hardly likely to persist, however, if his property was actually confiscated; and when Henry wrote to the municipal authorities, saying that the 'terres, possessions, rentes, meubles, debtes et biens' of d'Étables and de Malines were forfeit, he made no reference to de St. Genois.[2] Equally, when Mountjoy wrote to London on the same matter he referred to the confiscation of the property of d'Étables and de Malines, but the name of de St. Genois does not appear in his letter.[3] The property of the others was awarded to Christopher, James, and Anthony Knyvett in consideration of their good service in France and elsewhere; and it was no doubt hoped that the fact that de St. Genois had got off scot free would not be noticed in Paris.[4] In fact this seems improbable, for it was very easy for the French to keep their ears to the ground in Tournai. When Arnold Beaufitz was being examined he revealed that one of the French King's spies had visited him in Tournai.[5] There must have been many others, for there was no language problem and a Frenchman from Paris could no doubt easily pass himself off as a Tournaisien. There is no record, however, that Henry's stratagem was seen through by the French authorities.

Success in dealing with the aftermath of the conspiracy filled Mountjoy with confidence, although the real credit belonged to Poynings. When there were rumours of trouble in 1516, Wolsey urged that all arms held by the citizens should be impounded, but Mountjoy would not agree to what he now deemed a panic measure, in spite of his earlier alarm on this subject.[6] Although

---

[1] C 76/197, m. 20; Hocquet (a), xxxix; Rymer, p. 517; SP 1/11, f. 116; *LP* ii, 978.
[2] PRO 31/8/144, f. 255; Hocquet (a), xxxvii; *LP* ii, 534.
[3] Cal. E I. f. 83; *LP* ii, 1621.   [4] C 76/197, m. 12; *LP* ii, 1028.
[5] Cal. E I f. 62 b; *LP* ii, 824. This man was supposed to be bound for Scotland, and Mountjoy therefore considered that Henry should 'be advertised of his demeanour and to have tokens of his person'. He had a good sum of money in a bank at Bruges, 'and though his apparel be but base here, whereby he is nothing esteemed, yet being at Paris he goeth well be seen' (ibid. f. 63).
[6] See p. 61 n. above.

the King had ordered that he should 'take from the said inhabitants all their harness and habiliments of war, whereby we shall be out of danger of them if they intend anything prejudicial unto the city', he did no more than take a census, 'showing unto them that we would know in what a readiness they were to serve the King if need were'. This brought to light 600 habergeons,[1] 80 cross-bows, and 65 hand-guns—too few to worry about. If Henry insisted that they should be gathered in, it could be done, but it would cause a great disturbance. Indeed, it would be embarrassing, since the census had ostensibly been intended to measure the help the citizens could provide rather than their strength as a potential enemy. However, as an added precaution the Governor inspected the 'artillery house' where the public store of weapons was kept. He rated it 'no great thing'. It had strong doors and locks, however, to which four of the *Chefs de la Loi* had keys, and Mountjoy decided (rather belatedly, for he had been in office for more than eighteen months) that he should now have his own key and 'be the fifth with them'.[2]

---

[1] Sleeveless coat of mail.
[2] Cal. E I, ff. 115–16; Strype, no. 6; *LP* ii, 2353.

III · THE DEFENCE OF THE CITY

THE magnitude of the commitment that Henry had accidentally and foolishly undertaken is witnessed by the fact that both Calais and Berwick—vital frontier towns —were held with fewer than a thousand men each. The initial garrison in Tournai had 5,000 men, of whom 1,000 were expensive cavalry. It may be argued in the King's defence that he planned to invade France again in 1514, and that it would have been useful to have a substantial contingent in Europe which would join him on his return; but even from this point of view the occupation was an absurd luxury. It would have been far cheaper to pay off the army during the winter months in the usual way; and in any case it would have been impracticable to withdraw a large number of troops to join the new invasion army. The citizens, or at least the lower orders, would have lost no time in joyfully falling upon the depleted garrison and seeking to reclaim the city for France.

Part of the initial forces left to defend the city came from the Low Countries, Germany, and Spain; and some of them at least served in the hope that they would be enlisted in the proposed 1514 expedition. In February 1514 Sir Edward Poynings reported to Wolsey that five or six German captains were serving in Tournai 'for small wages trusting this next May, or at such time as the King shall set forthward, that his Grace will retain them'. He added that it was a point in their favour that when they had been discharged from Henry's army at the end of the 1513 campaign they had refrained from offering their services to the French; and he asked whether he was in order in keeping these men in service.[1]

It is not clear how many foreigners were actually in the garrison at the beginning of the occupation, but there were still over 1,000 in the months of April and May 1514. These men— and their leaders—were grateful for the employment Henry had provided in the 1513 expedition, and they were doubtless reluctant to leave his service. The garrison accounts show that

[1] SP 1/7, f. 94; *LP* i, 2657.

24 halberdiers and 50 Spanish infantry were commanded by
the Count of Nassau, 40 infantry and 200 cavalry by the
Bastard d'Aymeries, 12 halberdiers and 700 cavalry by the
Count of Faulconberg—a total of 1,036 men, with a monthly
wage bill of nearly £1,200. The rates of pay seem to have been
more generous than average. For example, the Count of
Nassau's Spanish troops were allowed 10 extra pays—which did
not necessarily reach their pockets; and the Count of Faulconberg's 12 halberdiers were allowed 9 cavalry pays, equal to 18
infantry pays. In short, the reckless expenditure which had
characterized the 1513 campaign still persisted in the early days
of the occupation.[1]

It was not long before the King and Council realized just how
costly the garrison was going to be. At the beginning of 1515,
when the huge drain on England's finances had been in force
for just over a year, they decided that something drastic must
be done to reduce the bill; and they armed Mountjoy with a
series of economy measures before he left for his new post. The
city was to be held 'by a far less number than in times past'. A
new 'ordinary'—that is, establishment—had been drawn up,
which meant that large numbers of men would be discharged.[2]
The soldiers were no longer to be paid in advance. The relatively highly-paid yeomen of the guard were to be allowed to
waste naturally. Guard duties, which required a large number
of military personnel, were to be partly undertaken by civilians.
Responsibility for the defence of the city was to be gradually
handed over to the municipal authorities. The salaries of the
principal officers were to be cut.

It may have been felt that to make such sweeping changes
necessitated changing all the senior men in the garrison.
Mountjoy took with him a new marshal, Sir Sampson Norton,

---

[1] E 36/3, ff. 37–45 b; *LP* i, 2995. This account shows payments authorized by
Margaret of Savoy to contingents in small garrison towns in the neighbourhood of
Tournai totalling nearly 1,000 men. These were part of the 10,000 Margaret had
agreed to provide at Henry's expense as part of the defences of Tournai during the
winter and up to the end of May 1514; and indeed they may have been the only
men she provided. Henry refused to pay the full amount that had been agreed
upon, and Margaret admitted that he had at least some right on his side, 'albeit
if all manner of things in that affair were well considered that it might be answered
somewhat to the contrary' (Galba B III, f. 227; *LP* i, 3014).

[2] Cal. E I, f. 42; *LP* ii, 148.

to replace Sir Anthony Oughtred (who was due to become Governor of Berwick),[1] and a treasurer, Sir Edward Bensted, to replace Sir Robert Dymock; and he was under instructions to replace the under-marshal when he got to Tournai.[2] On the other hand, it may simply be that the decision to reduce the salaries of the principal officers made it necessary to find new men. Poynings, for example, was paid £6. 13s. 4d. a day, whereas the new rate allowed to Mountjoy was only £1. 16s. 6½d. Poynings could hardly be expected to stay on at the new rate. Again, the post of treasurer dropped from 13s. 4d. a day to 5s. 5¾d.[3] Whether or not the simultaneous changing of the senior posts was fortuitous, it had disastrous results. Men usually eye a new leader with suspicion, especially when the man he replaces is exceptionally able and has earned respect and loyalty. When three senior men are replaced on the same day suspicion may easily blossom into something more dangerous.

As soon as he arrived in the city in the afternoon of 5 February Mountjoy called on the *Chefs de la Loi* and the Dean and Chapter of the Cathedral to present letters from the King. He was received 'in good and humble manner', and was able to tell Henry that the citizens 'made me offers, with faithful hearts apparent, to accept me and take me as your Lieutenant accordingly'.[4] Two days later, on Wednesday 7 February, he and the new marshal and treasurer were sworn in, in the presence of the retiring Governor.[5]

The Tournaisiens may have put on a show of welcoming the new Governor. The soldiers did not. Mountjoy summoned a meeting of his council, at which Poynings, Oughtred, and Bensted were present, to explain the plans he had brought from London and to discuss how they should be given effect. They were bound to be unpopular with the troops for precisely the reasons that they appealed to the King. At this stage of the occupation by far the biggest element in the cost of the garrison was the wages bill. If the cost was to be reduced it was the men who would suffer most.

The proposal to reduce the size of the garrison meant that

[1] C 82/421 $\frac{7}{55}$; *LP* ii, 572.   [2] SP 1/10, f. 43; *LP* ii, 126.
[3] E 36/256, pp. 342, 343, 349, 351.   [4] Cal. E I, f. 42; *LP* ii, 148.
[5] SP 1/10, f. 59; *LP* ii, 147.

large numbers must be discharged, since the King was not content to wait for natural wastage. Most of the men had settled down happily to their new life and they had no intention of being uprooted. In theory, the change from payment in advance to payment in arrear was of less consequence, as it did not mean that the total amount of money going into the men's pockets would be reduced. It did, however, mean that checks on their wages for breaches of discipline would be deducted a month earlier; and that it would no longer be possible for a deserter to disappear from the garrison, taking with him the whole of his next month's pay.

Nevertheless, it might have been possible to get the proposals accepted had the new Governor set about it in a sensible way. Unhappily the deliberations of the council were allowed to leak to the rank and file, who were particularly upset by one of the implications of the new method of payment. So long as they were paid in advance they were able to pay for their rations (which they had to provide out of their wages) for the greater part of the month. They might as a rule have to seek credit for only the last week or so. Now, however, they would suddenly be forced to rely on credit for an additional four weeks, until the new system of payment became effective. This would cause real hardship, for the tradesmen of Tournai were unwilling creditors at the best of times, and doubly so when they were dealing with the occupying forces.[1]

As soon as the garbled account of the council's discussion had percolated throughout the garrison 'the soldiers greatly murmured' and swore that they would continue to be paid in the usual way. In the evening of 6 February large numbers of them, including even some of the yeomen of the guard, who were supposed to be better disciplined than the ordinary soldiers, congregated in the market-place and demonstrated in front of the chamber where the council was meeting. They were led by one of the yeomen, Davy ap Howell, who convinced himself and many others that the proposed change would actually deprive them of a month's pay. The council came out to reason with the ringleader, but could make no headway. Mountjoy later told Henry 'And for anything that either Master Poynings and I or the old treasurer or any other of your council could say

[1] SP 1/10, f. 56 b; *LP* ii, 165.

unto him, we could not induce him but in any wise he thought he should lose a month's wages.'[1] The Governor did his best to assure the mob that they would be paid as soon as possible. Indeed, he could hardly say anything else, for they were in a highly explosive state; and if they did attack the council there was little prospect that anyone would lift a finger to save them. The Tournaisiens would have been delighted to stand by while the occupying force destroyed itself.

The Governor's assurance about pay seems to have pacified the men for the moment, but Sir Sampson Norton (with whom, according to Mountjoy, some of them had old scores to settle) provided the occasion for further trouble before nightfall. Thomas Tempest, the under-marshal, who was no doubt aware that it was proposed to replace him with one of Wolsey's followers, wanted to make a good impression on his new superior, perhaps in the hope that he would be given a reprieve at the eleventh hour. He suggested that Norton should inspect the watch being set for the night. Sir Sampson welcomed the proposal 'for his learning'; but no sooner had he entered the market-place than he was spotted by the crowds of soldiers still there. They made for him and, as he says, 'were very hot with me for money. I answered them, in as courteous a manner as my wit would serve me, they should have it'; but this was of no avail and the under-marshal urged him to make his escape. However, he bravely insisted on seeing the watch posted before rejoining his colleagues in the council chamber.[2]

He told them that if the men were not brought under control right away the situation must get completely out of hand; but it was too late to do anything that night. The council members 'mounted their nags' to escort the Governor across the market-place to his residence. They had difficulty in forcing their way through the angry mob, but when Mountjoy repeated his assurance that they would be paid as soon as possible, he was allowed to pass. The men still refused to disperse, however, and held a mass meeting at which they agreed to prevent the gates from being opened next day until they had been paid.

They were as good as their word. The keys of the city were deposited each night at the Governor's residence after the gates had been locked and the watch set; and they were collected

[1] SP 1/10, f. 148; *LP* ii, 325.   [2] SP 1/10, f. 59; *LP* ii, 171.

again each morning by an under-porter and his assistants, to be taken formally to whichever of the gates were to be opened that day. On this occasion, however, the path of the little procession was barred by the mob. Sir Sampson Norton, on his way to discuss the situation with the Governor, again found himself in the middle of the trouble. He has left his own record:

As soon as they saw me they cried all at once 'Money! Money! Money!' I answered them and said 'Masters, ye shall have money. It is a-telling for you. Your captains may go and receive it'. And so went I towards my lord. And on the midst of the press one said on high: 'Thou art come to hang us all! Go set gallows round about the market-place and if thou hang one, thou shalt hang us all!' with many more lewd words. And I let as I had not heard him and went to my lord's lodging.

Mountjoy was not yet dressed but he came out to speak to the men 'as fair as was possible'. This merely made them more angry, and incited them to 'the most horriblest mutiny that hath been heard'. The cry of 'Down with Sir Sampson!' was taken up on all sides, and an attack was launched on the house into which the Governor and marshal had hastily retreated.[1]

At this point the Governor decided that the only course was to sacrifice the new marshal. In their attempt to get their hands on him the men had broken into several houses, and Mountjoy believed that unless something drastic was done his own residence and his personal possessions would be destroyed.[2] As the men seemed to regard Norton as their main enemy it might appease them if he was sent back to England. If he remained, it was inevitable that he would be 'mischiefed'. Norton did not want to go, however, and he told Henry bitterly: 'My lord and the council suffered a trumpet to be blown to cause me to avoid the town, to my great dishonesty.' He did not depart at once, but spent the day in hiding; and that evening he went secretly to Mountjoy to ask what he wanted him to do. The Governor, who was under the impression that he had already left, was furious. He told him that unless he departed at once every member of the council was in danger of losing his life. Only then did Norton leave. He was naturally afraid of being made a scapegoat, and wrote from Lille to both Henry and Wolsey to show that he had acted honourably. If 'lord, councillor, or

---

[1] SP 1/10, ff. 59, 60; *LP* ii, 171, App. 4.   [2] Cal. E I, f. 42; *LP* ii, 148.

poor man' could prove him wrong he would willingly suffer death.[1] The mutineers thus won a resounding victory. They were given a month's pay and an assurance that they would continue to be paid in advance. In defending his decision to the King, Mountjoy claimed that the lives of all the council members had been in jeopardy, and that if they had not capitulated the men 'would have spoiled the town'. A stronger hand, however, might have prevented things from going so far. There is no sign in the accounts of the mutiny that any attempt was made to divide and conquer the mutineers: nor is it clear what part the captains played. It was to them that the commander-in-chief should have looked to have his authority enforced, but the noisy dialogue was conducted direct between the members of the council and the serried masses of the rank and file. The captains, who were just as much concerned with the method of payment as were the men, seem to have stood carefully on the sidelines, leaving it to their companies to fight their battles for them.

The soldiers were quick to capitalize on their victory. The plan to reduce the size of the garrison was no less objectionable than the proposal to alter the method of pay; and the day after they got rid of Norton they staged a new demonstration in front of the Governor's residence. In the course of it they delivered a second ultimatum. No one was to be discharged. All stayed, or all went. Their earlier slogan had been 'Money! Money! Money!' Now they chanted in unison 'All! All! All!' The council had no alternative but to give in again; and it only remained for the unhappy Governor to report his initial failures to London.[2] Poynings sent his version to Wolsey. The garrison had been greatly disordered because of the 'cassing' (i.e. dismissals); and the soldiers had banded together to ensure that not one of their number would be discharged.[3]

Seldom can a Governor's term of office have started less auspiciously. Exactly one week after his arrival in Tournai Mountjoy sent Lancaster Herald off to England with a comprehensive admission of failure, and with his proposals for the future. The 'ordinary' which Henry had approved was too

[1] SP 1/10, ff. 59–59 b; *LP* ii, 171.   [2] Cal. E I, f. 42; *LP* ii, 147.
[3] SP 1/10, f. 52; *LP* ii, 149.

small. He enclosed with his dispatch a statement of the minimum establishment—infantry and cavalry—which he considered safe, and without which he would be reluctant to continue to have charge of the town. Although the new treasurer had been instructed before he left London to issue pay to no more than the newly-approved establishment without a special warrant from the King, it had been necessary to ignore the instruction. Otherwise the town—and the treasurer—'had been thereby spoiled and utterly destroyed'.[1]

Henry demanded a full investigation 'both of the first beginners of this business and also of the causes which they pretended to the grounds of the same'; and the council in Tournai, using 'as good and politic ways and means' as they could devise, hastened to do his bidding. Their conclusion was that the stupidity of the Welshman Davy ap Howell had sparked off the whole mutiny. It led to a general fear 'of losing a month's wages because of the change of the treasurers as also because they would not take their wages at the end of the month'.[2] A number of recently discharged soldiers had also played their part. These unemployed men had it in mind to offer their services to the renegade Richard de la Pole, and they had tried to induce serving members of the garrison to join with them in their treasonable enterprise. The ringleaders had been taken into custody and their confessions obtained, 'as much as we think will be had of them both by fair means and foul'—an interesting commentary on the processes of contemporary justice—'and intend that they shortly shall have punishment according to their deserving'. The unemployed soldiers were clearly an embarrassment, and the council resolved to order them all to leave the garrison, except for 100 who would be retained to help with the duties of watch and ward in a civilian capacity. Any who were craftsmen or who were capable of acting as victuallers would be given permission to remain, but only if they provided sureties for their 'allegiance and true demeanour'.[3]

It seems that Mountjoy failed to carry out any of his initial instructions. One of the articles in 'his book signed by the King's hand' provided 'that in case be any of the guard deceased or

---

[1] Cal. E I, ff. 42–5; *LP* ii, 148.   [2] Cal. E I, f. 42; *LP* ii, 148.
[3] SP 1/10, f. 148; *LP* ii, 325.

departed from hence were in 8*d.* or 12*d.* by the day I should not admit any person in their rooms'; but he decided that it would be unwise to run down the yeomen of the guard so fast.[1] They played an important part in the watch and ward of the town, and he proposed instead that as any died or left Tournai they should be replaced by ordinary privates, who were paid only 6*d.* a day. This would keep the same number of men available for guard duty, but of course the wages bill, which was what worried the King and Council, would be only marginally reduced. There was some sense in Mountjoy's plan to keep the strength of the yeomen up, although with a lower status; but it seems likely that the real reason for his going against the King's wishes was pressure from the officers and men of the guard. If the contingent was to be allowed to waste away, it meant that for all practical purposes there would be no more promotion; and this was not a welcome thought to men who had decided to make their careers in the occupied city.

Another instruction required that 'for the more surety and best order all the garrison keeping watch and ward should be divided into constables and vinteners'—that is to say, the pattern of Calais was to be followed. It was cheaper than using military personnel, so that once again there would be a saving at the expense of the soldiers; and once again they objected. Mountjoy succeeded, however, in getting them to accept that the 'search watch' (the watch responsible for ensuring that the other watches kept on the alert) should be reorganized; but he failed to introduce the change generally. The other watches continued to be manned by soldiers, 'which was and is thought by us all of the King's council which now be here, and they that be gone, the best way, and so we find it'. Although the decision not to follow the King's instructions was thus attributed to the wisdom of the council in Tournai, there must have been a great deal of latent hostility to a proposal which would reduce the number of soldiers, and it may be that yet again the will of the men prevailed.[2]

The Governor defended himself to the King on the ground that if he had done what he was told, it would have meant

---

[1] Cal. E I, f. 43; *LP* ii, 148.
[2] Cal. E I, f. 43; *LP* ii, 148. For the watch arrangements in Calais see *Army Royal*, pp. 22–4.

complete disaster. He had prevailed on the former Governor and Sir Richard Jerningham to remain in Tournai until things calmed down, but when they left, his council would be 'very few'.[1] It was therefore important that Sir Sampson Norton should be replaced as soon as possible, 'for we think it not convenient for the said Sir Sampson to return hither'—a masterpiece of understatement that emphasizes the extreme weakness of the position of the Governor and his council. Jerningham resented having to remain in the city, for he was under instructions to proceed elsewhere. He wrote privately to the King, asking whether he should follow his instructions or obey Mountjoy's request to remain, which would greatly hinder the King's business.[2]

Henry accepted that most of the mutineers must be pardoned. Had all had their deserts the garrison would have been seriously depleted. He wrote to the Earl of Worcester, telling him that the Governor should pardon both the members of the garrison for their 'riots and unlawful assemblies' and the townsmen 'for their treasons and conspiracies';[3] but Mountjoy was not prepared to settle for this. He must have a formal commission from the King 'if the pardons should be of any value to the parties'; and he sent a form of words to London to meet the case. He also considered it necessary to extend the pardon to the motley crew 'of Englishmen and Welshmen and many thieves and murderers and such other' who had supported the soldiers in their mutiny. If they were outlawed, they would either 'make business' in the city before they left it, or appoint a leader and offer their services to the King's enemies.[4] Henry agreed, and the incident was closed, except for the issue of large numbers of individual pardons.[5]

For the next few months things were quiet in the garrison. There is no record that any of the mutineers was executed; and it seems likely that the council, in spite of the promise of appropriate punishment, took the easy way out, and simply dismissed the more unruly members of the garrison. This is borne out by

---

[1] Cal. E I, ff. 40–1; SP 1/10, f. 52; *LP* ii, 149.   [2] SP 1/10, f. 58; *LP* ii, 166.
[3] See Ch. II above.   [4] Cal. E I, f. 67; *LP* ii, 890.
[5] Cal. E I, f. 71 b; *LP* ii, 964. The pardon was given by means of a Signed Bill. The Governor sent a certificate addressed to the Council, saying that so-and-so had asked for the general pardon; and the certificate, if approved by the Council, was signed by the King.

the fact that 'one of the chief beginners of the business' who had been banished from Tournai turned up in England and re-enlisted as a yeoman of the guard. Henry could, of course, do as he liked, Mountjoy peevishly wrote to Wolsey, but this sort of thing made his position very difficult. How could he maintain good discipline when a discharged mutineer was welcomed back into the King's own bodyguard?

It is obvious from this letter that the Governor was far from happy in his post, and in constant fear for the security of the town, and probably for his own safety. He said that even if the new fortifications which were planned had been built, and the city were much more secure, 'this is not the place I take pleasure to abide in'. He could hardly tell the King that he thought the occupation was a great mistake, but he went as far as he could with Wolsey. 'You see what charge the garrison putteth the King to, what pleasure his Grace hath and may have thereto, what business is in the keeping thereof, what dishonour should be in the losing thereof, which God defend!' He concluded his letter, 'scribbled in haste at Tournai', with the reluctant admission: 'All these things I doubt not that you may and will do in your wisdom far better than my wit can serve me to remember you: wherefore I remit all to the King's pleasure.'[1]

Mountjoy had been in office for only five months when the Lord Chamberlain, the Earl of Worcester, came for talks with the citizens, the main objective of which was to reduce the cost of the occupation without impairing the security of the city. While he was in Tournai there was a second mutiny, about which little information has survived.

The first news of it is contained in a dispatch from the Governor of Calais, Sir Richard Wingfield, written on 24 October, in which he reports to Wolsey: 'as I understand on Sunday last there was a great misorder amongst the soldiers of Tournai, whereof as yet I have not the very great certainty and particularities; but tomorrow I trust to have it and incontinently after with diligence I shall advertise your Grace.'[2] Once again a misunderstanding about pay seems to have been the root cause of the trouble. A detailed report was sent from Tournai to the

---

[1] Cal. D VI, f. 306; *LP* ii, 701.   [2] SP 1/11, f. 134; *LP* ii, 1059.

King, but it has not survived, and we have to rely on the sentences passed on the ringleaders to get some idea of the mutiny. It was handled with much greater firmness than Mountjoy showed in February, which is probably to be attributed to his greater experience, and to the fact that the Earl of Worcester was on the spot to strengthen his resolution.

Mountjoy reported on 8 December that the ringleaders in the 'riotous assembly and rebellion' had been duly dealt with; and he enclosed details of their offences and punishments. He hoped that all had been done to the King's honour and 'to the terrible example of all other'; and he paid a tribute to the help he had had from the council, and on this occasion from the captains. The chief offenders were singled out and quickly taken prisoner, and contingents of loyal troops were kept in readiness to meet any general uprising. The decisive action against the ringleaders (which may have been due to Worcester's influence) took the heart out of the mutiny and the trouble quickly subsided. Mountjoy begged Wolsey to intercede with the King on behalf of those of the mutineers who had not been arrested, who were 'sore ashamed and in great fear'. Those who had been executed showed great contrition on the scaffold, and exhorted their fellows to beware of 'making of any such rebellious assemblies from henceforth'. Everyone had come to the conclusion that the episode was the work of the Devil rather than of the men themselves; but this did not prevent the council from passing sentence on the unfortunate individuals who had been the instruments of the Devil.[1]

Five men were executed on 3 December. John Blande had urged a number of discharged soldiers not to take 'the King's reward granted to bring them home', but to remain in Tournai in the hope that they would do better for themselves—a direct challenge to the policy of discharging men and encouraging them to leave the city, so that the garrison could be run down without creating an unemployment problem. Blande's head was set on St. Martin's Gate, near where the discharged soldiers had been living. Robert Dighton was 'adjudged to have his head stricken off and set on one of the gates of the town' for spreading a rumour that the Earl of Worcester had received from the town a year's wages for the whole garrison

---

[1] Cal. D VI, f. 308; *LP* ii, 1259.

without passing the money on to the men. Further, he had donned his armour on the day of the rebellion. Richard Thompson's offence was that he came with a group of men in armour to attempt to rescue a capper from the watch tower where he was imprisoned. This capper had started the rumour that Worcester had pocketed the men's wages. Thompson was duly beheaded and his head placed above the watch tower he had attacked. William Mitton and Percival Frankyns also lost their heads for being in armour and acting as the mutineers' spokesmen.

The other offenders were dealt with four days later. Christopher Johnson was hanged—a lingering and more unpleasant form of death than beheading—for maintaining 'rebellious opinions, not only among his company but also in the King's Lieutenant's presence'. He had proclaimed that the money Worcester was supposed to have received was due to the men, and that they must see that they got it. His body was fixed to a frame, and his head, which had been cut off after he had been hanged, was perched on a stake high above it. Richard Browne and John Bale went with Johnson to the place where he was executed, with halters round their necks, wearing only their shirts. They were then banished, 'never to come within Tournai nor Tournaisis upon pain of death'. Henry Werreschall was banished for trying to prevent the arrest of John Blande. He must have counted himself lucky to get off so lightly, for it was usual to inflict on the man who attempted a rescue the punishment due to the principal offender. William ap Jones was banished 'in his clothes only'. He had been among the rioters, but was saved by the fact that he was not wearing armour. Finally, two men who were no longer serving soldiers were banished. Their offence was that they had taken 'the King's reward' to return to England, but had secretly come back to Tournai, 'having no regard to their oath nor money'.[1]

A general pardon was issued to the other mutineers, except for a handful who managed to escape from the city,[2] including a certain John Packman, whom Henry ordered to be brought to justice at all costs. This man seems to have been a captain and the King may have deemed it necessary to make an example of him. Mountjoy made strenuous efforts to track him down, but he came back 'of his own mind' to seek sanctuary in the Abbey

[1] SP 1/12, f. 9; *LP* ii, 1255.   [2] Cal. D VII, f. 50; *LP* ii, App. 16.

of St. Nicholas des Prés outside Tournai. He asked if he could
safely enter the city, as he feared that he might be arrested for
debt. Mountjoy gladly replied that there were no charges of
debt against him but that he would, of course, have to answer
for any other charges. Packman surrendered, and as there was
overwhelming evidence that he had played a big part in the
mutiny he was sentenced to death.[1] In the course of his trial,
however, he revealed information about four Norfolk and
Suffolk merchants who were supposed to be in league with the
traitor Richard de la Pole; and the Governor suggested that his
life should perhaps be spared.[2]

Packman was unlucky. The King said he must pay the full
penalty. Mountjoy reported in May 1516 that according to his
demerits he had been 'put to execution, drawn, hanged, and
quartered'. Another of the ringleaders was more fortunate. John
Lacy returned to Tournai on the strength of the Governor's
promise that his life would be spared; and to Mountjoy's relief,
for his honour was at stake, Henry agreed that he should only
be banished.[3] It is difficult to see what purpose was served by
enticing Lacy back to the city for the express purpose of banish-
ing him, but perhaps Mountjoy hoped to extract some useful
information from him before his self-imposed exile was given
official support.

In spite of the disastrous consequences of the first attempt to
reduce the cost of the occupation Henry's objective continued to
be to minimize the garrison; but it was not easy. The only
people who could share the burden of defence were the Tournaisiens; but their obligations were clearly defined in the surrender treaty, and they were too astute to allow themselves to
be rushed into any new commitment. When they were pressed
for help they simply said that they were bankrupt. They were
merchants of great experience, well able to assess their bargaining position; and they saw that they now had the benefit of a
professional garrison, which had been denied them since the
treaty of 1478, and which would cost them nothing after the
first ten years of the occupation. The city was in a better defensive position than it had been for more than thirty years; and

[1] Cal. E I, f. 78; *LP* ii, 1509.   [2] SP 1/12, f. 163; *LP* ii, 1510.
[3] Cal. E I, f. 101; *LP* ii, 1894.

Henry, caught in a trap of his own making, was footing the greater part of the bill. The citizens could afford to sit back and leave the initiative to the English.

It was because of the weakness in the English position that the Earl of Worcester had to be sent to Tournai in 1515 to negotiate the future arrangements for the garrison with the city. The Governor and the leading members of his council— Whethill, Jerningham, Bensted, and Sampson—were included in his commission; and he was accompanied by John Young, the Master of the Rolls. The commissioners had two main objectives. First, to persuade the citizens to assume greater responsibility for the garrison; and second, to set in motion the building of a powerful new citadel which could be manned by a relatively small number of troops.[1]

The extent to which the citizens could be given control of their own defence was a matter of delicate judgement. If the balance of power was allowed to shift too far in their favour it might encourage them to try to throw out the English. It was therefore necessary to negotiate a parallel guarantee of good behaviour. But what form could the guarantee take? Forfeiture of goods and chattels, or the lives of the citizens (the sorts of guarantee that were written into the surrender treaty), would be valueless if the city brought off a successful coup; and there-fore the aim of the commissioners must be to allow the Tour-naisiens to exercise as much control as possible, and so to achieve the maximum saving to the English Crown, but not so much that they would feel strong enough to defeat the occupy-ing forces.

Worcester's detailed instructions have not survived (his com-mission is only in general terms—to treat with the Tour-naisiens for the safe-keeping of the city, their annual tribute, and so on); but a letter drafted in the King's name by his secretary Thomas Ruthal reveals the line which he was briefed to take.[2] The draft is, unfortunately, badly mutilated and it is difficult to get the whole of the sense, but it is at least clear that the commissioners were armed with three alternative proposi-tions.

The first, and the cheapest from Henry's point of view, was to get the citizens to agree 'to accept the charge of the city with-

<hr>

[1] C 76/197, m. 22; Rymer, p. 518; *LP* ii, 980.   [2] Cal. E I, f. 71; *LP* ii, 964.

out any garrison, like they did when it was under the obedience of France'. Presumably this meant that the defence of the city would be committed to some form of militia backed up by a small contingent of English soldiers based on the proposed new citadel. This was to be Worcester's opening demand; but if 'after long reasoning and debating' he failed to get the city to accept it, he was empowered to make a second proposal. The municipal authorities should become responsible for appointing a professional garrison of a size to be agreed with the commissioners, the cost of which would be met from the sums they were due to pay Henry under the surrender agreement. This was rather an optimistic idea, for the money in question would support only a handful of men.

The second proposition would be more costly to England than the first—which would cost nothing—but at least it had the virtue that the Tournai garrison would be a self-balancing item in the English budget. The annual tribute provided by the citizens would be ploughed back into their own defence. To conceal the English government's position Worcester was instructed to employ a well-tried diplomatic gambit in putting forward the second alternative: 'then ye as of yourself may make this overture to them'. If the Tournaisiens were prepared to accept the alternative, well and good. If not, Worcester had not revealed Henry's fall-back position—provided that he was a good enough actor to convince the Tournaisien delegation that the second alternative was in fact his own idea.

The third proposition seems to have been simply that the English Crown should continue to be responsible for the garrison, but that it should be much reduced in size, by agreement with the municipal authorities.

Quite early in the negotiations the citizens put forward the conditions on which they would accept greater responsibility for defence. The main proposal was that Henry should appoint a captain with 500 or 600 men who would take their orders from the four councils. In return the citizens would bind themselves, their heirs, and successors to be loyal to Henry. Jean Hacquart, the recorder, undertook to put this proposition in a 'minute of obligation' in both French and Latin, so that there could be no misunderstanding; but when he came back to the commissioners some days later he brought no minute. He explained that he had gone over the surrender treaty very carefully with the four councils, and they had decided 'that they were as straitly bound as they might be'—apparently implying that it was not open to them to make any suggestion, however constructive. Worcester guessed that they had come to the conclusion that it might be better for them not to volunteer proposals, but that they should leave it to Henry to issue orders, 'for the desire or the commandment of a prince made of his subjects implieth a coercion or compulsion'; and it might be to their advantage at some future date to be able to show that they had not co-operated in the matter of defence. He found it impossible to understand their thinking, however, and complained about the 'lightness and unstableness we find in them that their words and deeds agree not'. He had no idea what was the reason for their sudden change of heart, but he suggested to the King that they were playing for time to give the political scene in Europe a chance to become clearer.[1]

In any case, Worcester considered that the proposal, even if it had been put forward, was not good enough, mainly because the citizens could not give a satisfactory guarantee that they would stick to their part of the bargain. He also thought that they were in no position to give a better guarantee; and he pointed out that their proposal, if carefully examined, would be seen to have more advantage to the King than at least one of his own proposals. It would establish a position very similar to that which the city held when it was part of France.[2]

Mountjoy, for his part, expressed misgiving at handing over control to the city authorities too soon. He accepted that the wealthier classes were well-disposed. If they had the benefit of an English garrison 'for a season', he thought they would be able to establish a firm hold over the city as a whole, and it might then be possible safely to reduce the number of troops. But for the moment he had 'but small trust' in the common people, who were certain to rally to the French if they ever made a serious attempt against the city. In any case, if it was decided to 'minish' the garrison it must be done 'but by little and little'.[3] Nevertheless, Henry was not prepared to let the matter rest. He made it plain to Worcester and his fellow-

---

[1] Cal. D VI, f. 198; *LP* ii, 856.   [2] SP 1/11, f. 77; *LP* ii, 891.
[3] Cal. E I, f. 67; *LP* ii, 890.

commissioners that 'his determined pleasure' was that the inhabitants should become responsible for the safe-keeping of the city by one of the three ways he had suggested; and the commissioners, having no alternative, undertook to accomplish his wish.[1]

No agreement was reached with the municipal authorities and Worcester's mission failed. The next major reduction in the garrison came at the beginning of 1517, when the completion of the citadel was in sight, and Mountjoy was replaced by Jerningham. Nearly 500 were discharged at this time.[2] At the end of February Jerningham was instructed to dismiss 400 more forthwith, and another 500 on 1 May, on the assumption that by then the citadel would be 'enclosed and at a defensible height'. These numbers included 100 cavalry, half of which were to be English and the other half 'strangers'—the foreign mercenaries. These were to be chosen 'of them which be now already retained, and none other'. This rider foreshadows the malpractices common in the English army of the later sixteenth century. It was feared that men might be recruited into the garrison for the express purpose of being discharged, for which service they would receive a small payment, so that the total number in post—and the financial benefit to their captains, who issued their pay—would remain the same.[3]

The 'strangers' posed a special problem. They could not in equity be kept when Englishmen were being discharged. On the other hand, it was politically important to keep on good terms with the Low Countries' nobility, who retained these men, and who were in effect receiving pensions from Henry. Worcester and his fellow-commissioners had been well aware of this. It would have been simple to discharge all the foreigners, but they had served the King well in the 1513 campaign, and he must not forget his obligations towards them. 'It shall be expedient that we shall understand your determined mind what order shall be taken with the Bastard Aymeries, Thubianville, and John Sellier, your servant, with other gentlemen of these parts which have served your Grace the space of two years and more'.[4] Henry did continue to be mindful of his obligations, for in March 1517, when he became aware that d'Aymeries was

[1] SP 1/11, f. 77; *LP* ii, 891.   [2] Cal. E I, ff. 125–6; *LP* ii, 2825.
[3] SP 1/15, f. 16; *LP* ii, 2972.   [4] SP 1/11, f. 77; *LP* ii, 891.

not being paid, he promptly commanded the Governor to remedy the omission.[1]

Jerningham and the council ventured to suggest that the rate of dismissal should be slowed. If too many departed 'before the closing up of the citadel . . . much danger and casualties might ensue'. The King reluctantly agreed that a realistic view must be taken—'in doubtful matters the worst is to be feared, and the surest way chosen'—although he thought that at the moment there was no serious threat to the city. Nevertheless, on the understanding that the council would complete the citadel as soon as possible, he agreed that for the time being fewer men should be discharged.[2]

Sir Richard Whethill was particularly unhappy about running down the garrison. He pointed out that the King had come to the conclusion that the city could be garrisoned with 1,000 men, even without the benefit of the citadel, being under the impression that Tournai had only 10,000–11,000 inhabitants. In fact the population—men, women, and children—was more like 20,000. Whethill urged that the proposal to reduce the garrison should be abandoned. Neither his English, which is picturesque, nor his spelling, which is ingenious, nor his arithmetic, is easy to follow; but he says that the recent dismissals have caused much speculation in France, and in Tournai itself. The citizens were 'nothing sorry' at the departure of the men, 'for they think that the King is weary of his charges, so that by minishing and minishing they trust to return home again'. If the systematic reduction of the garrison continues, Whethill will ask for his own discharge.[3] Had the King's instructions been carried out the garrison would have been reduced to 1,000 men: in fact it was left at 1,200 until 'the closing of the citadel'.[4]

The citadel was virtually complete in August 1517. A draft letter of that month from Wolsey to the King says that it 'is now

---

[1] C 82/444 $\frac{8}{299}$; *LP* ii, 2977.   [2] SP 1/15, f. 36; *LP* ii, 3055.

[3] SP 1/13, f. 53; *LP* ii, 1664. This letter is dated 13 March 1516 in *LP*; but the correct date must be 13 March 1517, since Whethill clearly refers to the subject-matter of the King's instructions of February 1517 (SP 1/15, f. 16; *LP* ii, 2972). In August 1516 Whethill suggested to Wolsey that after the citadel was finished the establishment might be 400 soldiers and 600 'commoners' (i.e. private citizens); but he thought that this would be cutting it fine (SP 1/13, f. 266; *LP* ii, 2260).

[4] SP 1/16, f. 15; *LP* ii, App. 38.

closed in and perfected up to the battlements', and that the garrison is to be reduced to 600 men.[1] Jerningham lost no time in seeking to achieve one of the benefits which the King's works were designed to provide—the elimination of guard duties by English soldiers throughout the whole city. He summoned the four councils on 29 September to tell them that the 600 men who remained would shortly withdraw into the citadel, and that the municipal authorities must become responsible for watch and ward in the rest of the city. He also asked for a statement of the watch arrangements in force before the city had been captured, so that he could satisfy himself that they would be adequate. After discussing the matter among themselves the four councils said that they would gladly prepare a memorandum about the former arrangements, but there could be no question of agreeing to anything like this without first putting the proposal to the people as a whole.[2]

The Governor had earlier tried to get the citizens to take over guard duties. At the beginning of 1517 they had refused 'to retain [i.e. pay] a competent number of Englishmen for watch and ward to be kept within the city'.[3] Now that the citadel was operational it was easier for Jerningham to insist that the city authorities should look after their own defence, since the theory was that the citadel could hold out indefinitely against a siege; and if the citizens wanted to avoid the consequences of a successful attack on the town the remedy lay in their own hands. Nevertheless, in spite of this strong incentive, the citizens showed no great wish to defend themselves, which is hardly surprising, as any attack was most likely to come from France.

At the beginning of 1518 Henry began to show signs of extreme irritation at the municipal authorites' reluctance to co-operate. Wolsey told the Governor that the King was determined that they should be brought into line, and instructed him 'by all the politic ways ye can use' to induce them to make some effort to provide for their own defence. Henry intended that the watch and ward arrangements that had been customary before he captured the city should be reinstated, except that the Tournaisiens should now employ as many Englishmen as possible, to mitigate the problem of unemployment created

---

[1] SP 1/16, f. 15; *LP* ii, App. 38. [2] Hocquet (a), xliv.
[3] SP 1/16, ff. 123–4; *LP* ii, 3907.

by the discharge of soldiers from the garrison. To encourage the city fathers to agree to this proposition he was willing that they should impose taxes to pay the wages of the new force.[1]

The city refused point-blank to help, and the Governor decided that the only thing to do was for him to provide a body of 200 Englishmen for watch and ward. These men were charged with the duty of guarding all the city gates outside the area of the citadel, but they were still responsible to the Governor, and not to the municipal authorities; and they nightly brought him the keys, as had been done when the garrison had been dispersed through the whole of the city. The King accepted this as an interim measure; but he still hoped that the four councils would take over the financing of the guard. Wolsey told Jerningham that this would be put to a delegation which was due to come to England shortly—although he understood that they were trying to put off their visit because they knew that the King was displeased with them.[2]

The preceding paragraphs have been concerned with the attempt to reduce the establishment of the garrison without endangering the security of the town. The records of the successive treasurers, which would have revealed the effect of the policy in terms of numbers in service during the whole occupation, have mostly disappeared; but those that survive make it possible to examine the size of the establishment at different points during the occupation.

There is no precise information about the initial establishment. The over-all figure is generally put at 5,000, of which 4,000 were infantry and 1,000 cavalry. We can only speculate about the composition of the force during the early months of the occupation. The companies in the invasion army, from which the garrison troops were drawn, had not been uniform, since they were very largely the retinues of noblemen and gentlemen, and varied in size according to the wealth of the 'captain' who retained them. Sir Robert Dymock, who became the first treasurer of Tournai, had only 54 men. At the other end of the scale Sir Henry Marney was captain of 818. Between these extremes there were companies of every size, but most were round about 100, which suggests that there may have been

[1] SP 1/16, f. 110; *LP* ii, 3886.   [2] SP 1/16, ff. 123–4; *LP* ii, 3907.

an attempt to get this number recognized as being the standard.[1]

It is first possible to see the establishment clearly in 1515, immediately after Mountjoy had taken over as Governor. The accounts of the new treasurer, Sir Edward Bensted for a fortnight in February/March show the position very accurately. They record the sums paid out, and are receipted by either the captain or the petty-captain, and they therefore provide an exact record of the numbers actually in post. It has been presumed for this purpose that complement equals establishment; and where a post exists, or appears to exist, but is unfilled perhaps because the holder is on leave, it has been regarded as part of the establishment.

By far the most striking thing about the establishment is the size of the companies. Although they had varied enormously in the 1513 expedition they are now almost completely uniform. The treasurer's accounts show that in 1515 there were 29 infantry companies, of which 21 had exactly 78 men. It is probable that the other eight were temporarily a little above or below an establishment of 78.[2] The records do not show how the yeomen of the guard were grouped, but they had four petty-captains, which implies four companies. If these were standard 78-men companies, it implies a total of 312 men. In fact there were 314 yeomen in post.

The position of the cavalry is less clear. The Governor and the other principal officers had cavalry allocated to them, partly to act as a bodyguard—Mountjoy had 17 and Sir Richard Jerningham 13—and some of the ordinary captains had from one to five horsemen under their command. These totalled 134, and since they were all paid in 'Philips'[3] (at the rate of 8 a month, or about 10d. a day) they were probably mostly from the Low Countries.[4] Although Jean le Sellier was a civilian he was paid at the rate of 8 Philips a month, the payment being described by the treasurer as 'wages of war'; but le Sellier was a very special case.

The principal officers had their own separate establishments.

---

[1] *LP* i, 2053.

[2] The odd companies had 66, 73, 76, 76, 77, 77, and 79, in each case plus captain and petty-captain.

[3] i.e. Philippus guilders.   [4] E 36/256, pp. 355–63; *LP* ii, p. 1514.

The Governor had 60 infantry and 20 cavalry, and was also responsible for the clerk of the council, his assistant, and 2 drummers. At the time when the account from which these facts are drawn was made up there was no marshal in post—there having been no time to replace the unfortunate Sir Sampson Norton—but the under-marshal Thomas Tempest had a petty-captain and 59 soldiers, who would normally have reported through him to the marshal. He also had the heralds on his strength—Lancaster Herald, Hammes Pursuivant, and 2 trumpeters. The treasurer's establishment was reduced when Sir Edward Bensted took over from Sir Robert Dymock. The latter had a petty-captain and 57 soldiers to guard the money under his control, and he had 3 clerks to help with the accounts. Bensted, however, had to make do with 33 soldiers and 2 clerks, thanks to the economy campaign. The porter was responsible for 2 chief under-porters, and 12 under-porters; and he also had 29 soldiers at his disposal.

The two biggest individual establishments were those of the captain of the guard and the master of the ordnance. In 1515 Thomas Hert was master of the ordnance, with the rank of captain. He had a deputy—'the controller of the ordnance'—who was equivalent to a petty-captain, 10 master gunners, each with a servant, and 80 gunners—not enough, according to Sir Richard Jerningham, who told the King that because of the 'great compass and circuit' of the town they needed between 200 and 300 gunners.[1] The master of the ordnance also had a clerk, a 'yeoman of the ordnance', a bowyer, fletcher, master smith and master carpenter, and 22 pioneers whose job it was to prepare gun emplacements and so on. The captain of the guard had 14 ordinary soldiers in his retinue, 4 petty-captains, and 314 yeomen of the guard. He had also a chaplain, 2 drummers and 2 servants.

These figures add up to an infantry establishment of just under 3,000. Between them the Governor, marshal, treasurer, and porter had about 200; the captain of the guard, 330; and the master of the ordnance, 130. The ordinary infantry, with their captains and petty-captains accounted for about 2,300. Thus in the eighteen months since the garrison was installed about 1,000 of the original strength had disappeared, as a result

[1] Cal. D VI, ff. 303–4; *LP* ii, 2131.

of the policy of reducing the establishment when it seemed safe to do so. Again the cavalry's position is unclear. The account shows fewer than 200 horsemen scattered under numerous commands. There is no sign of a large single group, although it seems likely that there was such a group when regard is had to the numbers of cavalry discharged later in the occupation.

However, in the case of the infantry the effect of the economy measures can be clearly seen. A mutilated copy of 'The King's estate that Sir Edward Bensted paid the garrison by'[1] is in the Exchequer papers in the Public Record Office. The beginning of the document, which probably carried the date, has been torn off, but it must relate to the garrison as it stood about the middle of 1516. The main reduction came on the ordinary infantry, which fell from 2,237 privates to 1,200. The ordnance establishment was virtually unchanged; and the yeomen of the guard actually increased. The personal retinue of the captain of the guard went up from 14 to 20; and the yeomen went up from 314 to 329. Unfortunately, the establishments of the Governor, marshal, treasurer, and porter were dealt with in the part of the document which has disappeared; but given that the master of the ordnance and the captain of the guard suffered no cuts it seems unlikely that the other senior officers would do so, if only for reasons of prestige. It follows that the main reduction was among the ordinary infantry, who lost over 1,000 posts.

Henry took a special interest in the yeomen of the guard. Although they were posted in Tournai they were still his personal bodyguard, and had a claim to serve him in England should they want to come home. In the middle of 1518 there were more of them in Tournai than the establishment approved by the King provided for; and he sent Jerningham a list of the supernumeraries, with instructions to discharge them from the garrison, except that those who were paid 12*d.* a day could elect to remain at 8*d.* a day, and that those who were paid 8*d.* could elect to remain as ordinary privates at 6*d.* There was to be no increase in the total establishment, however, which meant that four ordinary privates had to be dismissed to make room for every three '8*d.* yeomen' who wanted to stay in the garrison at the lower rate.

[1] E 101/61/14.

It turned out that none of the higher-paid yeomen was prepared to step down. They all claimed that they had given long and faithful service and could not believe that Henry really meant to 'minish' their wages; and they sought permission to return to England. The Governor duly paid them their wages and enough conduct money to get them home. He was also careful to send a list of their names to Wolsey, so that there was no danger that any of them would be paid again in England for their Tournai service. Most of the lower-paid supernumerary yeomen also left, and Jerningham found that he had only 8 men over and above the agreed establishment. He was able to accommodate these by dismissing 12 ordinary privates.[1]

The interest which the King, or his advisers, took in minor administrative matters in the city has been referred to above.[2] This interest, and sometimes interference, in day-to-day management made the Governor's job more difficult; and it was repeated in the purely military sphere.

In 1515, for example, the post of chief bowyer, which carried the wage of 8d. a day, fell vacant. It might be expected that appointment to a post at this level, the second rung from the bottom, which was the ordinary soldier at 6d. a day, would be made by the Governor; and that he need do no more than notify London at suitable intervals about this sort of appointment. In fact, an elaborate bill, setting out the details of the post and the qualifications of Henry Spurr, the man earmarked for the job by Mountjoy, was sent to London for the King's approval and signature. The bill, when signed, was an authority both for the Governor to admit Spurr to 'the room of chief bowyer' and to the treasurer to pay his wages.[3]

This was very different from the position in Calais, where the Governor and council had authority to make the most senior appointments below the level of the council itself. The explanation may simply be that Tournai had not been long enough an English possession for the King to give it as much autonomy as Calais enjoyed. Nevertheless, this hardly justifies his interference in the management of the garrison, which must often

---

[1] SP 1/16, f. 309; *LP* ii, 4251.   [2] See pp. 51–56 above.
[3] C 82/432 $\frac{7}{273}$; *LP* ii, 1375.

have been bad for morale. For example, when a post of gunner quartermaster fell vacant the King himself authorized the replacement. The Governor and the master of the ordnance were commanded to receive John Clogge, one of the yeomen of the guard whom Henry wished to help because of his 'true and faithful service'. There was, of course, no guarantee that Clogge was the best man for the job.[1]

The Governor and council accepted that it was open to the King to make these minor appointments if he so desired. A signed bill providing for the appointment of Henry Lymster also to the post of gunner quartermaster (this time at only 8*d*. a day) speaks of the post as 'now being void, and in your gracious disposition'.[2] But this does not alter the fact that the garrison would have been more efficiently run had the Governor been allowed to use the powers contained in his commission.

Mountjoy complained to Wolsey in July 1515 that one of the members of the garrison who had been dismissed for his part in the riots five months earlier had gone to England and been appointed a yeoman of the guard, in spite of the fact that Henry was well aware that he had been 'one of the chief beginners' of the trouble. Of course the King could do as he pleased, but it would be bad for discipline if it was generally believed that dismissal from the garrison carried no real stigma.[3]

In 1517 someone, who is unidentified, was dismissed from the garrison, and went to London to appeal against his dismissal, apparently to Wolsey. After a sympathetic hearing (presumably he was the sole witness) he was given a letter to the Governor saying that he had been thoroughly examined. His only offence was that he 'in defending himself passed his bounds and limits'. He was now sorry that he had 'overshot himself upon this only occasion', and it seemed clear that he should never have been dismissed. It was therefore the King's pleasure that he should be reinstated; and that 'remitting all displeasures, both you and all the rest of his Grace's officers there shall use him from henceforth with indifferent entertainment and favour'. There is no record of the Governor's comment when the man re-appeared and revealed that his decision had been overturned; but it cannot have been very favourable. The rest of the

---

[1] C 82/441 $\frac{8}{200}$; *LP* ii, 2644.   [2] C 82/459 $\frac{9}{273}$; *LP* ii, 4079.
[3] Cal. D VI, f. 305 b; *LP* ii, 701.

garrison must have seen the incident as a weakening of the Governor's authority; and Jerningham must have found his future relationship with the man embarrassing, since even normal disciplinary action against him could be interpreted as a breach of the King's order that he was to have 'indifferent' treatment.[1]

There were two more instances of this in the following year. Wolsey told Jerningham that although he had dismissed Thomas Palmer from the garrison for some offence, the man had been pardoned by the King, and awarded the position of a man-of-arms in Tournai to replace Nicholas Crowe, who had died. If the place was already filled Palmer was to be given a position of equal value.[2] A less offensive interference with the Governor's authority came a month later, when it was brought to Henry's attention that Richard Donolte, a yeoman of the guard in Tournai, was 'greatly decayed in his substance as well by long continuance of sickness as also by the misfortune of the burning of his house and goods'. The King, moved by pity and gratitude for the yeoman's service in the past, commanded Jerningham to pay him three months' wages at 8d. a day, and to continue to pay him at this rate until further notice.[3]

It was not only the King's intervention that made life difficult for the Governor. Wolsey played his part, for example, by insisting that his nominee Richard Hansard should replace Thomas Tempest as under-marshal. Richard Sampson, who was also Wolsey's man, and watched his master's interests with the eye of a hawk, tackled Mountjoy about the appointment of Hansard the day after the new Governor arrived, only to be told that because of his experience Tempest would continue in office. Sampson immediately reported this to Wolsey, adding that Hansard was better qualified than Tempest, who 'had never before knowledge of no strangers', and spoke only English. Hansard, on the other hand, had knowledge of 'many parts and many conditions of men, which thing is here necessary'. He also spoke perfect French, which would become more important as time went on and Tournaisiens were given senior appointments.[4] Mountjoy tried to keep Tempest in the post, and to make things easier told Wolsey that he liked Hansard

[1] SP 1/16, f. 42; *LP* ii, 3749. [2] *LP* ii, 4380.
[3] C 82/468 $\frac{10}{144}$; *LP* ii, 4757. [4] SP 1/10, f. 43; *LP* ii, 126.

very much and had made him a captain with the same pay as the under-marshal;[1] but this was of no avail. In the end the Governor had to give the under-marshal's job to Hansard.

The Governors, however, were not always blameless in the matter of authority. Jerningham, for example, who on the whole seems to have been a competent administrator, hesitated to take responsibility for discharging men as part of the process of reducing the size of the garrison. He sent to Wolsey a draft letter of dismissal which he hoped the King would sign and he could then pass on to the troops affected: otherwise, he feared that they would not depart 'without great grouching'. He also asked that the letter should be rewritten before Henry signed it. It would do more harm than good if the men to whom it was addressed recognized the handwriting of Jerningham's clerk, and realized that in carrying out an unpleasant duty the Governor was sheltering behind the King's signature.

Wolsey's reply was in the nature of a reprimand. The King and Council thought that if the King signed such a letter it would not 'stand to his honour'. The Governor was the King's lieutenant and chief officer in Tournai, and he and the council there had every right to dismiss men. Further, if any of the men were 'obstinate, repugning against your doing', they were to be punished for their disobedience and contempt. 'For by too much favour and mild dealing many things have been done there to the derogation of the King's honour, which his grace would never have suffered but for eschewing of more inconvenience'. Henry would now have his commands obeyed without any contradiction or grudging of any of his subjects. In short, the King and Council were prepared to intervene in the affairs of the garrison when there was some kudos to be got; but when there was something unpleasant to be done it was for the Governor to do it.[2]

Pay caused little difficulty during Poynings' governorship. The first treasurer, Sir Robert Dymock, had been treasurer-at-

---

[1] SP 1/10, f. 56 b; *LP* ii, 165.

[2] SP 1/14, ff. 215–6; SP 1/16, f. 110 b; *LP* ii, 2826; *LP* ii, 3886. These letters are dated respectively in *LP*, 25 January 1517 and 16 January 1518, but the latter must have been written in 1517. It is thus clear that the Governor's entry into the completed citadel (which took place in October 1517) is still some distance in the future.

war with the rear ward in the 1513 expedition, and inherited £12,700 of the ward's treasure for the use of the garrison. There was also £50,000 that he took over from Sir John Dauncey, treasurer-at-war with the middle ward; in addition, during his term of office he received the lump sum of £10,000 due from the citizens under the surrender treaty.[1] These were very substantial amounts and they gave the garrison a good start; but they were all once-for-all payments. When they ran out it was left to the King and Council to provide funds from England, which they were no more anxious to do than they were to reply to correspondence.

Within a few days of his arrival in Tournai Mountjoy found it necessary to instruct Lancaster Herald 'to move my lord of York and the Council for money to be sent hither in haste'.[2] Nothing happened, and a few weeks later the Governor wrote again to both Wolsey and the King, beseeching that money should be sent with all speed. The next pay day was 6 May; 'and after that, as far as we can cast, we have not for another month.' It would be disastrous if the men's pay were only one day late, for there was nothing to be had without money. Food was very expensive, and for the most part the men were living 'hard and sharp upon their wages'. If something was not done quickly the whole garrison would be in jeopardy.[3]

A year later Mountjoy was again pressing the King for more regular payment. The treasure-chest was nearly empty—it had only enough for six weeks' pay, a fact to which the Earl of Worcester, who had just returned to London, would be able to testify;[4] and he had to write yet again in June 1516.[5] Jerningham found matters no better when he took over the governorship from Mountjoy;[6] and in 1518 he was still complaining to Wolsey. He assured him that 'the soldiers be the most poor that ever I was among'. A fifth of them had not had a single penny in wages for the last two months; and they were inevitably in debt.[7]

The large sums which the garrison started with were held in coin, except for part of the £10,000 paid by the Tournaisiens,

[1] E 36/256, p. 383; *LP* ii, 1512.   [2] SP 1/10, f. 51; *LP* ii, App. 3.
[3] SP 1/10, ff. 148 b, 150; *LP* ii, 325, 326.
[4] Cal. E I, ff. 78 b–79; *LP* ii, 1509.
[5] Vesp. F XIII (ii), f. 244; *LP* ii, 1995.   [6] SP 1/15, f. 38; *LP* ii, 3056.
[7] SP 1/16, ff. 168–9; *LP* ii, 4004.

which was in silver plate; but when this had been spent the problem of getting fresh supplies of money to Tournai presented itself. The practice at first was to send it by cart from Calais, which was both cumbersome and hazardous. Robert Fowler, an officer of the Exchequer, delivered £10,000 to Sir Robert Dymock in this way in June 1514, and suggested that it would be more satisfactory if in future one of Dymock's clerks came from Tournai. His own time was much too valuable to be wasted in accompanying the treasure-cart; and the clerk could be provided with a strong escort. Before he could send off his letter, with this suggestion, he received orders to take another £10,000 to Tournai, much to his disgust. He added a postscript to his letter expressing the hope that this was the last time he would be asked to make this tiresome journey.

One of Fowler's difficulties in handling the first consignment was that he was uncertain whether the treasurer in Tournai could make use of crowns; and he therefore took the precaution of providing all the money in 'sterling gold'. In Tournai, however, he learned that crowns would be quite acceptable. They could be issued at the rate of 4s. 2d., which he considered very reasonable. 'I know not where to make so much of them except in the town and marches of Calais. I do utter them there as yet for 4s. 3d. the piece with much business' (i.e. much difficulty). He therefore proposed to take the whole of the second £10,000 in crowns.[1]

It was, however, simpler and safer to use the exchange services of the merchant bankers to finance the garrison; and as a rule this was done in the later years of the occupation. In particular Jerome Frescobaldi, his son Leonardo, and Philip Gualteroti, merchants of Florence, were called upon. Jerningham at least was not always satisfied with their performance. Merchant bankers served him so badly that he had 'no confidence in no merchant's promise'. He considered that Gualteroti was not big enough to handle the large sums that the garrison needed,[2] and he hoped at one time that his services would not be used again.[3] The dangers of transporting cash were stressed by Jerningham in the summer of 1516, when he begged Wolsey to see that any money destined for Tournai was

[1] SP 1/8, f. 128; *LP* i, 2983.   [2] Cal E I, f. 147; *LP* ii, 3120.
[3] Cal. E I, f. 57; *LP* ii, 3141.

sent well before the winter set in, for at that season 'the carriage will be troublous and specially if it be white money'. Large sums of coin could not be carried secretly, and therefore they could not be carried without danger.[1]

In September 1516 he and Mountjoy complained that payments from the Frescobaldis were overdue. They sent a special plea to Jerome, who was in Bruges, that the money should reach Tournai in time for pay-day; but the only reply was that Jerome had no word from his son (who was presumably in London) that he was to make any payment at all. This meant that the King's honour and the security of the city were at risk, for the next pay was due in a few days and the treasurer had only half the money needed to meet it. If the other half did not come in time, 'what shift we shall make, God knoweth!' The council was also aggrieved by a breach of confidence on the part of Frescobaldi. He had been asked to keep the garrison's plight secret, but he disclosed the contents of the Governor's letter to the post, grumbling that 'it was a great sum of money and merchants must occupy money daily. Wherefore it is both to be feared that the matter shall be blowen abroad, and also that there shall be some doubt as to the continuance of the payment.' The Governor and treasurer besought Wolsey to do something to get them out of their constant difficulties over pay. They had recently written to him several times on this matter, but as usual they had had no reply.[2]

In the following year Jerningham, in forwarding a statement of the monies he had received from Jerome Frescobaldi on six dates between 21 February and 21 March, told Wolsey that the payments had been slow in coming forward, which was very worrying. Further, he understood that the Frescobaldis intended to ask a higher price than had been agreed upon, and he hoped that this would be resisted.[3] The money received on this occasion was in numerous parcels of different sorts of coin.[4]

On this occasion Wolsey must have been aware that the garrison was in dire straits, for he wrote on 10 September

---

[1] SP 1/13, f. 227; *LP* ii, 2097.   [2] SP 1/14, f. 16; *LP* ii, 2364.
[3] SP 1/15, ff. 73–73 b; *LP* ii, 3098.
[4] e.g., 'in crowns at 36¼ patars the piece, 1230 which maketh £249. 8s. 4d.; in angels 200 at 6s. 8d. the piece, *summa*, £63. 6s. 8d.; in gold guildens at 28 patars the piece 285 which maketh sterling £44. 6s. 8d.; in Philips at 25 stivers the piece 572 *summa* £25. 13s. 4d.; in money, £381. 2s. 8d.' (SP 1/15, f. 76).

instructing Mountjoy—with singular optimism—to see that Jerningham was in Calais on 13 September to pick up £6,000 from Robert Fowler. Jerningham politely drew Wolsey's attention to the fact that his letter had reached the Governor on 16 September (a fast postal service, but in the circumstances not fast enough), and that he could hardly be expected to be in Calais three days before he was told to go there. However, he left Tournai on 17 September and two days later reached Calais, where he took over the £6,000 'in pence and divers golds' from Fowler.[1]

It was convenient to use the merchant bankers, so long as they were efficient, but if the money for the garrison remained in English hands throughout it was possible for the treasurer in Tournai to make a profit on the exchange—at the risk, of course, of incurring a loss. In 1516 Jerningham suggested that it would be in the King's interest to send very large sums of money less frequently, which would be cheaper and little more risky than sending smaller sums at frequent intervals; and that he should send nobles and royals. He could issue these coins at the rate of 10s. 6d. the royal and 7s. the noble. He did not propose, however, to give them to the garrison as pay, but to sell them to merchants and use the proceeds as pay. The demand for nobles and royals was sporadic, however,—'some months there cometh merchants to search them and some months there cometh none'. So Jerningham still wanted some silver for wages, so that he could hold on to the gold until he had a chance to exchange it at a profit.[2] He was in fact proposing that the treasurer should take on the function of merchant banker.

Bulk supplies of money for the garrison's pay were transferred between the senior officers by means of indentures. These were documents in which the subject-matter of the transaction (for example, 'eight and twenty thousand and eight hundred crowns of gold of the sun at 4s. 2d. stg. the piece which doth amount unto the sum of £6,000') was written out twice on the same sheet of paper or parchment, which was then divided into two by means of an irregular cut. Each of the parties to the transaction signed one of the halves, which he handed over to the other party. If it later became necessary to verify the

---

[1] SP 1/14, f. 23; LP ii, 2383.   [2] SP 1/13, f. 254; LP ii, 2229.

indentures, perhaps because of a dispute over the amount involved, it could readily be done by fitting the two halves together again. If they fitted perfectly, the documents were well authenticated.[1]

Pay was issued by the treasurer and his staff to the captains, who were responsible for paying their companies. At the end of the sixteenth century, when the same system was in force, it was grossly abused. Captains pocketed pay due to their men and falsified the muster returns to enable them to draw pay for non-existent soldiers. There is no evidence of this during the occupation of Tournai. The treasurer's books were kept efficiently. They show the wages due company by company, the exact number of days covered, and the signature of the captain, or his petty-captain acting for him, to testify that the money was duly received. As a rule the books are also signed by the Governor and the treasurer. Another indication of the good behaviour of the garrison for the greater part of the occupation is the fact that the treasurer's accounts show few stoppages of pay for indiscipline.[2]

The company organization was still relatively simple. It consisted of a captain, who was paid 4s. a day, one petty-captain (2s.), who corresponded to the company lieutenant of the later-sixteenth-century army, and as a rule 78 privates at 6d. a day. Although there had been 'vinteners' (i.e. men in charge of platoons of 20 ordinary soldiers, who corresponded to the later corporals) as long ago as the reign of Edward III, and although there were vinteners in Calais,[3] there were none in Tournai at the beginning of the occupation. At least, if there were, their rank was given no financial recognition, for every man was paid 6d. They do make an appearance in the later stages of the occupation, but it is not clear that they were ever paid more than the private. They may have been no more than acting unpaid corporals, although it is difficult to see what

---

[1] Examples of indentures for the garrison's pay are to be found in SP 1/9, f. 40 (Jerningham–Dymock); SP 1/10, f. 198 (Mountjoy–Bensted); and SP 1/12, f. 74 (Jerningham–Bensted). The real security lay not so much in the wavy line of the indented cut, which could be traced out and imitated fairly accurately, as in the matching grain of the paper or parchment, which could not be imitated.

[2] e.g., E 36/256; *LP* ii, p. 1513. (Sir Edward Bensted's account.)

[3] See *Army Royal*, p. 21.

attraction this status can have had. It can hardly have been a stepping-stone to promotion, as the chances of promotion, both on statistical and social grounds, were very poor.

The yeomen of the guard were the crack infantry of the day. They were paid 8*d*. or 1*s*., compared with the ordinary private's 6*d*., and they had a special status, being the King's own body-guard. Their petty-captains were paid 3*s*. 4*d*. a day, more than half as much again as the ordinary petty-captain. The gunners were paid as privates, the master gunners had 8*d*., while the 'controller of the ordnance', who was second-in-command of the ordnance establishment, ranked as an ordinary petty-captain. The under-marshal was paid as a captain, as was Lancaster Herald. The pursuivants were equivalent to ordinary petty-captains. The chief under-porters had 1*s*. and the under-porters 8*d*. The treasurer had two clerks, one at 1*s*. and the other at 8*d*.; and the clerk of the Governor's council had 1*s*.—a surprisingly low wage, having regard to the responsibilities of the post. Much of the secret correspondence of the garrison inevitably went through his hands. The drummers were paid as private soldiers, but the trumpeters, whose calling required greater technical skill and who supported the heralds on formal occasions, were relatively highly-paid at 1*s*. 6*d*. a day.

Mountjoy's pay is shown in the accounts as £1. 16*s*. 6½*d*. a day[1]—a seemingly odd amount, which is in fact 1,000 marks (£666. 13*s*. 4*d*.) a year expressed as a daily rate. This compared unfavourably with the £2,400 received by his predecessor. The marshal and the captain of the guard each had 6*s*. 8*d*. a day; and the treasurer and the porter each 5*s*. 5¾*d*. a day, equal to £100 a year. The master of the ordnance was the lowest-paid of the senior officers, having no more than a captain's pay of 4*s*. a day.

At the beginning of the occupation payment was made monthly in advance, so that the men, who had to provide their own food, might have cash in hand for at least part of the month. The proposal to change to payment in arrear, which Mountjoy failed to implement on his first arrival in Tournai, seems to have been implemented at a later date (perhaps towards the end of 1516). When Jerningham took over as Governor in January 1517, the King, tired of the constant

---

[1] Not 36*s*. 6¾*d*. as shown in *LP* ii, 1514.

stream of complaints about the lack of money to pay the men, ordered him to change payment from monthly (presumably in arrear) to quarterly in arrear. The fact that this change 'was brought to pass in good and quiet manner' suggests that Jerningham was able to handle the men much more skilfully than his predecessor. His term as treasurer had made him familiar with the money troubles of the private soldier, and he had the good sense to announce that he was setting up a fund of £1,000 to help those who ran out of cash between pays, 'whereof the whole garrison be well content'.[1]

The King and Council were much impressed by the new Governor's success in implementing an unpopular measure; and within less than a year they were asking for more. On 26 March 1518 Jerningham and the council wrote to Wolsey, referring to a proposal that pay should be issued half-yearly, and claiming that it was not possible 'to bring it to so long a day'. Every kind of food and all other necessaries were at a premium. There was no baker, brewer, or butcher who would give the men credit, particularly now that they had moved into the citadel and were 'dissevered' from the town. But for the fact that Jerningham had advanced money to the victuallers and 'undertaken to answer to the brewers and bakers', it would not have been possible to pay the garrison even quarterly.[2]

In April the King returned to the charge. He told the Governor that the city must come into line with the other garrisons of the realm, which were paid half-yearly. There was no need for Tournai to have 'continually so hasty and speedy payment'; and in future there would be only two pay-days— 3 April and 3 October. It was admitted that this might strain the men's resources, so the Governor would be given an imprest of 1,000 marks to help any man in difficulty, it being understood that the sums so advanced would be deducted from the six-monthly pay. (Jerningham had allowed £1,000 a quarter for this purpose. The King authorized only two-thirds of that amount for a period twice as long, but the garrison was, of course, much reduced in size.) The council and captains were

---

[1] Cal. E I, f. 125 b; *LP* ii, 2825.
[2] SP 1/15, f. 38; *LP* ii, 3056. This letter, which has no year in the date, is shown in *LP* as 26 March 1517; but the correct date must be 1518, since the garrison did not enter the citadel until after September 1517.

required to declare themselves 'to be contented and confor-
mable to receive the payment in form afore rehearsed'.[1] There
was to be no mutiny on this occasion: the men were to sign for
their good behaviour.

This was the last straw; and it is a tribute to Jerningham's
leadership that there *was* no mutiny. The Governor must have
taken the leading groups into his confidence, and suggested that
the best course was to send to Wolsey a reasoned case against
the introduction of six-monthly payment. The men-of-arms
(the heavily-armed cavalry, who cannot have been numerous,
and make their appearance in the records only on this occasion),
the gentlemen of the garrison, the yeomen of the guard, the
constables, and the Governor lodged simultaneous protests.
All the letters survive, except that from the men-of-arms; and
they all seek to prove that conditions in Tournai are quite
different from those in Calais.[2]

Jerningham's official account of his action was that he summoned the leaders of the garrison and explained 'the whole
circumstance' of the King's command. The leaders went off to
tell their men, and to prepare their certificates. They came
back, however, with letters of protest, which the Governor
forwarded to Wolsey. In his covering letter he said he had no
doubt that the men's claims about their poverty were justified.
'All the articles declared in the said certificates be of truth and
unfeigned.' In his own view, six-monthly payments would be
disastrous for morale. Even as he was dictating his letter some
victuallers came to complain that a number of men had taken
their victuals by force. Jerningham made enquiries, and found
that the men, who had no money, had offered the victuallers
'to tally with them or set it upon their scores', but they were
not prepared to give credit, as they too were virtually bankrupt.[3]

It is not clear if six-monthly pay was introduced before
the city was handed back to the French; but it is notable that
the system towards which both the Governor and the King were

[1] Strype, pp. 12–14; *LP* ii, 3320.
[2] Cal. E I, f. 158; & *LP* ii, 3323 (the gentlemen); Cal. E I, ff. 156 b–157; & *LP*
ii, 3322 (the constables); Strype, pp. 8–12; & *LP* ii, 3321 (the yeomen); Strype,
pp. 12–14; & *LP* ii, 3320 (the Governor and council). None of these letters includes
the year in the date, nor is the internal evidence conclusive; but they must all have
been written in 1518, although they are shown in *LP* under 1517.
[3] Strype, pp. 12–14; *LP* ii, 3320.

feeling their way became formally established in the latter part of the century. Jerningham's imprest to tide the men over was given the name of 'lendings', which were regularly issued to all men throughout the six-monthly period; and at the end of the period the men had their 'full pay', which was the difference between their total entitlement and the sum they had received in the form of 'lendings'.

IV · THE KING'S WORKS

THERE were two main elements in the plan to reduce the cost of the occupation to England. It was hoped first that the Tournaisiens would take on part of the defence of the city, to reduce the number of Englishmen needed there; and second that the provision of a powerful citadel, which could be defended by a relatively small force, would reduce the wage bill still further. The citizens' reluctance to shoulder any part of the defence burden has been described in the preceding chapter. We are here concerned with the second element in the economy plan—the building of a new citadel.

The theory behind the proposal to have an impregnable citadel was perfectly sound. The city's first line of defence was the outer wall, which needed a minimum of 2,000 men to defend it, and ideally a good many more, if the same men were not to be kept at their posts twenty-four hours a day. If the main wall was breached and the besiegers entered the town in large numbers it was almost inevitable that the garrison would be split into small groups that could be liquidated without difficulty—unless they were able to withdraw into a heavily fortified place, where, given plenty of food and ammunition, they could hold out long enough to give their own side time to assemble an army to raise the siege. In 1513 there was a castle in Tournai, but it was of no great strength and had been allowed to fall into disrepair. Had the English troops found it necessary to fight their way into the town the castle would not have saved the citizens from total destruction.

One of Mountjoy's first tasks when he arrived in Tournai at the beginning of 1515 was to get the building of the citadel under way. It was first proposed that there should be two, one near the Abbey of St. Martin and the other by the Sluice on the river Scheldt at the east side of the town.[1] Within a day or two of his arrival the new Governor, accompanied by Sir Edward Poynings, whom he was replacing, and the master of the ordnance, Thomas Hert, 'devised two convenient places'

[1] SP 1/10, f. 51; *LP* ii, App. 3.

where they might be built, and later suggested to the civic authorities that they should help. This immediately led to trouble, as Mountjoy reported to the King. Nothing would induce them to co-operate; and they expressed great surprise that it had ever been assumed that they would allow the two citadels to be built.[1] The Governor met the four councils formally on 6 March, and again announced that the King intended to build one or two citadels. He pointed out that this would mean that the people would no longer have to billet the soldiers; and he asked what help the city would provide. The councils considered the matter, with the inevitable result. They instructed the *Chefs de la Loi* to draw the Governor's attention to their poverty, and to ask him to tell the King that they regretted they simply could not make any contribution.[2]

As soon as the Earl of Worcester arrived in Tournai as Henry's special representative, he summoned a meeting of the four councils, and told them first that because of the good reports the King had received about their loyalty—apparently the citizens' conspiracy was officially a thing of the past—he had again confirmed their privileges. Having thus sugared the pill, he went on to say that in the interests of the defence of the city and the safety of his loyal subjects the King proposed to construct one or two citadels, and that he would look to the four councils to provide timber, stone, and workmen for the job.[3]

This did not help much. In accordance with their instructions, Mountjoy and his colleagues 'practised' with the *Chefs de la Loi* to induce them to contribute towards the cost of the citadel, to provide materials, and to compensate citizens whose houses had to be pulled down to make way for the new buildings. They stressed that Henry would incur 'inestimable charge'—all for the wealth, profit, and security of the city; but the *Chefs* were unmoved. They repeated that they simply could not afford to help. Their representatives at the Westminster Parliament in 1514 had made it clear that they were very poor, and Henry had implicitly accepted the fact, for example by allowing them to waive the payment of annuities due to people living in enemy territory. Since then the town had been further

[1] Cal. E I, f. 43 b; *LP* ii, 148.   [2] Hocquet (a), xxxxvi (*bis*).
[3] Hocquet (a), xxxviii.

impoverished by 'the great loss and desolation' resulting from the plague; and it had been put to considerable expense in repairing the damage done to the walls in the siege of 1513.

The meeting then plunged into one of the great debates at which the Tournaisiens excelled. Mountjoy tried to show that the city was quite well off. Most of the people removed by the plague had not been important tax-payers. The city's income from taxes was still substantial, and if it did not all find its way into the municipal chest it was simply due to bad government. It was pointless to argue about the cost of repairing the walls. It was manifestly their own responsibility and in their own interest to keep them in good condition. However, if they would agree to go some way towards meeting the King's demands, Mountjoy would try to persuade Henry to settle for that. The city fathers replied at length, and, playing for time with their accustomed skill, asked for four or five days to set their difficulties out in a memorandum for the King. When the debate was resumed they were supported by two 'of the most discreetest' men from each parish, and they handed over a document which enlarged on all their reasons for not contributing one penny towards the cost of 'the King's works'.

Mountjoy told them that their memorandum was not worth the paper it was written on; and to try to get the people to see reason he arranged for a proclamation to be made in every parish, showing how good Henry had been to them and to what expense he was going in their interests. The reaction of the common people was favourable, and the Governor reckoned that if only the four councils had been equally well disposed there would be no problem. Some of the villages in the Tournaisis offered to supply free building labour, but even if every village followed suit the proposed contribution would not be worth more than £100.[1]

Worcester followed up Mountjoy's depressing account of the recalcitrance of the four councils two days later. He thought that the people were now willing to have the citadel, for which the ground had been staked out; and to help things along he had asked a dozen leading citizens to dinner. The result was disappointing. The *grand prévôt*, the recorder, and one of the *échevins* took Worcester aside and told him that there was a

[1] Cal. E I, f. 58; *LP* ii, 812.

general feeling that Tournai, which had been a great centre of commerce, would become 'a city of war' as a result of the proposed fortifications. They asked that the plan for the new citadel should be dropped; and they promised to submit a statement of the conditions on which they would themselves take over the defence of the city. It was not only the Tournaisiens who were worried about the implications of fortifying the city. The inhabitants of Ghent made representations to Prince Charles that there should be an embargo on the sale of timber and stone for Tournai's citadel throughout his dominions. This fact was gleaned by the indefatigable Jean le Sellier.[1]

Towards the end of August Worcester and his fellow-commissioners confessed to Henry that, despite their numerous attempts to persuade the citizens 'to be contributors to the edifying of your citadels', they had drawn blank. No argument could bring them to see reason, and it must now be accepted that they would not help of their own free will. Worcester saw a possible alternative in strengthening the Abbey of St. Amand some miles to the south of Tournai, where he had been well received. He believed that the Abbey could be made very strong at small cost. The Abbot, who was presumed to be loyal to England, had taken kindly to the idea and was even prepared to contribute to the cost of the work. The fortification of the Abbey would no doubt have marginally strengthened the English position in Tournai, but it was too far away to be of any real use, and nothing came of Worcester's idea.[2] Winter was fast approaching, and for the moment there was little point in bringing pressure to bear on the citizens to help with the building programme.

A new attempt was made in 1516. In August the four councils referred to the King's earlier demands that they should contribute to the cost of the new fortifications. Once again they said they could not help, and rehearsed all the old arguments. They were impoverished as a result of their wars with Burgundy, and the siege of 1513. They were saddled with their various payments to Henry, and annuities which they could not meet out of income. The plague had raged for two years and had carried off between 13,000 and 14,000 people. This had ruined

---

[1] Cal. E I, f. 60; *LP* ii, 820.   [2] Cal. D VI, f. 198 b; *LP* ii, 856.

trade and reduced income from taxation. (It must also have killed off an unusually large number of annuitants, but the municipal authorities had the good sense not to refer to this fact.) They had spent 16,000 *livres tournois* in repairing the damage done to their walls by the English guns during the siege; and they considered that they were already doing enough for the defence of the city. They begged Mountjoy to pass this on to Henry and to ask that nothing more should be asked of them.[1]

In January 1517 Mountjoy and Jerningham made yet another attempt to get the city and the Dean and Chapter to help; but the results were again disappointing. The most the four councils would offer was 50 labourers a day for five or six months. The Governor did not try to get them to improve this, as they had decided to send a deputation to the King. It was to be led by the second *prévôt*, Jean Thorow, a hard bargainer, who at this time did most of the talking for the city. Jerningham told Wolsey that if the deputation was 'well and sharply handled' in London it would be easier for the council in Tournai to bring the city to heel, and that the Dean and Chapter would then come into line very quickly. He thought that the city's minimum contribution should be 400 labourers a day for four months. He warned that the deputation were hoping that some of the King's Councillors would take their part, and that they were bringing gifts to buy their goodwill. They would have three or four pieces of tapestry for the Duke of Suffolk, 'which they say was promised him when the town was delivered to the King'. They had remembered this four-year-old promise at a very convenient moment. Jerningham passed this on, so that the King 'should not take no prejudice from the same'.[2]

The four councils met on 3 April to hear the report of the delegation on their return. They explained that it had seemed to the King to be for the common good and security of the city that they should agree to contribute to the fortifications. He was aware that they had offered 50 workmen, but, even having regard to the great charges the city had to meet, he thought

---

[1] Hocquet (a), xlii; SP 1/13, ff. 29–30; *LP* ii, 1607. It is true that annuities were often related to more than one life, but the fact remains that mortality at any point of time in excess of actuarial expectation meant a windfall profit to the city.

[2] SP 1/14, ff. 215–16; *LP* ii, 2826.

they could do better than this. Finally, it had been agreed that they should provide 100 workmen for a maximum of six months;[1] and it seems that this was the limit of the city's contribution to the King's works.

William Pawne, who had been in charge of the fortifications at Berwick, was transferred to Tournai in September 1515 to act as commissioner of works, with general responsibility for the construction of the new fortifications there. Almost as soon as he arrived he found himself involved in the sort of squabble which was to persist during the whole of the occupation. He reported his safe arrival to Wolsey, and reminded him that he had brought instructions from London to give first priority to the completion of the citadel. (By this time it had been decided to have no more than one.) All other improvements were to be postponed for the time being. He was therefore astonished to find that the Governor had taken it upon himself to embark on the construction of three bulwarks. Thomas Hert, master of the ordnance, was in charge of one to the south of the West Sluice gate; Sir Richard Jerningham had the second, to the north of the West Sluice; and Sir Richard Whethill and Richard Sampson were jointly responsible for a bulwark with a false braye[2] outside the Bruille Gate.

Pawne pointed out that it was impossible to make satisfactory progress on the citadel itself when so many men were engaged in these other works. If all the available labour were put at his disposal he would make the citadel defensible by St. Andrew's Day. (Presumably he meant 30 November 1516, since he was writing on 30 September 1515, and by no stretch of the imagination could the works have been completed within two months.) Not only was the labour denied him, but he got no support from the members of the Governor's council. He complained to Wolsey:

Notwithstanding that I was sent hither by your grace and your most honourable lordships with sufficient authority, instructions and plats signed with the King's most gracious hand to have the devising, making and enclosing of the said citadel with most hasty expedition that could be made and for the King's most profit. Yet oftentimes

[1] Hocquet (a), xlvi.
[2] 'An advanced parapet surrounding the main rampart' (*O.E.D.*).

neither my counsel, the master mason's ne the master carpenter's
(who have done the King right painful, diligent, and profitable
service in the foresaid business here) which we have thought to have
sounded most to the King's and your pleasure and commandment
and for the most profit could not be heard nor accepted to our great
trouble confusion and abashment.

The commissioner clearly felt all the irritation of the experienced professional who has to fight against amateur interference bolstered by greater authority.

The real trouble was that the council suspected Pawne
needed careful watching. They had therefore appointed
William Bartholomew and Hugh Say to be his 'comptrollers',
although he claimed that Henry himself had appointed Thomas
Hert and Jean le Sellier for this purpose. The Governor's
council had no right to change a decision of the King. When
Mountjoy asked him to sign a letter agreeing to the appointment of Bartholomew and Say, he refused at first, but, as 'the
council so importunately willed me to set my hand to the said
letter', he gave way, on the ground that his books were above
suspicion and he did not mind who examined them. Since then
there had been intolerable interference in his management of
the building operations.[1]

He was still under fire a month later. Mountjoy and the
council had assumed that the kilns which had been built to
provide lime for the masons would reduce costs—it was cheaper
to make their own lime than to buy it locally—but in fact costs
had gone up. Pawne's explanation was simple. The increased
rate of building called for much more lime than the council's
own kilns could produce; and in any case the ancillary activities
—the carriage of stone, and the de-watering of the site, for
example—had also been intensified and were therefore much
more costly. He would be glad to let the Governor have a full
statement of his accounts if only he had a moment's leisure to
prepare them. His books, however, were made up once a fortnight—240 pages of them—and his clerks had great difficulty in
completing one fortnight's account before the next was upon
them. The council had also been chivvying him about 'check-
money', that is to say stoppages on pay which were supposed to
return to the treasurer; but Pawne said that he regarded this

[1] SP 1/11 b, f. 106; *LP* ii, 961.

as one of the perquisites of the clerks who collected it.[1] The unfortunate commissioner was caught between two fires, for he had also to answer searching questions about the unsatisfactory progress of the citadel from the Council in London.[2]

Pawne seems to have had a genius for upsetting everyone he dealt with. About this time his servant Robert Russell brought news from London that Wolsey was 'not a little displeased' because he had not written privately to him about affairs in Tournai. Wolsey liked to have many sources of information, and perhaps considered that it was easier to arrive at the truth when he had several conflicting views of a situation. Pawne confessed that he was greatly 'abashed' (a favourite word of his) and 'discomfited' when he thought how good and gracious lord Wolsey had been to him in the past. His commands were among the most important things in his life—next to those of the King, of course. He felt that he should not trouble him with news of all his problems; but promised to write more often in the future. Finally, he said that a report (that Wolsey had received) that he was 'fumous' was untrue. He was only 'sharp in his prince's causes'; and even if he was fumous, his fumes hurt him more than they hurt others.[3]

Pawne was not slow to take up Wolsey's licence to write to him direct. In March 1516 he listed a number of points for Wolsey about 'the not so soon finishing of the citadel'—a pleasant euphemism. His main target was again Mountjoy, whom he accused of unwarrantable interference in matters he did not understand. The Governor was indulging his fancy devising foolish variations of the accepted plans, actually going so far as to have the ground staked out so that foundations might be dug; but none of this came to anything, presumably because Pawne was able to demonstrate that Mountjoy's amateur ideas were unsound. The Governor had also injured Pawne's professional pride by calling in a supposed expert—one Jaques of Douai—with whom he worked out new plans, all of which wasted time.

Some of his plans, however, had been adopted, in Pawne's view with disastrous results. The bulwark which Thomas Hert was building had an arc of 500 feet, whereas 200 feet would

[1] SP 1/11, f. 140; *LP* ii, 1082. [2] SP 1/11, f. 148; *LP* ii, 1118.
[3] SP 1/12, f. 75; *LP* ii, 1403.

have been ample. A great deal of material and labour, all of which cost money, had thus been wasted—a fact that the Earl of Worcester, who had seen the bulwark, would be able to confirm. Again, the citadel wall was being built 21 feet thick, although 16 feet was all that was needed. The walls of the towers need be no more than 20 feet thick, but they were being made 25 feet, and in his wilder moments the Governor had talked of making them even 30 or 40 feet thick. The plans approved by the King provided for the Minthouse tower to be built in a certain place; but Mountjoy had insisted that it should go somewhere else. This increased by a quarter the amount of stone needed. Moreover, one of its walls was 'set askew and out of compass'. The catalogue went on. 150 men had worked for four months building false brayes in various places, none of which were necessary. A wall between the Pont du Château and the west sluice narrowed from 35 feet at the base to 20 feet at the top. Half these dimensions would have been perfectly adequate. But for all these nonsensical things the citadel would be well on the way to completion.

After this devastating attack on the King's lieutenant, his superior officer, Pawne goes on to defend himself against his critics in Tournai. His payments had always been supervised by the comptrollers appointed by Henry. All purchases of materials had been properly made by Jean le Sellier, and the goods weighed or measured at the time of purchase. The many allegations—that he had refused to allow his account books to be examined, that he had kept secret the prices at which he bought the many stores needed for the King's works, that the workmen had not been mustered before being paid, that payments for the cartage of lime, stone, and sand had been rigged, and so on—were completely false. Pawne concludes by reminding Wolsey that he had loyally served Henry and his father for 34 years; and he begs that he should be discharged rather than continue to endure the slanders showered upon him.[1]

Mountjoy continued his campaign against Pawne. In May 1516 he sent to Wolsey George Lawson, who had been master mason at Berwick, and whom he regarded as his ally against the commissioner of works. Lawson was instructed to discuss a number of outstanding points on 'these great works of the

[1] SP 1/13, ff. 46–7; *LP* ii, 1656.

King's' and to bring back answers as quickly as possible. Further, and this is probably the real reason why he was sent to England at this time, Mountjoy hoped that Lawson might replace Pawne, or at least be given a position of responsibility in which he could be used to undermine him. 'I would gladly have George for to be sent over and to have a charge in furthering of this work.' He was old and wise and had 'good sight in such causes'. The Governor and his council unanimously agreed that he would do the King great service. In Mountjoy's view Pawne was still up to his old tricks. He was paying the workmen without inviting any of the council to be present at the monthly muster. Was this to continue, or might he be called to order?[1]

Mountjoy complained about Pawne's management of the works during the whole of his governorship. He wrote to the King in December 1516: 'there be certain misdemeanours in William Pawne which you shall perceive by a book of articles at this time sent to Sir Richard Jerningham. And if he be not reformed in them, and will take our advices more than he doeth it shall be much to your grace's disadvantage.' He was drawing the King's attention to this unsatisfactory state of affairs to safeguard his own position.[2] Pawne for his part kept protesting his innocence. He begged Wolsey 'to give no hasty credence . . . to any such complaints as may be made by such evil and light-disposed persons to be made unto your grace of me behind my back'.[3]

It was an extraordinary situation. The Governor and the commissioner of works must have met daily in the ordinary course of events, and they must often have discussed the progress of the King's works. Pawne was a member of the Governor's council, where more formal discussion took place. They both signed the council's dispatches to Henry and Wolsey. At the same time both had their own direct line of communication to London and their letters could not criticize the actions of the other severely enough.

Henry was well aware of the strained relations between the Governor and the commissioner. In February 1517 a dispatch went to Tournai saying that it was 'his express mind and pleasure' that Pawne should keep the Governor fully informed

---

[1] SP 1/13, f. 176; *LP* ii, 1940.   [2] SP 1/14, f. 128; *LP* ii, 2622.
[3] SP 1/13, f. 267; *LP* ii, 2265.

about all matters concerning the works, and in particular about the payments he was making, 'so that they being all in unity and concord may the better endeavour themselves for the accomplishment of the said citadel to the King's most profit and advancement'.[1]

Pawne also fell foul of the master of the ordnance, Thomas Hert, who had to remind Wolsey that the King had appointed him and Jean le Sellier to act as comptrollers to the commissioner of works. Pawne and le Sellier were making payments by arrangement between themselves without any reference to Hert, which was quite contrary to the King's instructions, and in Hert's view highly suspicious. Both Mountjoy and the Earl of Worcester had confirmed that he should have access to all Pawne's books, but the commissioner had refused to disclose any information about his transactions. Hert therefore could not guarantee that the King's affairs were being properly managed. Further, the checks on workmen's wages, which Hert said amounted to a considerable sum, were still going to the commissioner's clerks, with the King's approval, according to Pawne. Hert asked Wolsey to reinforce his authority 'by the mean whereby the things that I control may take effect'; and also to give him some clerks to make his job easier. If this could not be done he wanted to be relieved of the office.[2]

A month later Jerningham, who was now Governor, was still complaining about the commissioner. He was daily called upon to settle claims for payments due from Pawne, who was absent in London. This was particularly unfortunate, as the weather was beginning to improve and the completion of the fortifications should be tackled vigorously; but if uncertainty about payments continued it would mean 'a great unsurety and let' to the King's works.[3] It is perhaps surprising that Pawne was allowed to remain in his post for so long; but it was not the last time that a clash of personality would make difficult the conduct of the sovereign's business abroad. On this occasion, as in later times, personality was with difficulty subordinated to the needs of the job; but efficiency must have suffered.

It is difficult to say how guilty Pawne was by the standards of the age, or whether there was anyone who would have done

[1] SP 1/15, f. 16; LP ii, 2972.   [2] SP 1/15, f. 21; LP ii, 2984.
[3] SP 1/15, f. 38; LP ii, 3056.

a better job. A stronger man than Mountjoy might have had him replaced, and indeed the Governor was so critical of Pawne's performance over a long period that it is arguable that he should have insisted on his dismissal. It seems unlikely that Sir Richard Jerningham, who was a better administrator than Mountjoy, would have tolerated him had he been Governor at the time of his appointment; but when Jerningham took over from Mountjoy the King's works were nearing completion, and the new Governor probably decided that it was better to retain the devil he knew.

It was not until 1516 that real progress began to be made with the new fortifications. Building was seasonal, as it still is. It was possible to plan during the winter but not to make much headway with execution. Pawne wrote to Wolsey in January 1516, listing the materials and equipment provided for the spring offensive on the King's works. There were already upon the ground 24,000 quarters of lime, 60,000 feet of hewn stone, 8,000 tons of filling or rag stone, 700 tons of wood, and 1,000 loads of sand. There were also substantial quantities of the other necessary stores: iron and steel, wheelbarrows, hand-barrows, gins (for winding up heavy loads, for example stone from barges in the river Scheldt), hurdles, tools for the masons and 'rockyers', tubs for mortar, buckets for slaking lime, hods for carrying bricks, baskets for sand, and shivers (i.e. pulleys) of brass.[1]

Further, Mountjoy told the King that he had been studying what was needed for the fortifications, and had come to the conclusion that everything could be found locally, except iron and steel. It would, however, be necessary to send a great number of workmen from England as soon as possible. If they were competent, the works would make good progress to the King's honour and profit.[2] This proposal was accepted, and in March Pawne and le Sellier were authorized to recruit men in England.[3] The Governor of Calais heard what was in the wind, and quickly told Henry that without clear instructions to the contrary he had no intention of allowing any of the carpenters and masons in Calais to move to Tournai.[4] Sir Richard Whethill

---

[1] SP 1/12, f. 75; *LP* ii, 1403.   [2] Cal. E I, f. 78; *LP* ii, 1509.
[3] C 76/197; *LP* ii, 1636.   [4] SP 1/13, ff. 44–5; *LP* ii, 1655.

took a slightly less optimistic view than Mountjoy. He told Wolsey 'the works here goeth well forward but it shall not be so soon ended as your grace would'.[1]

In a later progress report Mountjoy confessed, probably with trepidation, that one of his main problems was how much compensation to pay for houses standing in the way of the new buildings and needing to be demolished. The Earl of Worcester had intended to discuss this in London, but 'I never had answer'. The Governor raised it again through Lancaster Herald, and yet again through Sir Edward Poynings, still with no result. It had become obvious in the spring that valuable time and labour would be wasted if the council continued to wait for instructions from London, and therefore, with the full approval of his colleagues, he had ordered that the houses should be pulled down. He had taken the precaution of having them appraised first—they had been valued at 13 years' purchase, 'which in these parts is reckoned great cheap'—but he had agreed that the owners should receive adequate compensation in due course. He was clearly worried about Henry's reaction to this unauthorized commitment, and to soften the blow he reminded the King that the houses would yield useful material for the new fortifications. In any case, when they were being demolished 'the bruit and murmuration were fervent', and the Governor, ever anxious to save his own skin, deemed it both right and expedient to provide compensation. He ended his dispatch with the anodyne sentence: 'And as to your works, so to advance them and conduct them by the advice of other your council here both to your honour and for diminishing your great charges here with all the speed possible that I trust we shall deserve largely your grace's favour thereby'.[2]

If the Governor hoped to get away with this, he was doomed to disappointment. Henry left no doubt about his view that he did not deserve his favour. He simply could not see why the fortifications were taking so long. He considered that the Governor and his council had slowed things up by departing from the plan approved by him. In particular, their variations had meant cutting some of the foundations into rock, which was slow and expensive, and they had also meant the demolition of

---

[1] SP 1/13, f. 76; *LP* ii, 1708.   [2] Cal. E I, ff. 102–3; *LP* ii, 1894.

more houses than was necessary. Nor was the King impressed
by the long catalogue of materials provided. The quantities
might seem to be immense, but they were not enough to keep
fully employed the vast army of workmen that had been
assembled. Above all, there was no question of paying compensation. It was well known that when houses were demolished
for the common good none was payable, witness the burning of
the suburbs before the English army laid siege to Tournai in
1513. Nothing had been paid then.

Mountjoy replied in detail to the King's charges in a dispatch
signed by the whole council, to make it clear that they all
supported him. They had been appointed 'masters, overseers
and devisers' of the citadel, and they considered that they were
authorized to depart from the King's plan when it seemed right
to do so. They had extended the buildings by only 40 feet, and
this had many advantages. Further, had the approved plan
been followed in every detail it would have meant pulling down
even more houses. The rocks quarried out of the new foundations had been used as building material. The council's failure
to lay in enough stores in advance was due to lack of money.
When Worcester left Tournai earlier in the year he had
promised to see that funds were made available, but no money
came until April, when the new building season was already
upon them.

The Governor admitted that Henry might have a valid point
in suggesting that compensation was not payable when the
common good was in view; but he could only repeat that he
had done his best to find out his wishes, and that the decision to
pull down the houses had been taken only after long debate and
reasoning. Searching desperately for arguments to justify his
position, he reminded Henry that when he captured Tournai he
promised 'by the word of a king' that all the inhabitants should
enjoy 'clearly and without interruption their goods, houses and
inheritances'. His honour was therefore at risk. Further, saving
the King's pleasure, the burning of the suburbs was not a good
precedent. It had been done at a time of great danger by
common consent—including the consent of the owners. The
walls and ground remained, so that all had not been lost. In
Tournai, however, the owners were left with nothing, as the
sites had been built over; and the materials from the houses

(worth about £1,000) had been incorporated in the new fortifications.[1]

Mountjoy was seriously worried about the King's attitude, and wrote privately to Wolsey, supplementing the defence put forward by the council as a whole. The King's Council seemed to have gained the impression that he alone was responsible for the decision to pay compensation, but this was quite wrong. Surely no one could think that such a major decision would be taken 'all upon mine own head'? The truth was that 'the most part and most discreetest' of the council had agreed; and if Wolsey had heard all the arguments he also would have agreed. If the King still refused to believe that they had acted for the best, he suggested that commissioners should be sent from England to make an on-the-spot investigation, to decide whether he and his council had done their job properly.[2]

Shortly afterwards Sir Richard Whethill volunteered his minority view to Wolsey, in his angular, painful, and sometimes incomprehensible hand. He agreed that bad planning had caused much of the delay. Pawne and the master mason should have surveyed the site much earlier than they did. They could then have got out an estimate of the quantity of materials required, and stocks could have been built up before the main body of the workmen arrived for the new season. The huge building programme demanded an unprecedented supply of lime, and the eight lime-kilns that had been built to supplement Tournai's normal production were totally inadequate. They could have done with another eight. Again, any hope that the old walls and towers would yield much of the stone needed for the new fortifications had proved false, exactly as Whethill had forecast. The material on the outside was quite good, but the filling was rubbish. Whethill had warned the Earl of Worcester about this, 'but a poor man might not be heard'.

He reckoned that, even when the fortifications were completed and the garrison reduced to the safe minimum, the English presence in Tournai would continue to impose a serious drain on the balance of payments. 'I think often upon the great charges the King has been at as also is and shall be by reason of keeping of this garrison here whereby has come and shall come good sums of money out of his realm, which will be always

---

[1] Cal. E I, ff. 108–10; *LP* ii, 2236.   [2] SP 1/13, f. 257; *LP* ii, 2238.

chargeable.' The thoughtful marshal went on to suggest a remedy. Henry must buy up all the substantial houses in the city, and build more houses and shops, which would provide an income to make Tournai self-supporting. The capital outlay might be as much as £100,000, but it would be worth it in the long run.[1]

The argument about compensation was still in progress in March 1517. Henry, who had just received a deputation from Tournai to discuss this and other matters, sent a formal reply to the city; and at the same time he wrote to the Governor and council, briefing them on how to handle the matter when the city's representatives came home. He had not finally committed himself to pay any compensation at all, but had provisionally suggested that the burden should be shared. The Governor must therefore 'enter into communication with the parties having their houses razed' and do his best to get the agreed value of the property reduced. He was to remind them and the civic authorities of the heavy cost of maintaining the garrison and building the citadel. This money was spent for the common good, and it was therefore 'right agreeable to law and reason' that the cost should be spread. This was the universal custom when houses were 'plucked down' for defence purposes. It happened in London, and it had happened in Tournai when the suburbs were destroyed in 1513. It was expected that after they had listened to this tough line the householders would be happy to settle for anything, and that the half-share that Henry had provisionally agreed to bear would be kept to a minimum.[2]

Finally, a compromise was reached whereby the King agreed that the outstanding instalments of the special annual tribute of 4,000 *livres* which the city had undertaken to pay him for ten years should be regarded as his contribution towards the compensation of the property-owners who had suffered damage.

As the weather improved good progress was made, even with the smaller number of workmen allowed by Henry; but at the end of May a major catastrophe was only narrowly averted. At eleven o'clock on the morning of 30 May fire broke out in one of the thatched houses inside the compound and quickly spread to about twenty others. Thanks to 'the provision of almighty God and the good diligence of your soldiers and

[1] SP 1/13, f. 266; *LP* ii, 2260.   [2] SP 1/15, f. 36; *LP* ii, 3055.

labourers here' the fire had been contained, and the only people to suffer damage were the householders and the soldiers who were billeted on them; but Sir Richard Jerningham told Henry that the citadel's powder store could easily have blown up. If that had happened it would have been a major disaster, and much of the effort of the last two or three years would have gone for nothing; and it was now essential that a safe building should be provided for gunpowder, which was at present stored with food and other necessaries in 40 or 50 'small several houses and those be right simple'. Not only was the natural fire hazard very serious, but the country was full of incendiaries who could easily cause havoc in the citadel: indeed a number of them had been convicted and executed in the *bailliage*.[1]

At last, on Tuesday 29 September 1517, the Governor decided that the new citadel was sufficiently far advanced for him to order the whole of the garrison into it; and at the same time to tell the four councils that from now on they would be responsible for the defence of the rest of the city.[2] After three years of tremendous effort and the expenditure of huge capital sums the King's works were operational, and England could look forward to a reduction in the heavy cost of maintaining a presence in Tournai—at a time when many were beginning to think that the only sensible course was for Henry to cut his losses and withdraw from the city.

Henry had hoped that the new citadel would be completed sometime in 1516, but it was obvious long before the end of the summer that he was going to be disappointed. Richard Sampson told Wolsey that 'to have the King's pleasure accomplished this year for the closing of the citadel, it is nothing like'; but he believed that if plenty of materials were stocked up during the winter there was every chance that it would be ready in 1517. If only there had been enough lime and stone to keep 500 or 600 masons busy in 1516, it could have been completed by the end of that year. Sampson reminded Wolsey of the enormous size of the project. The works were 'marvellous weighty', and if they were as well finished as they had been begun they would have no equal in Europe.[3]

[1] SP 1/15, ff. 141–141 b; *LP* ii, 3313.   [2] See below, p. 202.
[3] Cal. D VI, f. 301; *LP* ii, 2274.

On 1 December Mountjoy, whose term of office as Governor was drawing to a close, submitted a general report on the works to the King. He and William Pawne were about to discharge 1,050 workmen for the winter season. He was glad to say that those who had been sent from England earlier in the year had been most diligent, and he hoped that it would be possible to find them alternative work until they were needed again in the spring—surely a pretty tall order. At the same time he ventured to suggest further departures from the design which Henry had approved. He thought it necessary that the wall from the Bruille Gate to the West Sluice should be two carts wide at the top, but this would be so big a job that it should wait until the citadel was finished; and he added that it was essential that nothing should hinder the construction 'of your wall and towers, and especially of your dike'. Neither Tournai nor the Tournaisis was prepared to make a significant contribution to the works, but Mountjoy suggested that it was hardly worth while making a fuss about this, especially since any labour that was made available would be hampered by the short winter day.[1] The Governor had no intention of allowing the bad planning of the previous year to be repeated. He assured Wolsey that he and his colleagues 'shall be busy about the provisions, making to have everything ready against the workmen's coming'.[2]

The Earl of Worcester visited Tournai in January 1517, to make a thorough study of the problems of the fortifications in the light of local conditions and the plans which Henry had approved; and while he was there he prepared a memorandum 'for the more ripe and better instruction' of the two commissioners of works, William Pawne and Jean le Sellier. This is an interesting document, not only because of the light it sheds on the fortifications. The final draft attributes most of the main decisions to Worcester personally ('the said Lord Chamberlain hath ordained and commanded on the King's behalf'), but the signed version provides for collective responsibility with the Governor and the members of his council. It would be interesting to know if the revision was made because the council resented that Worcester, who was an outsider from London,

[1] SP 1/14, ff. 128–128 b; *LP* ii, 2622.
[2] SP 1/14, ff. 211 b–212; *LP* ii, 2820.

although he knew Tournai well, should lay down the law on
matters on which they ought to have been the more expert, or
because the Lord Chamberlain felt on reflection that he had
taken too much on himself, and might later be exposed to
criticism if things worked out badly; but it is impossible to
discover the reason for the changes.[1]

In doing their job the commissioners were to be guided by the
memorandum, by the advice of the council in Tournai 'as far
forth as it shall sound for the best and soonest expedition and for
the least cost of making the citadel', and by the 'plat' and
instructions signed by the King's most gracious hand. It was
not made clear who had the last word in deciding that any
particular step *was* for the best and cheapest expedition of the
works; and the confused responsibility which had earlier caused
trouble was formally perpetuated. The final design was to be
determined by the King's instructions, the council, and the
commissioners; and it was possible that all might be in conflict.

Certain aspects of the design were left to the discretion of the
men on the spot. It had been laid down by Henry how many
towers there should be, where they should be sited, and how
many storeys each should have; but their height was left to the
council and the commissioners. The tower between the Pont du
Château and the West Sluice was to have three storeys, 'containing from floor to floor ten feet or more as it shall be thought
meet by the said councillors and commissioners'. The White
Tower beside the Minthouse was to have three floors 'of such a
height as shall be thought needful'. This empirical approach
to the science of fortification may seem surprising, but there
were some matters that had to be settled in the light of local
knowledge. The ideal height of a tower could be arrived at only
by considering it in relation to nearby features both inside and
outside the town. An extra ten feet might enable it to command
an area outside the walls which would otherwise be masked;
and Henry and the Council in London could not possibly see
this sort of thing. Extemporization in the design of fortifications
had its parallel on the field of battle, where elaborate theory as
to how an engagement should be fought, evolved in comparative calm by the council of war, must often have been thrown to
the winds as soon as battle was joined.

[1] SP 1/14, ff. 205–10; Cal. D VI, ff. 309–14; *LP* ii, 2819 (1) and (2).

The Earl of Worcester planned that 2,836 men should be available no later than the middle of February. More than half of them were to be masons and their supporting mortar-makers and labourers. Worcester reckoned that 506 masons were needed (he arrived at this figure by allowing 3 masons to every 20 feet of wall to be built); and as each mason had his own team of three labourers and mortar-makers it meant that a total of 1,518 of these had to be found. At the time when these requirements were worked out there were in pay only 127 masons and 456 labourers and mortar-makers, so that no fewer than 379 masons and 1,062 workmen to help them had to be engaged.

The position was rather better with the other artificers. All the necessary 300 carpenters, 8 sawyers, and 22 smiths were already in Tournai, as were most of the 80 'rockyers' and hewers of stone. But of the 200 labourers needed to man the 15 'gins' for discharging boats in the river Scheldt and winding up stones to the towers and walls there were only 48 already in pay; and none of the 100 men 'to go in the water wheels, to keep pumps and other engines for the avoiding of water, and to cast water with scoops' had been recruited. There were 334 'dikers' in pay, leaving 66 to be provided; and of the 12 'piermen, lightermen, measurers of stone and tellers of lime' 9 were in post. Worcester's memorandum is dated 24 January, and the target date for the recruitment of the full complement is 15 February, which means that 1,785 men had to be found and engaged within less than a month. It was presumed that the greater part of the workmen would be found in England.[1]

Worcester also laid down rules for the men, which were proclaimed in French as well as in English for the benefit of those who had been taken on locally. No man was to be so hardy as to steal or take away any of the King's tools or materials—hammers, chisels, beetles,[2] mallets, iron crowbars, wedges and sledges, wheelbarrows, hand-barrows, hurdles, board, timber, or anything else belonging to the King's works— nor was anyone to receive any of these things by way of pledge or otherwise. No householder was to allow any workman to play

[1] SP 1/14, ff. 211–12; *LP* ii, 2820.
[2] 'An implement consisting of a heavy weight or "head", usually of wood, with a handle or stock, used for driving wedges or pegs, ramming down paving stones . . . a mall' (*O.E.D.*).

dice, cards, or any other unlawful game in his house by day or by night, or to sit drinking, or loitering during working hours. A separate order commanded the soldiers of the garrison not to 'intermeddle' in the King's works or mingle with the labourers so that they were encouraged to neglect their duties.[1]

The plans evolved by Worcester and the council in Tournai looked admirable on paper, and the authors must have felt a good deal of satisfaction with a job well done when they sent them off to Henry for approval. They must have been equally disappointed when the King made known his reaction. He had seen and 'well understanden' all the proposals, and had 'substantially debated and reasoned thereupon' with the Council. Alas, they had all come to the conclusion that they contained much that was 'superfluous and costly'. They would run the King into much greater expense than was necessary, partly because of the 'sumptuousness of the work' and partly because they would delay the completion of the citadel, and the consequent reduction in the size and cost of the garrison.

Therefore the King sent to the Governor and council his express commandments for the completion of the works, from which they were to deviate at their peril. The citadel itself and the surrounding wall must be completed as soon as possible, so that a large part of the garrison might be safely discharged. This work had the highest priority, but Henry selected some other buildings for speedy completion, for example, the new tower by the Bruille Gate, and the gate and drawbridge at the Pont du Château which was to be one of the approaches to the new fortified area. All other work was to 'stand and rest' until the citadel was enclosed, which the King hoped would be accomplished by May Day, at which date he considered that 500 workmen might be dismissed.

Although Worcester had planned for a labour force of nearly 3,000, Henry laid down that there were to be no more than 2,000, as many as possible being English, so that they would be 'a great succour and strength for the surety and defence of the said city as though that number were in the ordinary retinue of the same'. In short, every Englishman among the workmen was expected to double as a soldier in time of emergency. As soon as the citadel was 'enclosed to a defensible height' the whole

[1] SP 1/14, ff. 211–12; *LP* ii, 2820.

labour force was to be dismissed, except for '500 or 600 masons, carpenters, and labourers, Englishmen, who shall continue to perfect the finishing of the works'. There were to be other economy measures. The main wall was to be narrowed to a breadth of no more than 15 or 16 feet at the top, compared with the twenty feet that had been earlier contemplated; and for the present the towers were to be restricted to one storey, but to be finished off in such a way that a second storey could easily be added at a later stage.[1]

The citadel occupied an area, about one-twelfth the size of the city, in the north-west quarter where the old château had been. It was bounded by the river Scheldt to the south, and its walls were protected by a moat fed from the river. The only part of the fortifications which has survived to the present time is a massive tower, which still bears the name of Henry VIII, and as none of the plans has survived it is difficult to visualize exactly how the works looked in 1519 when the English garrison pulled out.

Some idea of the general layout may be gathered from the instructions which were provided for the commissioner of works at the beginning of 1517. There were to be five new towers. One was to be sited between the West Sluice and the Pont du Château—the bridge which led from the old château north across the moat. This was to be two storeys high, each ten feet or more from floor to floor. At the 'Minthouse corner' there was to be a three-storey tower—the White Tower, which was to be as high as was 'thought needfull'. A two-storey tower was to be built 'in the new dike between the White Tower and the tower at the corner of the citadel in the town wall', and the latter tower, 'which stands in great danger', had to be as substantially built as the White Tower. Finally, the tower at the south end of the Pont du Château has to be made 'massive with lime and stone'. The existing stairs in this tower were to be walled up, and new stairs to be made inside the tower. The height was to be increased, and the tower was to be given a flat roof 'to lay ordnance on'.

Other features in the area of the Pont du Château were Thomas Hert's bulwark, which upset Pawne when he first

---

[1] SP 1/15, f. 17; *LP* ii, 2972.

arrived in Tournai, and a new drawbridge, with a gate at the north end, protected by two small towers. Apparently the drawbridge was to lead from the existing bridge, which was itself to have new walls along its length 'as thick as thought needfull, and as the bridge can bear'.

There were to be a good many changes in the vicinity of the West Sluice. A new arch was to be made at the south side of the Sluice 'in the departing' of the bulwark of the citadel and the town, and a second arch at the south end of the Sluice. These arches were to be made 'sharp above with spikons of iron', according to the design proposed by the Earl of Worcester—or 'after some other device as it shall be thought best' by the council, commissioners of works, and the master mason. The bulwark on the south side of the West Sluice was to be made up 'after the manner and fashion that it is begun'; and the corresponding bulwark within the town was to be completed according to Worcester's plan. The West Sluice itself was to be fortified and 'made strong with lime and stone', its roof was to be heightened as the council and commissioners of works thought needful, and it was to be made flat for ordnance 'to scour all round about'.

In the area of the Bruille Gate a bulwark was to be made 'after the best device of the council and commissioners'. Inside the gate, which led into the citadel, two walls were to be constructed 'as jaws to the said gate' and vaulted or joisted with timber, so that the ordnance could be carried round about the wall 'for the more strength of the said gate'.

Other points touched on in the instructions to the commissioners of works were that the new wall of the citadel should be 'higher or lower as the council and commissioners shall think necessary for the safeguard of the same'. All towers and buildings that seemed to be prejudicial to the safety of the citadel were to be pulled down, including a gate standing on the inner ward of the city eastward from the citadel towards the church of St. Brice; a high tower east of the Marvis Gate, if it seemed to threaten the citadel; two houses on the south-west side of the Pont du Château, and three houses on the other side; two towers to the south of the West Sluice; the steeple of St. Brice's Church, which commanded the whole of the citadel; a gate with towers south of the Pont du Château; and finally another

tower to the east of the same gate, which Worcester thought
should be allowed to stand 'until the bulwark and citadel be
further advanced for their safeguard and defence'.

In general, the plat and instructions, 'signed with the King's
most gracious hand', supplemented by Worcester's proposals,
were to be 'inviolably observed' by the commissioners of works,
assisted by the Governor's council, whose advice they were not
to refuse.[1]

The Lord Chamberlain's instructions give some idea of the
magnitude of the King's works, if they do not make possible a
very precise reconstruction; and when all the many buildings
that went to make up the citadel are visualized on the scale of
the enormous Tour d'Henri VIII, which has survived four and
a half centuries of violent change and still stands on what was
the northern boundary of the citadel, it becomes clear what a
vast undertaking the new citadel was. It also underlines the folly
of embarking on such a costly enterprise without the absolute
certainty that it would be vital to England's defence for many
years. Had Henry been satisfied that it would be in his interest
to hold Tournai for perhaps the next twenty-five years, the
capital investment would no doubt have been worth while; but,
as it turned out, the citadel was handed over to his traditional
enemy before it had a chance to earn a dividend.

[1] SP 1/14, ff. 205–10; *LP* ii, 2819.

V · TRADE AND COMMERCE

IT may have occurred to some of the more far-sighted members of the 1513 expedition that the capture of Tournai might provide England with a valuable new trading partner. Certainly there was no doubt in their minds about the importance of the city in the commercial life of the region. Brian Tuke, who later became governor of the King's posts, wrote enthusiastically about the city and its manufactures. Tournai was 'large and beautiful, the wealthiest city in all Flanders and the most populous of any on that side of Paris'. It manufactured excellent carpets and table covers; and he thought that it would be particularly useful to the King, since Burgundian and Rhenish wines could conveniently be carried to England from the city.[1]

Although Tournai may have appeared prosperous to her conquerors by their own standards, the city was in fact in an economic decline, an innocent victim of the war between France and the dukes of Burgundy. She had gone from strength to strength in the fourteenth century and for most of the fifteenth, and in 1513 there was still a great demand for her manufactures, cloth and fine tapestry in particular, in the rest of France, the Low Countries, and in Burgundy itself; but the external pressures to which she had been subjected at intervals for nearly a thousand years were intensified in the latter part of the fifteenth century, and the results were now beginning to be felt.

The dukes of Burgundy were anxious to consolidate their territories east of France, and in 1463 Philip the Good tried to take Tournai by force. He failed, and his son Charles the Bold, thinking that economic sanctions might be more effective, forbade his subjects in Artois, Hainaut, and Flanders, who supplied much of her food to the city, to do business with the citizens. He confiscated property owned in his dominions by the merchants of Tournai, together with all rents and profits due to them; and he arrested any who dared to defy the ban on trading with his subjects. These measures greatly weakened the city's trading position. The purchase of raw materials and the sale of her manufactured goods became more difficult, because of her isolation from metropolitan France. Further, the war with Burgundy imposed an additional drain on her resources. It became necessary to increase taxes on goods entering the town—wool, thread, silk, beer, wine, and wheat, for example— which increased the cost of the reduced volume of goods she was able to sell abroad, and made them less profitable.

Charles the Bold's policy was continued by his successor Marie of Burgundy, but economic sanctions proved to be no more decisive in the fifteenth century than in later times; and when the citizens made overtures about peaceful coexistence Burgundy agreed to have talks. Louis XI gave the Tournaisiens permission to deal direct with Marie, and on 22 October 1478 an agreement was signed in Brussels under which Marie and Maximilian of Austria restored all property confiscated from the merchants of Tournai and guaranteed that henceforth they would be allowed to trade freely in their dominions. The price the Tournaisiens had to pay was an undertaking never again to allow a garrison within their walls, to give freedom of passage to military forces, or to make war on Burgundy.

The city was also a victim of the cupidity and maladministration of the municipal authorities,[1] but this did not become obvious to Henry and his advisers during their brief stay. In any case, it is unlikely that their decision to occupy the city would have been influenced one way or the other by its economic state. Once the decision to remain had been taken, however, it was clearly in England's interest that the city's trade should be encouraged to prosper. It would help the citizens to find the relatively small amount of money which they were liable to pay Henry year by year; it would make them better able to contribute to the financing of their own defence; and there was a better chance that two-way trade would develop between England and Tournai, to their mutual benefit, if the city's industries were maintained in a healthy state.

It was therefore the objective of English policy to ensure as far as possible that the manufacturing and merchanting of the city flourished. At the outset the Governor and his council must

---

[1] See Ch. II above.

have hoped that the municipal authorities who protested their loyalty to Henry over and over again would co-operate whole-heartedly in attempts to increase trade between England and Tournai; and there are some indications that the Tournaisiens recognized that mutual trade might have advantages for them. This attitude was shortlived, however. Their main purpose was to ensure that all their privileges were continued, so that their trading relationships with their immediate neighbours would be unimpaired. Trade with England might conceivably mean something in the long term; but for the time being the city depended on trade with the Burgundian territories, which in turn depended on the treaty with Maximilian. Whether they liked it or not, the Tournaisiens again had a garrison, in spite of the provisions of the treaty of 1478. Did this mean that trade with the Emperor's people must cease?

The municipal authorities set about clearing up this point right away. They must have derived some encouragement from a surprising document issued by Margaret of Savoy in the name of the Emperor on 3 September 1513, only a few days before the siege of Tournai began. It recites that numbers of 'compaignons de guerre et autres', both mounted and on foot, have been making attacks on the inhabitants of Tournai and the Tour-naisis, Mortagne, and St. Amand; and they have been taking prisoners 'contre nostre plaisir et intencion', as a result of which the friendly trading relationship that has long existed between the Emperor's territories and Tournai is being prejudiced. These depredations must stop in the interest of peaceful trading. The offenders are to be brought to justice and no one is to give them succour or shelter. If they cannot be arrested, they are to be banished and their goods confiscated. De Fiennes, Governor of Flanders and Artois, is to see that these instructions are carried out.[1]

It is difficult to find a rational explanation for this edict. Maximilian was at war with France, and even in July the Tournaisiens thought that there was a good chance that he and Henry would attack them. The Emperor must have made up his mind by the beginning of September to persuade Henry to lay siege to Tournai. Why, then, go to the trouble of issuing a statutory instrument, the avowed objective of which was to keep

---

[1] *Ordonnances*, pp. 272–3; Hocquet (a), iii.

the city's trade flowing without interruption? Would it not have been more sensible to encourage the raiders to do their worst, in the hope that the Tournaisis would be partly softened up before the English army arrived?

Margaret of Savoy, who signed the instrument, showed herself to be well disposed towards Tournai before the siege began, perhaps because she knew that the city was an important trading partner for her own subjects. She may have wanted to keep the relationship going as long as possible, in the hope that the siege would be averted. Alternatively, although it may be imputing too much cunning to the Emperor, his objective may have been to lull the citizens into a sense of false security, so that they would be caught unawares when the invasion army appeared beneath their walls. Henry and Maximilian went to a great deal of trouble to keep secret their advance against Tournai, by taking prisoner everyone they encountered *en route*, so that news of their movements would be delayed as long as possible. This lends colour to the suggestion that the purpose of the edict was to deceive, but there is no certainty about this.

Whatever the implications of the edict, new representations had to be made to Maximilian; and he could hardly refuse to take a generous line, since it was largely due to him that there was now a garrison in Tournai. On 8 October 1513 he signed letters patent referring to the fact that the high and mighty Prince Henry, sovereign of Tournai, has entered into an agreement with him, under which Henry's Tournaisien subjects are to be allowed to trade freely with the surrounding territories. He mentions that Henry has installed a garrison, which may seem to be a breach of the treaty of 1478; and he confirms that the Tournaisiens may continue to frequent his dominions for the purposes of merchanting and otherwise without let or hindrance,[1] so long as they continue to recognize Henry as their sovereign lord.[2]

It must have been something of a relief to the municipal authorities to get their hands on this document, for they were aware of the coldness that had sprung up between Maximilian and Henry, which might conceivably have made the Emperor

---

[1] 'pourront doresenavant hanter et converser es dits pays terres et seignouries marchandement et autrement, francement, sceurement et paisiblement'.

[2] PRO 31/8/144, f. 231; *Ordonnances*, p. 276; *LP* i, 2345.

hostile to the city that had slipped through his fingers—in spite of the moral obligation to be reasonable about the garrison. It is significant that the negotiations that led to this agreement were carried on by the municipal authorities direct with the Emperor. The new Governor, who should have been responsible, seems to have played no part in them. This foreshadows the independent attitude of the Tournaisiens that was to be so troublesome throughout the occupation.

The first sign that the English presence might harm the commercial standing of the city came within a matter of weeks. Under the treaty of surrender Henry had agreed that any who were reluctant to recognize him as their sovereign were free to leave, taking with them their goods and chattels, so long as they did not settle in enemy territory. He no doubt hoped that this and the other gestures he made while he was still in Tournai would be seen as evidence of his intention to be a generous and just ruler; and that manufacturers and merchants would feel confident enough about the future not to avail themselves of the licence to depart. In any case, it was sensible to give potential rebels a chance to clear out, rather than to compel them to remain and thus store up fuel for any dissident movement that might develop.

The King completely misjudged the situation. Many of the leading citizens gratefully accepted his permission to leave. They took all their movable property with them and went off to make a new life for themselves elsewhere, some in the Low Countries, where their trading connections were strong enough to make them welcome, despite the fact that they were aliens; and some in France. The stipulation in the surrender treaty that they must not move to a country hostile to England (that is to say France) was pointless, for once a man was on one of the many high roads leading from Tournai he could go where he liked. If he went to France it might be at the cost of business with Tournai, but at least he had the satisfaction of knowing that he was faithful to Louis XII, which might stand him in good stead when that king recaptured the city. Whatever their motives, large numbers of merchants left, in spite of all Henry's endeavours to make conditions as attractive as possible.

The news of the exodus reached Henry in England very soon

after his return from Tournai, and he was much displeased. He sent a pained letter to the city, saying that it was obvious that as people were taking all their belongings with them they had no intention of returning. Further, he understood that there were others who intended to leave, which led him to conclude that the citizens as a whole were less faithful than he liked. Or—and it seems an extraordinary alternative to put to the city in letters patent—it might be that the Governor whom he had appointed, and who had been instructed to treat them no less favourably than his subjects in other parts of the realm,[1] was failing in his duty. Poynings, who no doubt took a pride in his job, cannot have been very pleased at having to transmit the sense of this to the municipal authorities.

Henry went on to say that he was astounded, given his good-will towards his new subjects and his solemn promise that they would continue to enjoy all their former rights and privileges, that any should want to leave the city. He understood, more-over, that it was being rumoured that he intended to abandon Tournai to some other prince, although he had made it abun-dantly clear while he was there that he would not. He now reaffirmed this, and it would be reaffirmed yet again when their representatives came to England for the Parliament due to be held after Christmas.[2] He therefore hoped that his dearly-beloved subjects would use their best endeavours to induce those who had left to return, and that all those who were still in the city would remain and carry on their business in the ordinary way, as they had done under French rule. They might rest assured that he would have their interests just as much at heart as if they were native-born Englishmen. If anyone has the slightest grievance he must bring it before the Governor, who will see that justice is done.[3]

The city's representatives duly turned up in Westminster for the session of Parliament which ran from 23 January to 4 March 1514. There are no surviving records of the session, and we can only speculate about the part the 'members for Tournai' played. It seems likely, however, that they had a considerable say in the decisions reached affecting the city, whether it was

[1] 'bien favorablement, en toute amour faveur et bénévolence et non moings que tous les meilleurs de noz subjectz'.
[2] See above, p. 49.   [3] Hocquet (a), xxvii; *LP* i, 2450.

said in the Commons' chamber, or in the corridors, or in meetings with Council members. The most important outcome of the session so far as Tournai was concerned was an Act of Parliament, the main purpose of which was to provide machinery for enforcing contracts made in England and Tournai.[1]

The measure is entitled 'An Act concerning ministration of justice in the city of Tournai', but it is more concerned with fostering trade and commerce between England and her newly-won territory than with justice. The preamble follows the lines of a number of related instruments, and refers in resounding terms (which must have delighted Henry every time he heard them) to his recent highly successful invasion of 'the realm of France, his very true patrimony and inheritance'; and also, for good measure, to the 'right great and marvellous costs and charge' he has incurred. His great wisdom and singular policy have reduced the cities of Thérouanne and Tournai to due obedience, 'by reason whereof now shall follow and ensue great amity, familiarity, and intercourse in buying and selling of merchandises, wares and otherwise between the citizens of the said cities, towns and precincts of the same and the King's natural subjects, inhabitants of this his realm of England'. In order that 'true and indifferent justice' shall be available to the merchants of Tournai and of England alike, elaborate provisions have been made for the registration of contracts and the settling of disputes arising between the merchants of the two territories.

The King has appointed a number of officers in Tournai, including two notaries who are to 'accept, take and record the knowledge of all contracts, bargains, conventions, pacts and agreements' made within the *bailliage* and brought to them by the parties to be recorded. The notary's record of such a contract is then to be deposited 'with another officer of the same city and town, which our said sovereign lord hath there made and deputed to accept and take of them'. This officer must have been the keeper of the seal royal, who was appointed while Henry was still in Tournai, for he is required 'for the more affirmance' of the contract to seal it with 'the seal of our

----

[1] 5 Henry VIII, c. 1.

sovereign lord made and left in the keeping of the same officer for the same intent'.

The Act then sets out the procedures for enforcing contracts so recorded and sealed. Any of the King's subjects domiciled in England who has made a bargain with a merchant in Tournai, or any Tournaisien who has made a bargain with an Englishman, who finds that the other party is refusing to fulfil his part of the bargain may exhibit the registered contract in the Court of Chancery, whereupon the Chancellor is authorized to send a sergeant-at-arms to the other party to require him to comply with the terms of the contract. If the other party refuses, or claims that there is a good reason why he is no longer bound by the contract, he is to be immediately brought before the Chancellor to justify his claim. If he continues to maintain that the contract is no longer binding, he has the choice of paying into court 'sufficient gage and pledge to the very value of the contents of the same writing obligatory', or remaining in custody while the matter is tried.

The Chancellor 'by his wisdom and discretion' is to appoint a day for the other party to appear before him 'to prove his objection and allegation'. If he fails, then he is bound to complete his part of the bargain forthwith, on pain of forfeiting the bond deposited with the court—or, presumably, although the point is not covered in the statute, remaining in custody until he has given satisfaction to the injured party.

Provision is similarly made for the enforcement in Tournai of debts, contracts, and bargains arising in England and Calais. All recognizances made in the Chancery, King's Bench, and any other court of record in England, and all 'writings obligatory' lodged with the Mayor of the Staple of Calais, may be exhibited to the *Bailli* of Tournai under the Great Seal; and the *Bailli* is then empowered to examine the parties, and require that the terms of the contract be carried out, or appropriate compensation paid to the other party.

It was essential that all merchants should be made aware of the new arrangements for enforcing contracts in England and in Tournai; but an Act of the Westminster Parliament did not apply automatically to Tournai. The device used to make it effective there was a charter of *inspeximus*, in Henry's name, which states (in Latin) that he has examined and approved the statute, which is to apply just as much to the *bailliage* of Tournai as to the kingdom of England. Its remedies are available to his subjects in both territories who carry on trade and commerce with people in the other territory, while they themselves remain at home.[1]

There follows a French translation of the Act, suitably modified for Tournaisien consumption. For example, the Court of King's Bench, which in the Act is described simply as 'his bench', which would have meant little to the great majority of the citizens, is translated as 'son bank vulgairement appellé la banque [*sic*] du Roy'. The *inspeximus* concludes with another passage in Latin, expressing the King's hope that both the citizens of Tournai and any others living within the *bailliage* will accept that the terms of the Act, which has been designed to meet the request of the citizens (no doubt transmitted through their representatives, who had come to Westminster for the Parliament), are just and reasonable, and that they will not fail to observe them.

The delegation from Tournai also expressed anxiety at this time about the trading rights of their merchants. They admitted that Henry had generously confirmed all the 'privileges, franchises, statutes and ordinances heretofore obtained, enacted and ordained for the honour, profit and advancement' of their city, and that Tournaisiens were permitted to own land and houses in England, and to export goods from there on payment of the same customs dues as were levied on the King's native-born subjects; but they were afraid that English merchants might for their own purposes pretend ignorance of the fact that the Tournaisiens had equal rights. They might 'vex and trouble' them to such an extent that their vital cloth trade might be seriously damaged and large numbers of workpeople thrown out of employment.[2]

Henry, who was still anxious to do everything possible for his new subjects—a fact which they seemed to have grasped very

---

[1] PRO 31/8/144, f. 241; C 82/402 $\frac{5}{436}$; Hocquet (a), xli (wrongly dated 1516); *LP* i, 2699.

[2] PRO 31/8/144, f. 243; C 82/402 $\frac{5}{457}$; Hocquet (a), xxxii; *LP* i, pt. 2, no. 2728: 'entant qu'il pourroit touchier le fait de la drapperie qui causeroit la totalle destruction du vivre, substentacion et et entretenement de grant multitude et quasi la pluspart du peuple de nostredicte ville se vivant et entretenement soubz le fait et exersite du stille de la drapperie'.

quickly—agreed that the delegation had a good point; and to make the position quite clear issued letters patent setting out the rights of the citizens of Tournai. It was perfectly legal for them to come to England and to do everything that English merchants did; and their privileges were not to be called in question, especially where the cloth trade was concerned. No one is to challenge this on any pretext whatsoever.

It is significant that both these proposals—that the equal trading rights implicit in the surrender treaty should be spelled out by the King and that provision should be made for the registration and enforcement of contracts—originated with the delegation from Tournai. It suggests that the citizens recognized the potential benefit of trade between England and Tournai, and were at least as anxious to foster it as were the more enlightened members of the King's Council. There is little doubt, however, that most of the Tournaisiens were thinking only of their own self-interest in any attempt to develop trade with England. They did not regard themselves as members of a new 'common market' in which the partners would advance together towards greater prosperity.

Indeed, nothing that Henry and his Council did could win the loyalty of Tournai's merchants. Those who remained in the city barely tolerated English rule; and many of those who left worked actively against the new regime. At the beginning of 1516 Jerningham reported to Wolsey that numbers of these were living at Ghent and Bruges, and in his view were a source of danger. 'Their French hearts cannot be contented to dwell in Tournai as long as it is English . . . and after my poor mind their daily assemblies and councils together is to no good intent neither to the King's most noble grace nor to his city of Tournai.'[1]

One of the Calais precedents that Henry followed was the establishment of a mint. As soon as Edward III had captured the town in 1347 he set up a mint there.[2] The coining of money was of course a royal prerogative; and it may be that Edward regarded the Calais mint as one of the things that set the seal on his possession of the place. Henry may have had the same idea in Tournai. There is, however, something of a mystery about

---

[1] SP 1/12, f. 156 b; *LP* ii, 1498.   [2] Craig, p. 67.

the date when the English Tournai mint was established, and how it was operated.

The clues are the coins that have survived and one or two documents. The coins are silver groats or fourpenny pieces, of which a good many specimens have come down to the present day; and a single half-groat that came into the sale room for the first time in 1919, and which was acquired by the British Museum in 1930.[1]

There are two main types of English Tournai groat. One has on the obverse the head of Henry VII, which appears on Henry VIII's coins minted in England until 1526. It has a Gothic crowned Ƭ and the legend HENRIC DI GRA REX FRANC Z AGLIE. On the reverse the legend of the equivalent English coin, POSUI DEUM ADIUTOREM MEUM, is replaced by CIVITAS TORNA-CEN[s]. This type bears no date, and it has no numeral after the King's name. The Tournai half-groat that survives is of the same type.

The other type of English Tournai groat has a shield in place of the King's head on the obverse, the legend HENRIC 8 DI GRA FRANCIE ET ANGLIE REX, and the date 1513 in arabic numerals on the reverse. There are two varieties of this design. In one the reverse has the letter 'h' in the centre, while the other has a Tudor rose. Both varieties place 'France' before 'England' in the King's titles, and give precedence to the arms of France (thus following the earlier practice of English kings who wanted to stress that they were kings of France in their own right), whereas in the equivalent coin minted in England 'France' comes after 'England'. The most important difference, however, between the groat with Henry VII's head and the 'shield groat' is that the latter is dated 1513 while the former has no date.

There are two surviving documents which augment the evidence of the coins themselves. The first is an instruction of March 1514 from Henry VIII to William Stafford, 'warden of mint within the Tower of London and elsewhere within our realm of England'; Lord Mountjoy, 'master of our moneys and coins there'; Sir Henry Wyatt, comptroller and assayer of the mint; and Sir John Sharp, the engraver, that

ye or your deputies of such bullion of silver as hereafter shall be

---

[1] R. Carlyon Britton, 'English coins from the Wheeler collection', *The British Museum Quarterly*, vol. v, p. 54, and Plate xxv (10).

brought unto you or any of you unto our mint within our said city of Tournai make or do to be made by authority hereof our money of silver according to the several prints and forms of several pieces of metal to these our letters annexed, that is to say groats of four pence and pence of two pence.

This money was to be of the same fineness as the coinage of England, and for every pound of silver coined twelve pence was to go to the master and all his officers.[1]

The same letters patent authorize the warden and his colleagues to recruit 'as many gravers, finers, smiths and all other persons' as are needed to staff the mint in Tournai; and also to acquire all the 'things and stuff necessary and requisite for the said mint'. The Lieutenant General and council of Tournai are commanded to provide 'their good advice, favour, aid and assistance' to the officials of the mint at all times.

This last provision is of particular interest, as it has some bearing on the conclusion arrived at above[2] that Mountjoy was not appointed *Bailli* of Tournai at the beginning of 1514, as the dating of his commission in the French Roll implies. If he had been *Bailli* in March 1514, while Poynings was Governor (which was theoretically possible), it seems inevitable that in the letters patent the title of *Bailli* would have been used; and if he was both *Bailli* and Governor, the letters patent would hardly have commanded the lieutenant general of Tournai (i.e. the Governor) to help the 'master of our moneys and coins' in England, since they would have been one and the same person. The lieutenant general in question must have been Sir Edward Poynings, and Mountjoy comes into the picture simply as master of the mint.

Almost the only other surviving document dealing with the English mint in Tournai is a receipt by Stafford for £40, 'for the costs going and coming of me the said William Stafford and of such coiners and officers of the said mint sent by my said sovereign lord to his city of Tournai for the ordering and exercising of the King's mint there', dated 7 April 1514.[3]

---

[1] E 159/293; *LP* i, App. 27. (*LP* has 8 March, but the manuscript appears to be dated 7 March.)

[2] See p. 42 above. Mountjoy's commission as Governor empowered him to appoint a master of the mint in Tournai, but, since it was issued in 1515, it does not throw light on the dating of the 1513 Tournai groat.

[3] SP 1/230, f. 144; *LP* i, 2788.

The documents suggest that the English mint in Tournai was set up in the spring of 1514, and that it is therefore unlikely that Henry's coins were struck in Tournai in 1513, or even in the old-style 1513, which ended on 25 March 1514. All the evidence shows that the administrative processes during the occupation moved very slowly—it took years to set up the court sovereign, for example—and it seems improbable that Sir Edward Poynings could have made the mint operational within a few weeks in 1513, not because of technical difficulties, which were relatively small, but simply because of the length of time needed to make decisions in any field.

The instructions to the officials of the London mint to start up operations in Tournai refer to 'our mint within the said city' almost as if it is a going concern; but if it had been a going concern, it is arguable that it would have been unnecessary for the King to provide the warden and his colleagues with specimen coins to work from in Tournai in March 1514. Further, if the mint had been functioning for some time at that date, one would expect to find some reference to the fact in the King's instructions. Finally, the receipt dated 7 April 1514 for the expenses of the warden going to and coming from Tournai, and of the 'coiners and officers' sent to Tournai, confirms that something new was done in the spring of 1514. What then is the explanation of the 1513 date on the 'shield groat'?

There are two possible explanations. The first assumes that the absence of any documentary evidence about the establishment of a mint before March 1514 means that the English mint did not begin operations in Tournai before the late spring of that year. The English officials and craftsmen brought with them dies with the head of Henry VII—the only ones available—and produced coins which corresponded to the equivalent coins being struck in England, with no date, as was customary. It then occurred to Henry VIII and his advisers not only that a great opportunity to mark his capture of Tournai had been missed, but perhaps even that posterity might take the evidence of the image of Henry VII on an undated English Tournai coin to mean that the credit for the glorious event belonged to the first Tudor and not to the second. Therefore in the course of 1514, or even later, the position had to be clarified by the issue of a coin which was clearly Henry VIII's, which bore the figure 8 and the date of the year in which he became immortal, and from which the likeness of his father had been removed.

This explanation can be supported by a letter written by Martin Pirry, comptroller of the mint towards the end of Henry VIII's reign, when he was advocating the establishment of a mint in the recently captured town of Boulogne. He says that it had been customary when the Kings of England conquered any foreign country or town shortly afterwards to 'set up in the places won a mint to the intent that the coins there printed might have course throughout the world for a perpetual memory of the winning thereof'; and as evidence of this he refers to the 'moneys yet remaining' that had been coined in Gascony, Normandy, Tournai, Calais, and other places.[1] On the other hand, the fact that Henry VIII left his father's portrait on English coins for another thirteen years after the capture of Tournai suggests that he did not regard the absence of his own image as being particularly important; and on the whole it seems that the possibility that coins minted in 1514 or later were 'back-dated' to 1513 must be discounted.

The second and less fanciful explanation to fit the facts is that the instructions of March 1514 related to what was in effect the second English mint in Tournai, and that the first coins of the occupation were struck by Tournaisien craftsmen in the last quarter of 1513. These men did not have access to a die with Henry VII's head, but using their own tools made dies for the 'shield groat' in which the numeral 8 is incorporated and which bear the date 1513. This explanation is supported by the fact that the 'shield groats' are continental in style, which suggests that the dies were the handiwork of local men. The undated coins with Henry VII's head are presumably the work of the craftsmen brought from England by William Stafford in 1514. They are 'English' in style, and they are also 'English' in that they bear no date. The dies for these coins were almost certainly

---

[1] SP 1/12, f. 179; *LP* xx, pt. 2, App. 16. This may be no more than the comptroller's inference from the fact that such coins existed. It was often convenient to set up mints in captured territory so that foreign coins, plate and so forth could be quickly turned into coin of the realm. Mr. Philip Grierson has called my attention to the fact that in late medieval Italy a city would sometimes set up a mint in a conquered territory or even in the cathedral of a captured town as a token of victory (W. Heywood, *Palio and Ponte*, pp. 20–22: London, 1904), but there is no surviving evidence that any English government followed such a policy.

engraved in the London mint. Although the French mint in Tournai does not seem to have been very active in the years immediately before Henry captured Tournai, coins had been struck in the city over a long period, and there were probably skilled craftsmen available to undertake the minting of the 1513 English coins, who were replaced by Englishmen in 1514.[1]

Dating was not at this time employed on the royal coinage of either England or France. Its use on the Tournai groat (which makes it the first English coin to bear a date) was perhaps influenced by the fact that Flemish coins had been occasionally dated since the 1470's but the prominent position given to the figures on the coin may well have been intended to emphasize the date of the capture of the city and the beginning of the coinage.

There are still some unanswered questions. For example, were there any types or denominations of English Tournai coins that have not come down to us? One authority takes it for granted that Henry VIII must have minted 'nobles, angelots, et autres' in Tournai;[2] but this seems unlikely. The instructions to the officials of the London mint referred to above[3] speak only of the minting of 'bullion of silver', so there were probably no gold coins. It is true that when Gaspard de Rebecque, an employee of the mint in Amiens, sought permission in 1516 to transfer to the English mint in Tournai (which was refused by his superiors), he said he would be working in silver and gold;[4] but that does not necessarily mean that the Tournai mint was in fact producing gold coins. However, if the output of the English mint was limited to groats and half-groats, it is still possible that the 'shield groat' was accompanied by a half-groat of the same design, although there is no known surviving specimen.

[1] This is the conclusion arrived at by Marcel Hoc ('Le monnayage tournaisien de Henri VIII roi d'Angleterre', *Revue belge de numismatique* (1952), pp. 65–75, and Plate IV), mainly on the evidence of the coins. The few documents strengthen this conclusion.

[2] C. P. Serrure, *Notice sur le cabinet monétaire de S. A. le Prince de Ligne* (Ghent, 1847), p. 375.

[3] See above, p. 138.

[4] F. de Saulcy, *Recueil de documents relatifs à l'histoire des monnaies frappées par les rois de France depuis Philippe II jusqu'à François I* (Macon, 1892), p. 157.

VI · THE BATTLE OF THE BISHOPS

WE do not know when Wolsey first reckoned that he could get his hands on the lucrative bishopric of Tournai. The possibility can hardly have occurred to him while he was organizing the 1513 expedition. If it had done, he would almost certainly have tried to persuade Henry to make Tournai his primary objective, and Henry would no doubt have agreed. All that he wanted was honour and glory and it mattered little where he found them. In any case, the see was held by the ailing Charles de Hautbois until shortly before the English expedition sailed. It is unlikely that the news of his resignation through ill-health would have meant much to Wolsey in England, when he had so many other things on his mind; but the implications of his replacement by someone who was now an enemy alien must have occurred to the Almoner in Tournai.

Nevertheless, even after the English garrison had been established there, no one else seems to have thought that Wolsey might fall heir to the see. Although he enjoyed far greater influence than his office normally carried, there was no reason to think that within a few months he would be dominating the affairs of state and collecting offices and wealth at a remarkable rate. When the Milanese ambassador, in a dispatch to the Duke of Milan (written on 27 September, two days after Henry had entered Tournai), speculated as to who would become Bishop of this 'great, handsome, and powerful city', Wolsey's name was not in his short list of candidates.[1] Da Laude kept his ear close to the ground, and his dispatch suggests that as yet neither Henry nor Wolsey saw the bishopric as a reward for the Almoner's contribution to the success of the expedition.

De Hautbois died soon after his resignation,[2] and on 19 June Pope Leo X appointed Louis Guillard to the see. This was a political appointment of the most blatant kind, for Guillard, the son of the vice-president of the *Parlement de Paris*,[3] was only twenty-one and still in minor orders. Because of his youth the

---

[1] *MC* 664.   [2] On 10 June.   [3] Cousin, p. 270.

Pope could only designate him Bishop elect. He would have to wait until his twenty-seventh year to become full Bishop. In the meantime he was allowed to enjoy the revenues of the see, so that the distinction between being Bishop and Bishop elect was for financial purposes academic.

The appointment was finalized in a flurry of bulls, all issued on the same day. The principal made Guillard administrator and 'Bishop elect'; but it had to be backed up by a second bull, giving him absolution from ecclesiastical censures in respect of his unusual appointment, a third providing dispensation for 'deficiency of age', a fourth dispensing him from a rule made by Leo himself that the grant of a benefice should be nullified when it followed on the resignation of a sick man who died within twenty days, and a fifth and sixth commanding the Dean and Chapter of Tournai, and the clergy, to accept the young man as administrator of the diocese. The Bishop elect took the oath on 26 July 1513, and he was formally admitted into possession of the bishopric on 24 August, the day after Thérouanne fell to the English invaders.[1]

The stage was now set for a fascinating paper battle, in which for the next four years Wolsey exploited the whole armoury of ecclesiastical law in an attempt to have Guillard removed. This was nothing new for Tournai. Before de Haut-bois took office there had been litigation about the see for the greater part of the preceding twenty years.[2] The youthful Guillard had the advantage of technical possession of the see, and the financial resources that went with it, for his tax collectors were already active. He countered every move made by Wolsey with consummate skill, and indeed carried the war into his opponent's territory. Meantime neither protagonist was resident in Tournai. Guillard, who refused to take the oath of loyalty to Henry, manifestly dare not show his face in the city, as he would have been deemed a traitor and dealt with accordingly. Wolsey, who became in quick succession Bishop of Lincoln, Archbishop of York, Cardinal, and Lord Chancellor, was much too busy shaping the affairs of the nation in London to visit Tournai, despite the fact that it might have swung the battle in his favour. During this period while the two adversaries hurled at each other's souls the deadliest instruments of

[1] SP 1/230, ff. 26–35 b; *LP* i, 2197.   [2] Cal. D VI, f. 289 b; *LP* ii, 29.

the canon law, with one of the richest bishoprics in Europe as the spoils for the victor, the many thousands in Tournai and the district had to take care of themselves without the benefit of the presence of their spiritual overlord—whoever they took him to be.[1]

The business of the diocese—and it was big business[2]—had of course to be carried on, whether or not there was a resident Bishop. Revenues had to be collected, stipends paid, travelling expenses met, the fabric of the cathedral and the numerous parish churches maintained, prebends allocated, and so on. Any surplus after these payments had been settled was no doubt smuggled as unostentatiously as possible into the pocket of the absentee Guillard. There was a strong undercurrent of loyalty to France among the clergy, many of whom looked ahead to the days when the city would be restored to the French Crown, and reckoned that their careers would suffer if they showed themselves to be willing collaborators with the English regime. So long as Guillard appeared to be their lawful Bishop they were perfectly happy to accept him, and indeed to lend him their active support.

The battle for the bishopric began in earnest when Wolsey sent Dr. Richard Sampson to be his vicar general at Tournai in September 1514. At the instance of Henry VIII, Leo X had appointed Wolsey administrator of the see of Tournai while he was Bishop of Lincoln, on the ground that the Bishop elect had refused to take the oath of loyalty to Henry and had deserted his charge. It is not clear when the appointment was actually made, but on 17 June the Bishop of Worcester, the English representative at Rome, wrote to Wolsey that he would not delay 'the present messenger, who carries the brief of the

---

[1] Cavendish's account of these events is compressed and inaccurate. He suggests, for example, that Wolsey was invested with the see of Tournai, that Richard Sampson was appointed his vicar general, and that Mountjoy became Governor, all before Henry left the city (*The Life and Times of Cardinal Wolsey*, 1743 edn., vol. ii, p. 189).

[2] There is in the Public Record Office a volume of the accounts of the bishopric in the time of Charles de Hautbois (E 36/82). It seems likely that this was called for by Wolsey, along with copies of the bulls referred to above (p. 350), which are also in the Public Record Office (SP 1/230, ff. 26–35 b), to enable him to assess how much the see was worth, and whether there was a loophole in the bulls which he could take advantage of in his campaign against the Bishop elect.

business of Tournai'. This must refer to the proposal to make Wolsey Bishop there.[1] On 13 July Henry wrote to Margaret of Savoy, telling her that he had given Wolsey the bishopric because of Guillard's attitude, and asking her to help him to get the revenues in accordance with the Pope's bull.[2] When Wolsey was translated to the Archbishopric of York in August 1514 it was technically possible that the promotion nullified his appointment to Tournai; but this was clarified on 16 September, when the Pope confirmed the appointment.[3] It was, however, to lapse if the Bishop elect came to the diocese to take up his duties and swore allegiance to the English Crown.

The fact remained, however, that Louis Guillard was the man in possession; and he was not going to withdraw without a struggle. He had the support of Louis XII, who had put him forward in the first place, and who also wrote to Margaret of Savoy asking her to ensure that Guillard, 'qui est vrai et indubit évesque', was left in undisturbed possession of the bishopric, to which he had a just and reasonable title. To do anything else would endanger the conscience and souls of those of her subjects who lived in the bishopric; but if she helped Guillard she and her people would derive great spiritual benefit, and it would incidentally also be 'trèsagréable à Dieu et à moy'.[4]

Wolsey for his part was under no illusions about the weakness of his position, and in selecting Sampson as his vicar general he probably found the best man available to fight his battles.[5] It is doubtful, however, if there was anyone in England who could have coped with the forces ranged against Wolsey's champion. He arrived in Tournai at the beginning of September to begin his impossible task. His first move was to meet the four councils. They assembled on Saturday 2 September to hear this 'notable docteur en théologie' explain in Latin that he had brought letters closed from the King their sovereign lord and the Bishop of Lincoln to inform them that the Pope had appoin-

---

[1] Vit. B II, f. 79; *LP* i, 3011.   [2] Le Glay, ii, p. 191; *LP* i, 3075.
[3] PRO 31/9/1, f. 230; *LP* i, 3284.   [4] SP 1/9, f. 104; *LP* i, 3217.
[5] Sampson was certainly eager to serve his master to the best of his ability. He incurred his displeasure for some reason in 1514, and wrote a grovelling letter saying that he was shocked at having offended Wolsey, for nothing gave him greater pleasure than to perform his commands. To increase his usefulness he proposed to intensify his study of civil and canon law (SP 1/8, ff. 154–154 b; *LP* i, 3071).

ted Wolsey to the see of Tournai, until such time as the Bishop elect was prepared to reside in the bishopric and take the oath of loyalty to Henry. Having heard Sampson's statement and studied the letters, the four councils withdrew, as was their custom, into their separate colleges to consider the line they would follow. They came back to report unanimous agreement to obey the Pope's decree and the King's commands; and they asked the learned doctor to give them a copy of the documents for their own records. In return they showed him copies of the papal bulls which had appointed the Bishop elect, and asked for advice how to deal with them in the light of the latest developments.[1]

This was a satisfactory start, but it could hardly have been otherwise when there were some thousands of English troops in Tournai to encourage the citizens to follow the line laid down by Westminster. Sampson now had to show his credentials to Margaret of Savoy and Prince Charles's Council and seek to enlist their support. He went to Brussels, where he found Margaret very cordial and willing to help, in spite of the fact that Henry's sister Mary, who until quite recently had been expected to marry Prince Charles, was now going to marry Louis XII.[2] When he set off for Ghent to see the Prince's Council he was told that he was very foolish, as the citizens there were furious about the marriage. The common people in particular were 'so provoked that a little thing without fail would stir them and cause a commotion'.[3]

Undaunted, however, he went to Ghent and showed his documents first to the Prince's Council and then to the municipal authorities. He was well received, but the town council, being not quite sure of their ground, suggested that it would be more appropriate if he saw de Fiennes, the Governor of Flanders, whose residence was 'four Dutch miles' from Ghent. The Governor gave him a good hearing, after apologizing for not being able to put him up, as he already had a houseful of guests. However, he sent three gentlemen who spoke Latin to keep him company in his lodgings, and also half a dozen dishes of good meat 'and of wine plenty, both white and claret'.[4]

From Ghent Sampson went to Bruges, where the town

---

[1] Hocquet (a), xxxv; *LP* i, 3231. [2] SP 1/9, f. 107; *LP* i, 3246.
[3] SP 1/9, ff. 121–121 b; *LP* i, 3296. [4] SP 1/9, ff. 118–19; *LP* i, 3283.

authorities scrutinized his credentials very carefully, and showed themselves 'nothing favourable'. This brought him to a crucial meeting with the officers of the Bishop elect. Would they transfer their loyalty to Wolsey? The officers had made their headquarters in Bruges, ostensibly because of the 'fervent plague' raging in Tournai, but no doubt also because there they were less vulnerable to English pressure. Sampson showed them the Pope's brief in favour of Wolsey, and explained that he was empowered to act as Wolsey's agent in the administration of the see. They at once 'raised their bristles', and asked for time to think things over before they gave 'a reasonable answer'. Thinking it wise to treat them gently to gain their goodwill, Sampson agreed at first that they should have until St. Martin's Day (11 November), but then, guessing that they were temporizing, insisted that they should meet again on 28 September. Meanwhile, they were free to discuss the position with the Bishop elect, on condition that he did not return to Tournai to take possession of the see.[1]

This condition shows Wolsey's true attitude towards the bishopric. Hitherto his claim had been founded on Guillard's failure to come to Tournai, and it was on this ground that the Pope had made him temporary administrator. Now the English plan was to keep him away as long as possible. There was, however, some right on their side. Louis XII had at one stage promised to support Wolsey, and now, as Sampson reported bitterly, the French support on which the success of his mission depended had been withdrawn. Moreover, the Bishop elect, being well aware that the English were about to mount an assault, had made his dispositions with great skill. He had been clever enough to equip himself with a dispensation for non-residence *studii causa*, so at least for the time being he had every right to be absent from the bishopric. He had appointed a vicar general who could fight his battles for him in places where he dared not appear in person. He had instructed his officers, who were mostly Flemings, that when Sampson put his cards on the table they must be ready with theirs; and in fact they confronted him with all the documents supporting Guillard's claims.[2]

The officers' efforts to protect Guillard's interest (and there-

[1] Cal. E I, f. 33; Galba B V, f. 368; *LP* i, 3285, 3299.
[2] Ibid.

fore their own) did not stop here. They had contrived to get the high court of the diocese moved to Bruges.[1] This meant that if the dispute came before the court the proceedings would take place in an atmosphere of neutrality, or even of hostility to English interests. Moreover, the officers had done what they could to increase the wave of anger against England which had followed the decision to match Mary with Louis XII instead of with Charles.

Most important of all, Guillard's receiver had wisely remitted the recent profits of the see to France for the account of the Bishop elect. Sampson pointed out that at no time had Guillard's officers been subject to a lawful inhibition (except for Wolsey's commandment, which carried no weight—a good point, which cannot have pleased Wolsey when he read it), and there had therefore been nothing to stop them from collecting the revenues. He had examined the receiver's accounts, which had been closed up to midsummer (St. Thomas's Day), and the profits to that date had gone to Guillard long before Sampson came on the scene. If anything had remained he would have claimed it under spiritual law; and if that had failed he would have invoked the temporal law. But the money was gone, and not even an unanswerable legal case would bring it back. There would be no more to argue about until Christmas, when the accounts were next made up.[2]

The money may have been spirited away but the expenses remained. Not only were there no profits for Wolsey, but cash had to be found from somewhere for essential expenditure. Sampson bravely pointed out that the costs of the diocese arose mainly in Tournai itself, and that over a recent period the revenues he could control by virtue of the occupation of the city were about a hundred marks less than the costs in the same area. This, he thought, had far-reaching implications. For example, unless tenants saw that Wolsey was providing for the maintenance of the property they rented from the diocese, they would have no incentive to pay their rents to his agent, but would be tempted to continue to deal with those of the Bishop elect.[3]

---

[1] SP 1/9, ff. 121–121 b; *LP* i, 3296.
[2] Galba B V, ff. 432–432 b; *LP* i, 3287.
[3] SP 1/9, ff. 121–121 b; *LP* i, 3296.

Sampson suggested that the fact that there would be no money at stake until Christmas would give a breathing-space, in which Louis XII might be induced to lend Wolsey his support. There would then be no problem, 'so much they regard the French King and not greatly their own Prince'.[1] On the other hand, the Bishop elect had lodged an appeal with the *Parlement de Paris*, the usual procedure in cases like this. As Wolsey well knew, his father was a leading member of the *Parlement*, and if that body considered that Guillard had right on his side, they would pay little attention to anything that Louis had to say. In fact, the only certain way of winning was to get a favourable decision from the Pope, which neither the French King nor the *Parlement* could question.[2] An appeal had also been lodged in Rome.[3]

At the beginning of October Sampson appealed for help to Sir Richard Wingfield, the English ambassador at Margaret's Court. Although the letters he had received from the Archduchess appeared to be as strong as could be drafted, it now seemed that they 'be not so special as was necessary'. Something stronger was called for, and he hoped that if Wingfield could persuade Margaret to provide it she would also agree to have the letters proclaimed along with the apostolic brief. In telling Wolsey this, Wingfield expressed surprise at the attitude of the French King. He was supporting and comforting the Bishop elect 'to put your worship to all the business and trouble that may be'. Only if Louis could be persuaded to withdraw his support would Wolsey enjoy the fruits of the bishopric 'without any business'.[4]

Sampson was outmanoeuvred and overwhelmed by the forces arrayed against him. He was one against many, and his opponents had right on their side. They were well versed in the subtleties of ecclesiastical law, and they were probably confident he could make no move to which they did not have a simple and effective counter-move. He thought of acting on the strict letter of the Pope's brief and demanding action against the Bishop elect; but rejected the idea on the ground that if the matter was referred to the law it would be very troublesome, and the profits of the see would be swallowed up in legal costs.

---

[1] SP 1/9, ff. 121–121 b; *LP* i, 3296.   [2] Galba B V, f. 432; *LP* i, 3287.
[3] Galba B V f. 435; *LP* i, 3418.   [4] SP 1/9, f. 132; *LP* i, 3329.

He was also afraid that if he took a strong line he might be assaulted, so ugly was the mood of the common people. In any case, Guillard's position seemed to be very strong. He hoped that he had been right; but if Wolsey considered that the ecclesiastical court should be confronted with a demand that he should be recognized as the lawful Bishop of Tournai, he would see that it was done, however dangerous it might prove to be.[1]

The Bishop elect had won the first round decisively, and Wolsey deemed it necessary to take a hand in the game himself. On 22 October he wrote to the Earl of Worcester, ambassador in Paris, seizing on the Earl's boast that he could make the French King do anything he liked. Would he now cause him to forbid the Bishop elect to meddle any longer in the affairs of the bishopric of Tournai, perhaps by giving him some other suitable see? Given Worcester's skill as a mediator and the services Wolsey had rendered to Louis (which were surely worth the best bishopric in his gift), it should not be too difficult to transfer Guillard—especially if Louis is as open in deeds as he is in words. At the least, Louis must command him neither to participate further in the business of the see, nor to employ an agent to act for him. Louis should also be asked to write to Margaret of Savoy, making it clear that Wolsey had the 'occupation and administration' of the see according to the Pope's brief—and 'let this be your sheet anchor'. Worcester is to settle for nothing less than the second alternative.

Wolsey goes on to say that he has heard secretly from his friends in Rome that the French ambassador there is daily supporting the Bishop elect against him in the name of the French King. If Louis is party to this, it is astonishing: if he is not, then will Worcester make him aware of the position and see that his representative desists? The whole Court at Rome knows well that he does not deserve to be laboured against by the French ambassador, or anyone else speaking in the French King's name. He sees no real difficulty if only Louis can be induced to co-operate. 'I doubt not but the Pope's holiness will be glad to give it [i.e. the see of Tournai] and the same *in commendam*[2] with my archbishopric.' He concludes with an

---

[1] SP 1/9, ff. 121–121 b; *LP* i, 3296.
[2] Tenure of benefice in absence of regular incumbent.

apology for putting Worcester to so much trouble, and assures him that he will in return look after his interests at Court.[1] Wolsey also wrote at this time to Margaret of Savoy, asking her to mediate in the matter of the bishopric.[2]

Wolsey's letter reached Worcester on 2 November. Four days later the ambassador proudly replied that he had accomplished all that had been asked of him. He had already sent off the letter from Louis to Margaret of Savoy for onward transmission to her. The Bishop elect had been told to meddle no further in the affairs of the diocese. The French ambassador in Rome had been instructed to desist from his attacks on Wolsey's claim to the bishopric. Louis had agreed to compensate the Bishop elect, and had ordered the Treasurer Robertet to get Guillard's father to agree the terms of compensation. This was to be done next day. Finally, the King had asked him to say that the Bishop elect would 'make as full a release' as Wolsey could wish for. Before Worcester left Paris everything would be settled to Wolsey's complete satisfaction.[3]

This optimistic dispatch was followed by another, written in haste from Paris on 8 November, in which Worcester says that he hopes to bring with him to England the resignation of the Bishop elect, for he has been definitely promised it that morning. However, a note of caution creeps in at the end of the letter. He will do everything possible in Paris with the utmost diligence; nevertheless, 'methinketh ye might send to Rome to make your suit in the meantime'. In other words it will do no harm if Wolsey continues to seek satisfaction direct from Rome.[4]

It seemed, therefore, that Wolsey had by means of a single letter achieved a great deal more than Richard Sampson had done in all his meetings and negotiations in the Low Countries; and his success was apparently confirmed by a letter from the Bishop of Worcester in Rome to the King's Latin secretary Andreas Ammonius, in which he reported that the Pope was glad that the French King had promised Wolsey the 'resignation' of the bishopric. Further, Leo X agreed (as Wolsey con-

---

[1] SP 1/9, f. 151; *LP* i, 3378. (This is the second of two draft letters on the same subject.)

[2] *LP* i, 3388.

[3] Cal. D VI, f. 201; Ellis, 2nd Ser. i, pp. 239–43; *LP* i, 3416.

[4] SP 1/9, ff. 156–156 b; *LP* i, 3427.

fidently expected) that he should hold the diocese of Tournai in addition to the archdiocese of York.[1]

Wolsey, who left no stone unturned, was in fact keeping in close touch with the Bishop of Worcester at Rome. He thanked him extravagantly for all that he had done to obtain his bulls for the archbishopric of York and for Tournai, and also for his efforts with the Pope over the cardinalate.

And if by your politic handling the Pope can be induced shortly to make me Cardinal ye shall singularly content and please the King. For I cannot express how desirous the King is to have me advanced to the said honour to the intent that not only men might thereby perceive how much the Pope favoureth the King and such as he entirely loveth, but also that thereby I shall be the more able to do his Grace service.

He goes on to say that he does not know how he can repay the Bishop, but he will in all respects advance his honour and profit.[2]

Meanwhile Sampson struggled on as best he could, reporting with great assiduity his repeated failures to bring the officers of the Bishop elect to heel. They were stubborn and obstinate, waiting hopefully for the return of their master to claim his rightful position, and 'little favouring' Wolsey's claim to the administration.[3] If anything, the attitude of the clergy in general tended to harden as time went on, for in June he recorded that 'as touching the jurisdiction to be exercised in Tournai, there is no man dare adventure that thing'. They needed freedom to visit France and the Low Countries; and if they agreed to act on Wolsey's behalf there was a good chance that they would find themselves banned from both countries. They would rather suffer imprisonment for the time being than 'meddle with the jurisdiction'.[4]

Sampson followed this up with a request to Wolsey for a confirmation of the original brief in his favour, 'for it is a thing of great effect to have a grant for the second time confirmed. It taketh away all supposition, if any be.' He would have been in a much stronger position in dealing with the Bishop elect's officers if he had had the reaffirmed brief in the first place. The position was now so confused that it had been decided that he

[1] SP 1/9, f. 128 b; *LP* i, 3496.   [2] SP 1/9, f. 130; *LP* i, 3497.
[3] Galba B V, f. 435; *LP* i, 3418.   [4] Galba B III, f. 367; *LP* ii, 612.

and some of the Bishop elect's officers (who refused to believe that Guillard had surrendered, despite the documentary evidence) should ride to Paris to get clarification from the Bishop elect himself. Sampson could not make up his mind whether the officers were genuinely ignorant of their master's decision, or were simply pretending that he was still clinging to his rights. This could only be settled if they visited Paris together for a confrontation with those most directly concerned.[1]

Sampson met Guillard's officers on 15 November. He told them that Wolsey had Margaret's support, and that the French King had promised not to stand in his way. They said that that was all very well, but they had just received fresh instructions from Guillard to defend his jurisdiction; and they also showed Sampson a copy of a new appeal to Rome. This, he thought, made it essential that he should go to Paris. If he did not, the officers would doubtless bring back false reports of what happened there. He reminded Wolsey that his claim to the see was founded on 'certain causes which is but momentary' (that is, the temporary absence of Guillard from Tournai). If the Bishop elect came to the diocese and these causes were thereby removed, Wolsey's administration automatically ceased. In that event those of Wolsey's officers who had been fighting for him (the principal being Sampson himself, who made it abundantly clear that he had a deep interest in saving his own skin) would be in for a bad time. Sampson did not add that if the Bishop elect dared to set foot in Tournai itself he also would be in for a bad time.[2]

When Sir Thomas Spinelly, the English ambassador in Flanders, discussed Sampson's proposal to go to Paris with the Prince's Council in Brussels, the president expressed the view that his journey was unnecessary, as Wolsey's claim to the revenues of the diocese was undeniable. There was every justification for using force to ensure that his dues were paid, without going through any further pretence of negotiation. Nevertheless, it was agreed that Pierre Cottrel, the Bishop elect's former vicar general, and Sampson should proceed to Paris, 'there to know whether the Bishop . . . would prosecute the appellation against the Pope's brief'.[3]

[1] SP 1/9, f. 159; *LP* i, 3439.   [2] Cal. D VI, f. 288; *LP* i, 3445.
[3] SP 1/9, f. 194; *LP* i, 3493.

Sampson spent an unprofitable few days in Paris. He was back in Bruges on 15 December and reported the result of his mission. He had cut short his visit because Christmas was approaching, and he feared that the six-monthly revenues of the see would find their way into the hands of 'the other party' unless he was there to prevent it. For several reasons he still had not taken action against the Bishop elect's officers. It seemed likely that Wolsey would shortly get possession of the see, and if he could do it 'with quietness and favour of the country' it would be to his great honour and profit. On the other hand, if formal proceedings were instituted, the officers and their friends would so arouse the people that it would take a long time to calm them down. Once they were 'in a rumour and moved, they neither regard God nor King'. He had come to an agreement with the officers, however, that the revenues of the diocese should remain in their hands until Wolsey's title was clearly established; and when it was, the money would be handed over.[1]

There was more to it than this, however. Sampson counselled caution also because

the temporality in these parts be so minded against the spirituality so that if there should be any schism there should immediately be many things taken from the spiritual jurisdiction which were hard ever to recover, for the spiritual law in these parts hath knowledge in pecuniar and civil causes whereupon resteth great advantage to the Bishop.

Therefore nothing must be done to disturb this happy state of affairs.[2]

Whatever Louis might have promised, Sampson was satisfied, after talking with the Bishop elect's father and others in Paris, that his promises were 'but colours and words'. It was true that if a suitable French bishopric fell vacant Guillard might be prepared to resign Tournai; but the Bishop of Paris said that the vacancy would have to materialize before Tournai was renounced. Sampson thought it would help if Wolsey was represented at the French Court by 'a diligent solicitor', not only because Guillard's friends would try to slow things up as much as possible, but also because when the formal renuncia-

---

[1] Galba B V, f. 365; *LP* i, 3545.   [2] Ibid.

tion came 'it shall not be counsel for your Grace to trust to the crafty and subtle Frenchmen'. They would be clever enough to arrange for a technical error to creep into the documents, so that in due course they might be declared null and void. To forestall this he should send to Paris someone 'who knoweth perfectly the experience of renunciation *in curiam Romanam*'. Louis himself might be well disposed, but he was in the hands of his Council, 'which be good Frenchmen and so necessarily ill Englishmen'.[1]

There were other reasons why Sampson decided not to force the issue with the Bishop elect's officers. In his own view Wolsey's translation to the archdiocese of York nullified his claim to Tournai, no doubt because of the Lateran Council's ruling about plurality; and in support of this he had the temerity to cite the view of the Bishop of Paris, with whom he had discussed the matter. There were also practical difficulties in taking the see over. Had it been a question of filling two or three positions, 'I should long ere this have made sharper process'; but, as Wolsey well knew, it took many people to govern a diocese, and he doubted whether he would be able to find three others to help him. Finally, Wolsey's trust in the officers of Tournai was misplaced. Almost without exception they favoured the Bishop elect; and none was more fervent against Wolsey than his own receiver, Jean Villain. Nevertheless, if the Pope would provide a brief that got round the plurality difficulty, Sampson was prepared to run the diocese almost single-handed, although he feared that it would make him a laughing-stock.[2]

Wolsey's reply to this comprehensive and complacent record of failure has not survived; but there is a draft reply in his own hand, a masterpiece of invective in which his fury stands out in every line. This was almost certainly enshrined in a letter to his unfortunate vicar general. He first disposes of a suggestion made earlier that to seek to enforce his rights could lead to a breach between Prince Charles and his subjects and Henry by saying curtly 'ye wat not what ye mean'. There was not the slightest danger that this would happen, for had not Charles concurred in the recent treaty between England and France? If any resisted the enforcement of Wolsey's rights, Margaret would

---

[1] Galba B V, f. 365; *LP* i, 3545.　　　[2] Ibid.

doubtless see to the punishment of the offenders. It was nonsense to suggest that the Bishop elect had the slightest hope of having Wolsey's title to the diocese revoked.[1]

The Archbishop, warming to his task, proceeds: 'Ye need not doubt thereof the Pope would not offend me for one thousand such as the elect is, nor is there no such thing spoken nor intended. I would not have you to muse so much on the moon but to go straightly and wisely to my matters and not to be moved with every wind and frivolous report.' Sampson's suggestion that Wolsey's claim would vanish if Guillard returned to Tournai is disposed of equally forcefully. 'Do ye suppose the said elect shall be admitted or suffered to dwell in Tournai without the King my master's licence, which I am sure he will never obtain?' He would have to become the King's subject, utterly renouncing the French King, and that would never happen. Everything that Sampson has done so far has been wrong, especially his proposal that rents should be frozen until the dispute is settled. This would be prejudicial to Wolsey's rights, and Sampson is commanded immediately to set about collecting everything that is due at this holy time of Christmas, brooking no opposition. Finally, Wolsey hopes that he will attend to his interests in future better than he has done so far, otherwise he will have recourse to other means, 'for that ye have hitherto thought for the best is clearly turned to the worst'.[2]

We do not know if Sampson received a letter on the lines of this devastating draft, but it seems likely that he did, for Wolsey was not in the habit of sparing the feelings of those who let him down. If the letter was sent, Sampson's Christmas cannot have been very happy; and he must have looked forward to 1515 with apprehension.

In fact, 1515 began even worse than Sampson can have expected. Two events occurred on New Year's Day which affected the campaign to make Wolsey undisputed master of the see of Tournai. The young Prince Charles 'entered his government' in the Low Countries, and the direct influence of his aunt, Margaret of Savoy, and his grandfather, in the region was at an end. The removal of Maximilian from the immediate scene was no great loss. Margaret, however, had been a good

---

[1] SP 1/9, f. 216; *LP* i, 3546.　　　　[2] Ibid.

friend of Tournai and of England,[1] and it seemed inevitable that Wolsey would find it more difficult to attain his objective with her influence withdrawn, particularly as the membership of the Prince's Council was changed so that it became more favourable to France.

Louis XII died on the same day. This event was less predictable than the accession of Charles, but it was potentially more dangerous. It led Sampson to conclude that all his hard work had gone for naught. He sadly told Wolsey 'the Bishop and his father hath now by the French King's death all their desire. For as I have written to your Grace in divers letters before, all their craft was to defer for this change.' He had had it on the best authority that if Louis died before Wolsey's claim was established beyond all question he would never get his way.[2]

The first positive sign that Francis I was going to be difficult came very quickly. A bull of Leo X dated 10 January 1515 committed the case of his beloved son Louis, Bishop elect of Tournai, against his venerable brother, Thomas, Archbishop of York, to the officers of Paris, Amiens, and Rouen. These men were unlikely to give judgement against the known wishes of the French King, and indeed the tone of the bull suggests that the Pope believed that the Frenchman had the better claim. It sets out his case in detail, maintaining that he has been duly appointed to Tournai and that he has peaceably enjoyed the goods of the church there for over a year. It goes on to say that Wolsey's claim to the administration of the diocese is based on certain apostolic letters 'obtained from us on false pretences'; and, further, that he has relied on letters from certain lay persons, and the efforts of 'our beloved son Richard Sampson, his vicar', in his attempt to deprive Guillard of the fruits of the see and to convert them to his own use. He has harassed, disturbed, disquieted, and threatened the Bishop elect, who, believing that his life is in danger, has now appealed to the Holy See.[3]

---

[1] She continued to be a good friend. In September 1515, after she had helped to settle in Henry's favour a claim for wages due for the 1513 campaign, Dr. William Knight spoke of her 'manifold kindness and perseverance in good mind toward the King which is more great than commonly hath been found in any woman and very seldom among men' (SP 1/11, f. 94; *LP* ii, 945).

[2] Cal. D VI, ff. 289–90; *LP* ii, 29.

[3] Vat. Arch. A.A. Arm. I–XVIII, 1901.

The bull commands the chosen officials to summon before them Wolsey, Sampson, and Guillard to hear what they have to say. They are to decide in the light of the evidence who is in the right, and to impose ecclesiastical penalties on the guilty parties, who are apparently presumed to be Wolsey and Sampson. Should the Englishmen refuse to appear in person, the citations of the court may be affixed in places where they will come to their notice, and they will be fully effective, in spite of a ruling of Boniface VIII that no one is to be called to judgement outside the boundaries of his own country. Further, if either Wolsey or Sampson should happen to be entitled to an indult[1] of interdict, suspension, or excommunication, the Pope rules in advance that for the purposes of the present case it will have no effect. It looks in fact as if the Pope did everything he could to make it easy for the Bishop elect to win his case.

In spite of this apparent alliance between the Pope and Francis, Suffolk reported from Paris in February that the French King agreed that Wolsey should have the bishopric of Tournai and even the best bishopric in France, if he wanted it.[2] About the same time Clarenceux King of Arms told the Earl of Worcester that Francis had desired the Duke of Suffolk 'to satisfy my lord of York (i.e. Wolsey) that he will in any wise he have the bishopric of Tournai'.[3] Suffolk himself said a few weeks later that Francis 'promised yesternight on his faith in my hand that he would make the other give it up to Wolsey in all haste'. The King had added that 'he would not stick with Wolsey for ten of the best bishoprics in France'.[4] Louis XII had said much the same thing a few months earlier, no doubt with equal sincerity.[5]

Sampson told Wolsey that, while the main difficulty was still to control the officers of the Bishop elect in Flanders, he was now beginning to have trouble even with the clergy in Tournai. Part of the trouble was personal. Like almost every other diplomat in the history of international relations, he considered that insufficient attention had been paid to his own accommodation problems. He thought that he should have first claim

---

[1] Pope's licence for thing not sanctioned by common law of Church (*O.E.D.*).
[2] SP 1/10, f. 49; Cal. D VI, f. 221; *LP* ii, 140, 176.
[3] SP 1/10, f. 66; *LP* ii, 183.   [4] SP 1/10, ff. 88–9; *LP* ii, App. no. 7.
[5] See above, p. 152.

on the Bishop's palace in Tournai, but alas it had been taken over by the Governor. He had been unable to find any other permanent residence, 'for the gentle Canons of Tournai, some for malicious mind will not lodge me, and some for fear dare not, lest the Bishop should return'. He did, however, have his eye on a house that had been confiscated and which the marshal had promised him. 'It is but a little house, and not fully builded, but it should be sufficient for this thing.' It would not cost very much to complete it.[1]

One of the reasons why the clergy were being difficult was that Henry had gone out of his way to confirm their privileges through letters patent issued in the middle of 1514. It seems extraordinary that this should have been considered necessary, for during his stay in Tournai he had confirmed in the most generous fashion the 'privilèges, droicts, seignouries, franchises, possessions, dismes, tonlieux, forraiges de bouvrages, jurisdictions, rentes, exemptions, admortissemens, libertéz, acquestes, coustumes prérogatives, dons, grâces et octrois' of the Dean and Chapter, both in Tournai and elsewhere—a catalogue which shows among other things how multifarious the financial interests of the Church were.[2] Since then, however, a number of royal decrees had been promulgated in the interest of the lay government of the city,[3] and it was suggested that, as nothing more had been done for the Church, it was somehow left at a disadvantage. This was wholly unreasonable, but, in order that justice might be seen to be done, Henry again let it be known that his Church in Tournai and all her members were to enjoy 'plainement et pacifiquement sans aucun contradiction' all the privileges they had enjoyed under the Kings of France his progenitors.[4] In Sampson's judgement the result of this unnecessary gesture was 'that if anything be contrary to their pleasure they be immediately ready to plee their privileges and the confirmation of the same. They be so bolded with favour. . . .'[5]

It might be expected that relations between Wolsey and his vicar general would have become strained after the blast of

---

[1] Cal. D VI, ff. 289–90; *LP* ii, 29.   [2] *Ordonnances*, p. 277.
[3] The levy on grain entering by water, waiving of annuities due to enemies, and so on.
[4] C 82/404 $\frac{5}{518}$; *LP* i, 2862(2).   [5] Cal. D VI, ff. 289–90; *LP* ii, 29.

invective which Sampson probably received in December 1514, and indeed that Sampson might have found it difficult to carry on as the Archbishop's agent. It is true that the flow of reports from Sampson suddenly diminishes at this time, and that in one he appears to throw his hand in. He has just had a meeting with Margaret of Savoy, whom he considers to be as loyal to Wolsey's interests as ever; but she has told him that her authority is 'now but little'. He has also spoken to de Fiennes, who promised 'reasonable favour', provided always that Charles saw no difficulty; and he intends on the following day to appear before the Prince's Council to demonstrate the validity of Wolsey's title to the administration of the see. 'Nevertheless, what furtherance I shall have I know not.'[1]

So far so good. But then, at this point, half-way through his letter, he becomes dispirited. Since the death of Louis XII two months ago he has heard nothing from Wolsey; and in that time everything has gone wrong. The new French King has been troublesome and has come out in favour of the Bishop elect. The Prince has 'entered into his lands' and appointed a new Council that is 'full French'. Above all, the Bishop elect is strong enough to take up residence in the diocese—not of course in Tournai, but the mere fact that he dared to reside anywhere in the see was enough to bring Wolsey's administration to an end. The Pope's brief left no doubt on this point. Sampson believed that his mission had failed and said that 'there is no man that hath greater sorriness than I'. This was an apology to Wolsey, but he was no doubt just as sorry for himself. He knew that victory in Tournai would mean his own rapid advancement; and this had now vanished into thin air. Indeed his career might take a step backward. Nevertheless, he concludes his letter by praying that it may be his good fortune to serve Wolsey in some other sphere 'where my hold shall not be so momentary'.[2]

Sampson, however, was not to escape so easily from the Low Countries. In March events took a surprising turn when Guillard sent a message to the vicar general, then in Ghent, offering to come to a settlement, why it is not clear. It is unlikely that the French officials appointed to settle the dispute would have found against Guillard, but he may have feared that the case

---

[1] Galba B V, f. 430; *LP* ii, 197.   [2] Galba B V, f. 431; *LP* ii, 197.

would drag on so long that it would pay him to come to a private arrangement with Wolsey. His proposal was so unattractive that it suggests he believed he was negotiating from a position of great strength. He offered to enter into an agreement which would comprise 'all things past and for to come . . . so that after, he should quietly obtain all the parts of the bishopric'. This probably meant that he wanted to be left in undisputed possession of the see, in return for a financial contribution to Wolsey to cover the preceding eighteen months, in which he had had some sort of a claim to the revenues. Sampson pointed out, however, that Wolsey was in no position to waive a claim to the temporalities (whatever might happen to the spiritualities). They belonged to Henry, having been confiscated when Guillard refused to take the oath of loyalty to the English Crown. Nevertheless, he agreed to put the proposition to Wolsey.[1]

He hoped to meet the Bishop elect in Ghent to explore a settlement, but Guillard was equally anxious to avoid a confrontation. He moved on to Bruges. The time for drastic action seemed to have arrived, partly because the Prince's Council, which had great influence in religious matters in the Low Countries, and which had been encouraging Wolsey to stand up for his rights, now decided to recognize Guillard. Sampson concluded that he must screw up his courage and for the first time invoke the spiritual power. This was a gamble he had been reluctant to take, for he realized that it might be his last chance. If the spiritual power proved to be no more effective than the temporal, then indeed he had come to the end of the road.[2]

He told Wolsey that he would forthwith 'monish' the Bishop elect, and require him to hand over the fruits of the see within fifteen days, on pain of incurring the wrath of the Church. The admonition could not be carried out in Guillard's presence, since he was taking great pains to keep out of striking distance, but it would be done before a notary and a witness, and the terms posted in all the main centres of the diocese. He also proposed to admonish the Bishop elect's officers, threatening them with excommunication if they continued to receive the

---

[1] Galba B III, ff. 359–359 b; *LP* ii, 239.
[2] Ibid.

revenues for Guillard and did not render to him (Sampson) the whole account of the see.

He urged Wolsey to invoke the aid of the Pope again. It should be easy enough, he reckoned, to have the Bishop elect suspended from office until he had given satisfaction over the revenues; and he might also be required to appear in person at Rome to answer for his conduct. If the matter was diligently handled and the Pope favoured Wolsey's cause, it should be possible to deprive Guillard of the see, or at least to induce him to resign and accept some other benefice; but it would call for careful negotiation, since the Bishop elect had enjoyed from the outset the dispensation for absence *studii causa*.[1] Spinelly wrote independently that he had been helping Sampson, and had found the Bishop elect 'totally proud, obstinate, not willing to hearken to anything but only to have the full revenues of the said bishopric'. No progress could be made locally. It was up to Wolsey to find a solution.[2]

Any breach between Wolsey and his vicar general seems to have healed quickly. On 16 May he graciously thanked Sampson for his efforts, and admitted that, although he had had no success in the struggle with the Bishop elect, he had done everything possible. He could be no more grateful if he 'had brought all things to good process'. Further, he will be writing shortly to tell him about the promotion he has earned. Wolsey also approved the aggressive line which his vicar general proposed to follow. There is to be no question of a compromise. It is to be 'all or no part'. The French King has clearly broken his promise, and Sampson is to pay no more heed to threats from that quarter. The bishopric is outside Francis's jurisdiction, and he will not harm Wolsey for twenty such as the Bishop elect or twenty such as his father. If Guillard initiates any spiritual process against Wolsey, Sampson, or any of his loyal officers, then 'spare not to take him if you may, and send him to prison'. If the Archbishop of Rheims takes any action against Sampson, then he is not to lose a moment in taking the same action against the Archbishop. Wolsey concludes with the encouraging command 'Viriliter age et tandem omnia vincas'. If Sampson goes to it with a will, all will come right in the end.[3]

[1] Galba B III, ff. 359–60; *LP* ii, 239.   [2] SP 1/10, f. 95; *LP* ii, 262.
[3] Cal. D VI, f. 347; *LP* ii, 469.

Sampson must have been overjoyed. He received Wolsey's letter on 19 May and replied enthusiastically the following day, thanking him for his great generosity, which he had done nothing to deserve. In particular, he was grateful for the promise of promotion, not of course for his own sake, but because it would enable him the more easily to do his master honourable service. He would now wield the spiritual sword more sharply in the campaign against Guillard, and call in the temporal as it seemed desirable. He knew that he could rely on Mountjoy and the leading captains of the garrison to give him all the backing he needed, and, indeed, he had already enlisted the co-operation of Richard Hansard, the under-marshal. Hansard had apprehended three of Wolsey's farmers [i.e. revenue collectors] 'an English mile from Tournai', although he allowed 'two or three which were of the fattest' to slip through his fingers. This was a step in the right direction, and Sampson hoped that the example would encourage other collectors to deal with him rather than with the Bishop elect's officers.[1] This was particularly important, for shortly afterwards Guillard was clever enough to send some of his men into the Tournaisis to collect from some curates a tax which he claimed he had promised to pay over to Charles. By this means he not only maintained his own standing in the Tournaisis but also helped to keep Charles well disposed towards him.[2]

There was no chance, however, of pursuing such a strong line outside Tournai and the Tournaisis. For several reasons it would be neither for Wolsey's honour nor for his profit. Prince Charles's Privy Council had forbidden Sampson to campaign against the Bishop elect in Flanders, and he feared that in any case he would arouse the common people, 'which of their own nature be malicious' and would resent anything done for the honour and profit of an Englishman. Again, there was the Bishop elect's sound argument that, as long as he was resident in the see, the revenues were his. If Sampson sought to exercise spiritual jurisdiction in Flanders he would appear to be 'very sore blinded', and no one would pay the slightest attention to his pronouncements. It was different in Tournai, where, because of 'his obstinacy and homage not offered or done', the Bishop elect was in a weak position; but if Wolsey wanted

[1] Cal. D VI, ff. 294–295 b; *LP* ii, 480.   [2] Cal. D VI, f. 305; *LP* ii, 701.

Sampson to exercise 'spirituous jurisdiction' in Flanders he must ensure that he had a 'more clear title'. But by far the simplest solution, to Sampson's poor mind, was to provide a pension for the Bishop elect. He and his friends would be ready enough to renounce the see if he could be given 'an honest living' elsewhere. A pension of 300 or 400 marks until he found a bishopric in France would show that Wolsey wanted the bishopric not for his own profit but for the honour of the King; and if Francis failed to find an alternative see, say after a year or so, then Wolsey could quietly forget the pension.[1] Four days later Sampson wrote from Bruges, again begging Wolsey to offer compensation to Guillard.[2]

He was still urging the same course at the end of May. He suggested that Wolsey was in a strong position now that most of Europe had 'made a faithful league against the French King'. Francis might be willing to find another see for Guillard, intending to make Wolsey, and therefore England, well-disposed to France. He must 'diligently solicit' the French King. Alternatively, it might be wise to compensate the Bishop elect. Unless something was done quickly, the small number of loyal people—for example, 'the learned doctor of Bruges', one of the few members of the clergy who recognized Wolsey, and Jean le Sellier—would withdraw their support.[3] Spinelly introduced a new element into the debate by claiming that Guillard had 'clearly counterfeited the tenor of certain bulls apostolic whereby it is said that he hath deserved to be deprived'. He and Sampson would try to get chapter and verse on this.[4]

Wolsey now acted on the advice he had received and tackled Francis direct. Sir William Sidney's brief for a mission to Paris instructs him to remind the French King that he had promised that the Bishop elect would make no trouble for Wolsey and his officers, and indeed that he would resign. In spite of this, Guillard was now in Flanders, seeking to frustrate all attempts to collect the revenues of the see. Further, he had obtained inhibitions against Wolsey's officers from the Archbishop of Rheims; and, but for Francis's promise, Wolsey would long ere this have taken steps to protect his rights. The Pope had 'largely confirmed and granted' him the administration, partly in token

[1] Cal. D VI, ff. 294–295 b; *LP* ii, 480.   [2] SP 1/10, f. 192; *LP* ii, 499.
[3] Cal. D VI, ff. 290, 298; *LP* ii, 512, 528. [4] SP 1/10, f. 194; *LP* ii, 521.
12—E.O.T.

of his efforts to maintain peace between France and England. Wolsey set great store by the bishopric, not of course for its revenues but simply because Henry and the Pope had appointed him to it.[1]

If anyone had suggested to Francis that denying Wolsey the revenues of Tournai would encourage Henry to leave the city, or, alternatively, that allowing him to enjoy them in peace would make Henry want to keep it, then Sidney was to make it plain that 'they be far deceived'. The opposite was nearer the truth, for there was a better chance of reasonable discussion about the future of Tournai if Guillard were removed from the scene. Sidney is therefore to suggest that Francis should 'revoke and call home the said elect, putting him to silence, and give him straight commandment to desist and clearly forbear from any intermeddling in the said bishopric of Tournai, or the receiving of any profits of the same', and to allow Wolsey and his officers peaceably to enjoy the administration. An interesting feature of this brief is that in the earlier passages, which deal with other matters, it is the King who is speaking, but when the section on Tournai is reached it is clearly Wolsey who is issuing instructions to the ambassador in his own name.[2]

Sampson himself was given diplomatic status in May 1515. His name was included in the commission issued to Cuthbert Tunstal, Thomas More, and John Clifford when they were sent on an embassy to Prince Charles.[3] It may have been considered that his experience in the Low Countries would make him a useful member of the team, whose main purpose was to negotiate the continuance of a commercial treaty of 1506; but his new status had the incidental advantage that it strengthened his personal position. The accredited diplomat then, as now, enjoyed certain immunities, which on the whole were faithfully observed by the host country; and this was of particular importance to Sampson because of the hostility his activities as Wolsey's vicar general had attracted to him, both in Tournai and in Flanders. Wolsey must have been well aware of this, and his main purpose in including Sampson in the embassy may have been to strengthen his position as vicar general. He told him: 'Ye being the King's ambassador, your adversary shall be

---

[1] SP 1/10, ff. 174–6; *LP* ii, 468.   [2] Ibid.
[3] C 76/197, m. 30; Rymer, pp. 497–8; *LP* ii, 422.

the worse ordered to attempt any thing against you and ye shall be the more able to advance my causes.' He also sent an allowance of £60, to be used at the rate of 20s. 0d. a day, so that Sampson should be 'the better furnished as well in your apparel as in other expenses as accordeth the King's ambassador'.[1]

The more positive line which led Sampson to threaten the Bishop elect with the wrath of the Church and his officers with excommunication was bound to provoke retaliation. It was all very well for Wolsey to cry 'Handle the matter boldly and fulminate the censures according to the brief, not fearing excommunication of any man.'[2] The other side was well equipped to fulminate back, and their target would be Sampson rather than Wolsey. The vicar general may also have been thinking of his own skin when a few days later he said that the French King would never make Guillard resign. On the contrary, he would give him all his support, as it was very much in France's interest to have a Frenchman in possession of the see. It might be possible to induce the Pope to depose the Bishop elect, but this would be a dangerous precedent for bishops in general.[3] Perhaps Sampson had his eye on his own career when he made the latter observation.

At the beginning of July Sampson had to announce to Wolsey that the ultimate blow had been delivered. He had been excommunicated by the Archbishop of Rheims, the metropolitan of the see of Tournai. Further, he had been ordered to appear before the Archbishop to answer a number of charges.[4] This could be expensive, for, as he pointed out, 'the manner of spiritual process in these parts is not only to make comminations with spiritual pains, but also with pecuniary pains'.[5] He had at once replied by 'executing denunciations' against the Bishop elect's officers, as they had done against him, but there was little consolation in this gesture. 'It shall rather be to them a laughing sport than pain.'[6]

Wolsey had earlier urged that if the opposition played the trump card of excommunication, Sampson should have no hesitation in following suit; but this was more than he could stomach. He wanted above all to carry out Wolsey's commands,

[1] Cal. E III, f. 100; LP ii, 534.   [2] Ibid.
[3] Galba B III, f. 361 b; LP ii, 553.   [4] Galba B III, f. 372; LP ii, 769.
[5] Galba B III, f. 363 b; LP ii, 566.   [6] Galba B III, f. 372 b; LP ii, 769.

when it could be done to his master's honour, and he would not hold back for dread of any man; 'but in this cause, my lord, most humbly I beseech your Grace to consider that the effect of your brief is extinct, clearly without any colour, especially in all Flanders by the residence of the elect'.[1]

The only action he could contemplate was to appeal against the sentence; and here he might be on good ground, for the Archbishop of Rheims was a 'very suspect judge'. 'But an appellation is of no strength nor defence except he [the Archbishop] be prosecuted: wherefore, since this appellation is not prosecuted the process made by the Archbishop is of full strength.'[2] Sampson admitted that if his appeal succeeded the sentence of excommunication would be meaningless; but if the appeal failed, what then? It was, of course, open to the Pope to quash the sentence, irrespective of what happened about the appeal, but that would cost a great deal of money, and however devout Sampson may have been there was a limit to the price he would pay for his soul.

If Wolsey had no standing in the diocese, Sampson was faced by three unpleasant consequences. He was left with grave doubts about the efficacy of his own denunciations, but this was relatively unimportant. More serious was the danger that if Wolsey's authority was not there to back up his own, the sentence of excommunication against him might be valid in the eyes of Heaven. He could only speculate as to where his soul actually stood in the midst of the exchange of fulminations.

Above all, however, his professional pride was at risk. He was deeply versed in the elaborate ramifications of the canon law, and he could not agree with Wolsey that the Archbishop of Rheims had no jurisdiction, or even bring himself to argue on these lines. The debate would be conducted 'in face of princes, great learned men and wise men which beholdeth daily the doings in this business', and he could not expose Wolsey to the criticism that his vicar general was 'without learning, discretion and so beastly blind that he knew neither learning nor reason'. The matter of his professional reputation was clearly uppermost in his mind, for he comes back to the point. Like so many documents in Sir Robert Cotton's collection, the letter, alas, has had its margins eaten away by fire, but enough sur-

---

[1] Galba B III, f. 372; *LP* ii, 769.   [2] Galba B III, ff. 363–4; *LP* ii, 566.

vives to reveal the strength of Sampson's feelings. He repeats
that he must not show himself as a blind beastly fellow without
learning. Without fail learned men will despise him and point
the finger of scorn at him as he goes in the streets; and although
the opinions of the common people do not matter, they will take
their cue from their betters and become even more difficult to
govern.[1]

Tunstal took pity on his fellow ambassador and wrote
separately to Wolsey, commending him for the 'painful service'
he was rendering in these parts in spite of all the difficulties laid
in his path. 'And now of late, notwithstanding that he is in
commission'—this refers to his diplomatic status—'he was
openly in all the churches of this town accursed, which shows
the malice of your said adversary towards you ... I beseech you
to continue good to him in helping him in this business.'
Tunstal added that the feeling against Sampson was so strong
that if it had not been for the immunity afforded him by the
King's commission the secular arm would have been brought in
against him.[2] The campaign against Sampson, however, was
not entirely due to the dispute over the see. Charles and his
Council were reluctant to make progress with the renewal of the
treaty of 1506, and they were no doubt glad of any opportunity
to embarrass the English commissioners. 'The Prince, your
Grace knoweth, as a child is governed by his Council, which for
a great part is good French, and I dare say glad of this displeasure . . . to the King's highness or your Grace.'[3]

A position of stalemate was now reached. The friends of the
Bishop elect had gone as far as they could in their spiritual
attack on Sampson; and he for his part had gone as far as he
dared in retaliating. The temporal power which Sampson could
summon up to help him did not extend beyond Tournai and the
Tournaisis; but the Bishop elect and his officers took good care
not to set foot there. It was necessary for Sampson to make
frequent visits to Flanders, not only for the purposes of the
embassy but as part of the campaign to get Wolsey's authority
accepted. The Bishop elect could no doubt have prevailed on
the authorities in the Low Countries to put a stop to Sampson's
activities by arresting and imprisoning him; but he was pro-

---

[1] Galba B III, f. 372; *LP* ii, 769.   [2] Galba B III, f. 293 b; *LP* ii, 679.
[3] Galba B III, f. 371; *LP* ii, 686.

tected by his diplomatic immunity. So far as Wolsey was concerned the relative importance of the revenues of the bishopric must have declined when he obtained his Cardinal's hat in September 1515. They had seemed worth a great deal at the beginning of 1514, when he was King's almoner, but they had already become less significant when he became Bishop of Lincoln, and then Archbishop of York. This meant that he was content to let things remain as they were.

At the beginning of 1516 Sampson accepted that for the moment there was little to be done about dispossessing Guillard. He became more concerned with the affairs of the diocese within the city of Tournai, and in particular with the Benedictine Abbey of St. Martin, the Abbot of which had been giving trouble. In August 1515 Mountjoy had begged Wolsey to persuade the King to put his 'true subjects' into the abbey. If this was done it would be worth a thousand soldiers in the garrison.[1] Sampson shared this view and now directed his energies towards throwing out the Abbot.

The Abbot, Jean de Bois, proved to be just as tough a nut as the Bishop elect. He was pro-French, and did not trouble to conceal it. He was also a worthless character, if half what was said about him was true. He led a vicious life and was 'abominable for his own person'. He was frequently absent from his charge and had appropriated for his own use most of the abbey's valuables. 'He wastefully and viciously spendeth and dissipateth the goods and rents of the said abbey, doing no reparation but suffering the houses to decay and fall down.'[2] Unfortunately he enjoyed Charles's favour—in spite of the fact that he had committed enough crimes to depose ten abbots[3]—which made things more difficult. Had he been well disposed to the new regime his sins would no doubt have been forgiven. His real crime was that he was a loyal Frenchman.

In the middle of 1516, when the Governor tried to act against the Abbot, he cleverly side-stepped by inducing Charles to send him as one of his ambassadors to Denmark. This gave him diplomatic status and also took him a safe distance from Tournai. He realized, however, that this was only a temporary

---

[1] Cal. E I, f. 64 b; *LP* ii, 825. [2] SP 1/12, f. 149; *LP* ii, 1492.
[3] SP 1/11, f. 75; *LP* ii, 889.

respite. If he was to enjoy the fruits of the abbey he must sooner or later return to Tournai and face the English authorities. Therefore before leaving for Denmark he instructed friends in Ghent to arrange to 'permute' his abbey for one in Hainaut, which would enable him to live in the manner to which he was accustomed, beyond the clutches of the Governor of Tournai. As an alternative, he thought of resigning the abbey in favour of the nephew of Chièvres, Prince Charles's Chamberlain, no doubt in return for suitable compensation.[1] Sampson considered that if an exchange was permitted the new Abbot would 'without fail have as strong provisions from the Pope as may be, so that the King's highness shall have little of his pleasure in this matter'. The best remedy was to start a process of deprivation against him at Rome, which would automatically suspend the proposed exchange.[2]

The council in Tournai urged Henry to find out from Rome if such an exchange was likely to go through, and to ensure that if it did the abbey should go to an Englishman. It was just as important 'to have a good Englishman Abbot, which is a discreet man and hath this language, or else some other good man English of heart', as it was to have an English Bishop of Tournai. Further, Henry's hold on the city would be much strengthened if the see was made responsible to Canterbury rather than to Rheims, just as Calais and the Pale were.[3] Sir Richard Jerningham agreed. It would be much to the King's honour for Wolsey to have both the bishopric and the Abbey of St. Martin, especially if Sampson could hold them under him. 'I would reckon it should be as much strength as one of the best towers of the citadel when it shall be made.'[4]

In December 1515 the Earl of Worcester told Wolsey that he really must do something about the Abbot. He had 'meddled therein so sore' that it would be neither to the King's honour or Wolsey's to admit defeat at this stage.[5] Shortly afterwards Sampson so arranged matters that it seemed to be only a question of time before de Bois was removed. He got the monks to agree to make a formal complaint against him; and, being satisfied that they were ripe for rebellion, brought in from

<hr>

[1] SP 1/12, ff. 114, 152; *LP* ii, 1434, 1496. [2] SP 1/11, f. 75; *LP* ii, 889.
[3] Cal. E I, ff. 63–63 b; *LP* ii, 824. [4] SP 1/12, f. 150; *LP* ii, 1499.
[5] Cal. D VII, f. 50; *LP* ii, App. 16.

Flanders a notary 'which hath great experience for expedition of matters at Rome', who was to record and certify the monks' allegations against their superior. A meeting was duly arranged. The notary sat 'with paper and ink ready to write their desire'; but before he could begin to take down the first complaint a representative of the Abbot burst into the room and 'letted clearly the intent and purpose'. The wretched monks were terrified, for their plot was now laid bare. The Abbot's agent persuaded them that Prince Charles, with whom de Bois was on the best of terms, would induce Henry to allow him to 'enjoy peaceably the abbey, and then punish them at his pleasure'. As his scheme had failed miserably, Sampson suggested that the King should complain to the Pope about the Abbot's conduct and ask that he be removed.[1]

The plan to transfer the abbey to Chièvres' nephew misfired, because Prince Charles's Chancellor surprisingly decided that he dare not become involved in 'so contrarious a thing to the King's displeasure'. The Abbot believed, however, that he had found someone else who would co-operate, and Sampson feared that the new man would also be well disposed towards the French. He repeated what he had said many times: if only the whole see were loyal he would be strong enough to move against the Abbot, but with the Bishop elect standing complacently in the wings stern measures 'should have none effect but ridiculous'. Further, Guillard's father had just been made French ambassador to the Low Countries, which was a feather in the cap of the Bishop elect and his officers. 'I pray God,' exclaimed the despairing Sampson, 'there may come such a wind that may cause them to vail a bonnet of their mainsail.'[2]

In fact, the Abbot abandoned his plan for an exchange, probably because he could not persuade his chosen replacement that the English authorities in Tournai would necessarily accept him as the new Abbot. Something had to be done, however. De Bois had come to the conclusion that Henry would remain indefinitely in Tournai, mainly because no one could be so stupid as to pour enormous sums into building a vast

---

[1] SP 1/12, ff. 7–8; *LP* ii, 1254.

[2] SP 1/13, f. 2; *LP* ii, 1530. Bonnet: 'An additional piece of canvas laced to the foot of a sail to catch more wind' (it appears to have been formerly laced to the top of the sail, or to have been itself a top-sail); to vail: 'To lower . . . (a sail)' (*O.E.D.*).

citadel simply to hand it over to the French; and if he was right, he must take this fact into account in making his dispositions. He was in a much weaker position than the Bishop elect, whose rule went beyond the boundaries of Tournai and the Tournaisis.[1] His abbey was within the confines of Tournai, where English authority was supreme. If he was to continue to enjoy the fruits of the institution he had to live there and conduct himself according to the wishes of the Governor and his council. This was a bleak prospect, for he had no intention of mending his ways. He came to the conclusion that it would help to have an influential prelate made coadjutor in the abbey. By taking into partnership someone above suspicion he would increase his security of tenure, at the cost of sharing the revenues of the abbey. The more elevated his chosen partner the better; and he therefore sought advice from a theologian in Louvain about the best way of putting his abbey 'by way of renunciation or coadjutory' into the hands of a Cardinal who would be sympathetic to his cause, of course at price.[2] Spinelly, who knew his man, warned Wolsey that he would not cease till he had made 'some bargain of his abbey'.[3]

Sampson began proceedings against the Abbot in May 1516, but de Bois, who was no less expert than Guillard in those branches of the canon law which had a bearing on his standard of living, promptly lodged an appeal in Rome. In reporting this Sampson said that de Bois had styled himself 'the Pope's messenger and receiver of his money in these parts', which was nonsense. He simply pretended these things to justify his absence from Tournai. The Pope should be asked to appoint a commission, which might include the Abbot of St. Nicholas des Près and Dr. Baltasare de Cordis, one of the Canons of Tournai, to enquire into the Abbot's conduct.[4]

Shortly afterwards Spinelly told Henry that he had it on the

---

[1] He was however just as skilful an exponent of the canon law as Louis Guillard. There survives in the Cottonian manuscripts a notarially-attested instrument appealing on technical grounds against a citation made against him by an officer of the Tournai diocese. His case had been referred to the Pope before the proper interval had elapsed. Further, the citation had been affixed to the door of the abbey church without the name of the executor and was therefore in contempt of the Holy See. The Abbot lodged an appeal with the Pope on these grounds (Cal. E I, ff. 148 b–149; *LP* ii, 3167).

[2] Galba B V, f. 190; *LP* ii, 1766.   [3] SP 1/13, f. 127; *LP* ii, 1823.
[4] Cal. D VI, f. 292 b; *LP* ii, 1849.

authority of a merchant acquaintance that the Abbot had taken a Cardinal as his coadjutor, and that he was expecting the bulls to come through from Rome within a fortnight.[1] The Bishop of Worcester, who was probably unaware of the political implications, wrote to Henry recommending that Louis de Rossi, a relative of the Pope, should have the coadjutorship.[2] The Pope had a special affection for him and had approved the appointment.[3] De Rossi himself asked Henry and Wolsey for their support.[4]

While the English ambassador in Rome was doing his best to unite the Abbot of St. Martin's with a coadjutor of his own choice and thereby increase his security of tenure, Sampson was doing his best to throw him out. He suggested that although the Abbot was still absent from Tournai he could be taken prisoner for a very small sum. Henry had merely to give the order to the Governor and the job would be done. He added that if both abbey and bishopric fell into Wolsey's hands he would be the richer by £1,000 or £1,200 a year, 'all charges honourably borne'.[5]

In October 1516 Tunstal, writing to Wolsey from Bruges, told him that a Canon of Antwerp had seen the bulls sent from Rome appointing de Rossi coadjutor. If this was true, no doubt the Bishop of Worcester had already reported it.[6] A month later Cardinal de Medici wrote in support of de Rossi,[7] and the Bishop of Worcester again added his support. He hoped that Wolsey would persuade the King to agree to the appointment. It was understood that de Rossi was to be made Cardinal in the very near future and he was sure that it would be wise to help him.[8] The Pope himself also wrote to Henry in support of the proposal.[9]

Nothing happened, however. There was no reply from Henry or Wolsey, and in April 1517 the Pope wrote a pained letter saying that he had assumed that he would have had their agreement by now. He trusted that they would take a quick decision in favour of de Rossi, whose many services deserved a

[1] Galba B VI, f. 43; *LP* ii, 1895.   [2] SP 1/13, f. 163; *LP* ii, 1898.
[3] SP 1/13, ff. 261–2; *LP* ii, 2243(2).
[4] SP 1/13, ff. 166, 167; *LP* ii, 1911, 1912.
[5] Cal. D VI, f. 301 b; *LP* ii, 2274.   [6] SP 1/14, f. 56; *LP* ii, 2484.
[7] SP 1/14, f. 104; *LP* ii, 2572.
[8] Vit. B III, ff. 89, 90; *LP* ii, 2579, 2580.   [9] *LP* ii, 2502.

generous reward.[1] He even held out the hope that he might recall the bulls in favour of the Bishop elect if Wolsey would comply with his wishes. Further, he no longer insisted that de Rossi should be appointed to Tournai. He would be quite content if some other suitable provision was made for him.[2] The Bishop of Worcester, however, said that the Pope considered that Wolsey was being obstructive in the matter of the coadjutorship, and further that the benefices in Tournai had always been in his own gift.[3]

A fortnight later the Governor, Sir Richard Jerningham, wrote in the King's name to the Abbot, ordering him to come to Tournai by a given date to be informed of the King's pleasure about the affairs of the Abbey and its convent. De Bois promptly fell back on the defence he had used the year before. He again prevailed on Charles to 'send for him in haste for certain business of the King's, like as in my Lord Mountjoy's time in semblable wise he purchased to be sent into Denmark with other the King of Castile's ambassadors'. Only this time Jerningham had no doubt that the business was fictitious and that Charles's letter was only 'to colour his absence'. To make matters worse, de Bois had the effrontery to refer to the King of Spain as 'his sovereign lord and master', adding that he was 'not bounden to obey any temporal man's commandment in no manner of wise, nor would not'. Jerningham begged Wolsey to ensure that the Abbot got his deserts. There was not a single soul in Tournai who less deserved the King's favour.[4]

Sampson was asked by Charles, Maximilian, and Margaret to delay proceedings against the Abbot, and he felt that he must comply with their wishes, at least until Wolsey had had a chance of seeing their letters. Later, however, Margaret told him to go ahead, and the comedy of ecclesiastical thrust and parry was resumed. Sampson formally accused the Abbot. De Bois formally rejected his accusation on the ground that the Abbot of St. Martin's was outside the jurisdiction of the diocese of Tournai. Sampson forwarded his defence to Wolsey, adding his opinion that the Abbot in fact had always been subject to the Bishop. If he had obtained exemption it had been done without his knowledge, and therefore it must be regarded as 'surrep-

---

[1] SP 1/15, f. 95; *LP* ii, 3146.   [2] Vit. B III, f. 121; *LP* ii, 2890.
[3] Vit. B X, f. 70; *LP* ii, App. 53.   [4] SP 1/15, f. 112; *LP* ii, 3202.

titious'. His conduct was quite intolerable, and the King's representatives at Rome must revoke and annihilate any concession which de Bois might have obtained direct from the Pope. He was in a weaker position than the Bishop elect, for he had taken the oath of loyalty. He was safe so long as he remained in Charles's territories, but if he ventured beyond them he could be taken prisoner and brought to justice in Tournai. He was, however, planning to go to Rome to win privileges from the Pope to help in his campaign against English interests in Tournai. This could be frustrated if the English ambassador in Rome was properly briefed and kept his ear close to the ground.[1]

The records for the next year are scanty, perhaps because even the indefatigable Sampson had decided that he was fighting a losing battle against the wily Abbot. Certainly during the latter part of 1518 everybody knew that before long the occupation would end. This must have strengthened the resistance of those Tournaisiens who were hostile to the new regime and who had been waiting patiently for the English to leave; and it made pointless the pursuit of any long-term plans by the English authorities, whether in the civil or ecclesiastical sphere. In December the Abbot who 'for his immoralities ought rather to be expelled from his monastery' finally succeeded in getting the coadjutor of his choice appointed.[2] Two weeks later the Bishop of Worcester reported from Rome that he was still doing his best about the process against de Bois; but since the coadjutor had now been appointed there was no point in pursuing the matter further.[3] The persistence and ingenuity of the dissolute Abbot had won the day. The problems which his worldly behaviour posed for the community would have to be solved by the French when they returned.

The Bishop elect was on far stronger ground than the Abbot of St. Martin's. De Bois had to content himself with defence. Guillard could attack. He could go only as far as the Pope would allow him to, however, and Leo's attitude was much coloured by his relations with the French. When they were good he sided with Guillard, when they were bad, with Wolsey. At

---

[1] SP 1/16, f. 32; *LP* ii, 3720.   [2] Cal. E I, f. 200 b; *LP* ii, 4627.
[3] Vit. B III, f. 309; *LP* ii, 4681.

the beginning of 1516 he found himself backing Wolsey, and on 12 March Sampson received by the hand of William Bartholomew 'an inhibition, citation and letters compulsory' against Guillard. He promised Wolsey that these documents would be published in the Cathedral on the following Sunday 'in the best manner', and that copies would be displayed in Bruges, Lille, and Courtrai, if it might be done safely. He was unhappy, however, about carrying out the procedures within the diocese. It would have been far better to execute the measures in Rome, and to have the resultant decisions—preferably against the Bishop elect—transmitted to Tournai.[1]

The chances, however, of getting a clear-cut decision in favour of Wolsey in Rome were slight. It is true that at the beginning of August the Bishop of Worcester was able to send him a brief 'about the Tournai matter', which he had extracted from the Pope with the greatest difficulty. It had been prepared some time earlier, but the French ambassadors, who had been bombarded with letters from Paris instructing them to plead the Bishop elect's cause, had objected to its release. The Pope held it back as long as he dared, being unable to make up his mind which side to favour. At last, in response to the Bishop of Worcester's 'great and persistent pressure', he allowed it to issue, on condition that it was kept secret for the time being. When he had further considered the political situation he might agree that it should be made public. The French ambassadors, who knew what was going on, were 'greatly raging and threatening', as they considered that they had been defeated.[2]

In fact, this was only a minor triumph for Wolsey, for later in the year France and Guillard were back in the Pope's favour. Sampson told Wolsey in August that the Bishop elect had come to Flanders 'to enter into the towns of the diocese, as is the manner for the taking of his possession', in spite of the inhibition and all the rest. He had not ventured into Tournai or the Tournaisis, where he would have had short shrift, but if Wolsey still wanted 'to pursue the title of this bishopric'—and Sampson's tone clearly suggested that he should not—it would be necessary to obtain a new inhibition from the Pope with speed and diligence. It would also help if Wolsey wrote to Margaret of Savoy and her Council to ask them to do what they could to

stop Guillard's progress round the diocese.[1] The Bishop of
Worcester confirmed from Rome that the influence of the
French there had much increased. He also referred to a proposal
that Sampson should go to Rome, to help him to get the bulls
that would leave no doubt as to who was the true Bishop of
Tournai. He would be prepared to listen to any ideas that
Sampson had, but he added peevishly that he would deprecate
Sampson's mission as being derogatory to his own dignity.[2]

Some time earlier the Pope had committed the dispute
between Wolsey and Guillard to two Cardinals, but this did not
stop the Frenchman from seeking to establish his rights by his
own efforts. Not only did he appear in person in as many of the
towns of the diocese as he dared, but he also answered Sampson's publication of the inhibition against him by affixing documents in defence of his title to the church doors in all the places
where his tax farmers were active, and where the bishopric
owned temporal lordships. Sampson promptly sent his own
officers in the wake of the Bishop elect, with instructions to pull
down his 'affixions' and replace them with copies of an inhibition supplied by the Cardinals charged with investigating the
dispute, to which he added a footnote claiming that Guillard's
documents were in contempt of the Cardinals' jurisdiction.

Sampson suggested to Wolsey that the Cardinals should
designate someone to visit Flanders to see what the Bishop elect
was up to; and he added a plea that reveals that he had quickly
become a highly professional diplomat. He was afraid that 'for
poverty I should be little able to do your Grace either any good
service in these parts profitously or honourably, for in doing
your Grace service here I must meddle with some great
personages, and daily with such as (if I were not in your Grace's
service) passeth my poor degree'. In short, if he was to make a
success of the job entrusted to him, he must be enabled to mix
with the wealthiest in the land; and this meant the provision of
a generous living allowance.[3]

Except for this skirmish, 1516 passed quietly enough. Sampson visited England in December, and before he returned to his
post was made King's 'procurator, attorney and representative',
with extensive powers, presumably to strengthen his position

[1] Cal. E I, f. 112; *LP* ii, 2242.   [2] Vit. B III, f. 90; *LP* ii, 2394.
[3] Cal. E I, ff. 113–14; *LP* ii, 2289.

in Wolsey's interests.[1] At the beginning of 1517 he once again embarked on interminable paper processes against the Bishop elect.[2] Jean le Sellier, whose enthusiastic collaboration gave him a strong vested interest in the success of the occupation, and who probably stood to lose more than anyone if the English were forced to withdraw, was particularly worried by Guillard's success. He told Poynings that he should have struck while the iron was hot. The longer the Bishop elect remained on the scene the stronger became his hold. There could be no argument about the fact that Henry owned the temporalities by right of conquest. Guillard had done nothing between his appointment and the arrival of the English to give him the slightest claim to the see; and his proposal to bring the dispute before the ecclesiastical court at Bruges was out of order. But while his opponents debated, the Bishop elect brought off a brilliant coup that caught them quite unawares.[3]

He contrived secretly to obtain a bull from the Pope which gave him a clear title to the bishopric, empowered him to call on the secular arm to help him to obtain his rights by force, and specifically excluded Wolsey. This was most serious. Hitherto it had been a struggle between two individuals to win the valuable revenues of the see. It mattered a great deal to both, for substantial sums were at stake; but, except that the divided loyalty of the clergy had some bearing on the standing of the English authorities in Tournai, the personal contest between the two clerics hardly affected the security of the city. Now that the Bishop elect had the Pope's authority to enlist the aid of any government willing to help him, the position was quite different. The prize for Guillard was still the bishopric: but possession of Tournai and the Tournaisis was dangled before anyone who wanted to take up the licence which the Pope had given to Guillard. Henry and Wolsey were quick to see the new threat and they reacted with a mighty explosion.

As soon as he heard the news of the Pope's action Henry sent his ambassador an immediate dispatch, a majestic reprimand which can seldom have been surpassed in the field of diplomacy. Its furious terms must have made de Gigli rue the day when he

[1] C 76/197, m. 6; Rymer, p. 579; LP ii, 2770.
[2] SP 1/14, ff. 199, 217; LP ii, 2807, 2827.
[3] Cal. E I, ff. 117–18; LP ii, 2695.

became English representative at Rome, for it threatens the direst action against him if ever again he is guilty of such carelessness. It is prefaced by an interesting statement of the duties of the sixteenth-century ambassador:

We of special trust and confidence have deputed you to be resident in that Court as our orator not only to solicit and execute all such causes and matters as we have and shall commit unto you from time to time but also vigilantly to intend and foresee that no such thing be impetrate or obtained there prejudicial or hurtful to us and this our realm or derogatory to our dignity royal.

The ambassador, however, has miserably failed in his duty. A bull contrary to all law and justice has been 'lately passed and sped' at the instance of the pretended Bishop of Tournai, which redounds greatly to the King's dishonour, completely undermines his position in Tournai, and even makes possible war between him and his friends and allies—yet de Gigli had not even noticed its publication.

Henry goes on to say that he is astonished that the Pope should launch such an attack on English sovereignty without giving the King a chance of defending his position. He is sovereign lord of Tournai. The 'said pretended Bishop' owes him homage there because of the temporalities he holds from the King, if for no other reason. But he positively refuses to take the oath of loyalty, and has also 'traitorously conspired sundry enterprises for the taking and surprising of our said city'. Now he has succeeded in getting a clause inserted in the bull invoking the aid of the secular arm, which is an invitation to the Kings of France and Castile to declare war on Henry. Further, if the citizens of Tournai are to accept Guillard's authority under pain of excommunication, it is tantamount to discharging them of their allegiance to the English Crown. This is 'exorbitant and contrary to the laws of God and man, justice and reason'. It is the greatest dishonour to the Pope to be a party to such wrong and injury to a Prince; and it is a shameful return for all the help Henry had given the Papacy.

The King then enlarges upon the iniquities of the Pope over several closely-written pages; and having done so, turns his attention to the ambassador, who had apparently been caught napping. The singular trust and confidence which he has always had in de Gigli had been gravely misplaced, for by his 'negligence and inadvertisement' the bull had slipped through without let or hindrance, with consequent 'dishonour, prejudice, danger, damage, and displeasure' to his royal person. If de Gigli gives no better service in the future, he can rest assured that he will be replaced by someone who will be rather more vigilant and look after the King's interests with greater success. As it is, the ambassador must now set about persuading the Pope to revoke the bull, 'with sufficient clauses to extinct all processes and sentences made and to be made by authority and virtue thereof against us, the said Cardinal, or any of our subjects'.[1]

The Bishop of Worcester lost no time in seeking an audience with the Pope. He spoke forcibly about the grave damage which the bull would cause 'if his holiness should not shortly provide of a competent remedy to so great an error by him committed'. Leo had promised that he would never do anything that might be prejudicial to Henry's interests without first discussing it with de Gigli, but in the present case he had 'occulted' the whole business. De Gigli first heard of the bull from Henry in London, to his 'great rebuke'. Leo's actions were not the tokens, signs, and indices of the paternal affection that he admitted he owed Henry. Rather they were evident and manifest demonstration of 'capital and odious inimicity' against a Prince who richly deserved the gratitude of the Holy See.[2]

In speaking on these lines de Gigli was caught between two fires. He was the Pope's fellow-countryman, and no doubt hoped for further promotion. Therefore he must have been reluctant to make a full-scale offensive on behalf of Henry. On the other hand he was the English King's ambassador and held from him the valuable see of Worcester. He could not please both his spiritual and secular masters, and he must have found it difficult to achieve the balance in handling the problem that would maximize the benefits he would receive at the hands of both.

We have only his word for what he said, and in reporting to Henry he naturally made it sound strong. He had delivered his protest to Leo 'under such manner that I marvel greatly how

---

[1] SP 1/14, ff. 247–50; Vit. B III, f. 122; Harl. MS. 297, f. 69; *LP* ii, 2871.
[2] Vit. B III, ff. 130–134 b; *LP* ii, 2886.

the same rejected me not with his great displeasure'; but he was ready to give his life for the 'defension' of his Prince, and therefore did not hesitate to attack. The Pope admitted that he had agreed to the bull without considering the implications for England; but the French King had been 'presumptuously molesting' him, and because of his treaty with France he had given way too easily. It would be embarrassing to reverse the decision now, and he hoped that Henry would not press the point. There was a good chance that 'with mutation and changing of the time' the fortunes of France would change for the worse, and it might then be easier to accede to Henry's wishes.

This was not good enough for the Bishop, however. He boldly refuted the Pope's arguments, and said that 'great words and long promises' would not extinguish the conflagration which he had kindled. Leo, 'with a sorry and full displeasant heart', replied that the fact of the matter was that he could not suggest any remedy that would not seriously damage his own position. So he sent Sampson off to discuss the technicalities with the Cardinal of Ancona, 'an excellent man of doctrine', who spent two days studying the case before providing what he claimed was the only possible solution. This was that the bull should be suspended for four months.

In the same dispatch de Gigli defends himself. He is shattered by the King's implication that he has been guilty of 'perfidy, infidelity, and negligence'. This has upset him so much that it 'shall not little abbreviate the days of my life'. However, it was not his fault. The Pope had made 'this exorbitant revocation without any my knowledge, being sure that if thereof any understanding had comen unto me I had made such exclamations and protestations that either I had retarded or impeded the same or else I had been banished with disgrace and displeasure from his holiness'. In short, the bull had been prepared 'craftily, secretly and separately', and it was not surprising that he had no inkling of what was in the wind. The Bishop's account does not square with Leo's. Clearly the bull had been prepared with the utmost secrecy, and this would not have been deemed necessary had Leo really believed that the reaffirmation of Guillard's rights was simply a routine matter.

De Gigli concluded by offering his resignation. Although he was 'greatly discomforted' by the King's imputation of infidelity and negligence, which he considered to be quite un-deserved, he must take whatever his Prince might say in the best part. If Henry decided to replace him in Rome with 'any other person more sufficient'—and the Bishop had no doubt that there were plenty better men available in England—he would accept the decision with a good grace, and his loyalty to the King would continue unabated. 'The principal remedy of all my dolor shall be and is the satisfaction of your high commandments, noble pleasure, and desire.'

Leo, who must have known all along that his effort to help the Bishop elect would provoke a storm in England, sent a mollifying letter to Henry. He freely admitted that the King had rendered valuable services to the Holy See, and agreed that Wolsey had been given the administration of Tournai on the ground that Guillard had refused to take up the appointment. But when France and England were at peace there was no longer a case for excluding the Bishop elect. It was open to the King to appeal against the bull, especially if he thought it had been obtained on false pretences. If Leo had known that Guillard had tried to stir up rebellion he would never have granted the bull, nor would he have deprived Wolsey of the administration. Finally, the clause allowing Guillard to summon the secular arm to his aid had not been deliberately inserted. It was common form, and Henry must not take it too seriously. In any case, Leo had now agreed to suspend the bull for four months, to give him time for further consideration of the case.[1]

Julius, Cardinal de Medici, came to the Pope's rescue. He wrote to both Henry[2] and Wolsey,[3] saying that in the circumstances Leo had no alternative but to issue the bull in favour of Guillard. De Medici had done everything in his power to safeguard Wolsey's claim to the administration, although in fact there was little he could do, as the Pope had insisted on handling the matter himself. The Bishop of Worcester would be able to give the inside story of the affair, and in particular to confirm that de Medici had done his best.

Wolsey must have decided that he and the King had been too

[1] SP 1/14, f. 254; LP ii, 2873.
[2] Vit. B III, f. 119; Rymer, p. 604; LP ii, 2879.
[3] SP 1/14, ff. 256–7; LP ii, 2880.

hard on the unfortunate ambassador, for in March he wrote him a long comforting letter. He was sorry to find that de Gigli had taken the matter so much to heart. He must realize, however, that it was very difficult for Henry to understand how the infamous bull had gone through without the Bishop's hearing anything about it. It was to be presumed that his day-to-day contacts with the officials of the Curia would keep him abreast of such an important development, and naturally it had been concluded that he had failed in his duty; but if the Pope had deliberately kept the bull secret it was quite a different matter. There was no question of accusing the Bishop of perfidy. His rank, his long service, his past rewards, and those yet to come made this quite impossible. Henry, however, had not been sorry to learn that the Bishop so dreaded his displeasure; and the knowledge had strengthened the King's friendship for him.[1]

Wolsey went on to say that where the bishopric of Tournai was concerned it was important only so far as the King's honour and the security of the town were affected. It meant nothing to him personally, for he had not received a single farthing from it. For the moment the Pope's excuses and his promise to review the position would have to suffice; but the Bishop must not allow the dispute to drag on, for it was beneath the King's honour to be involved in such a petty squabble, when the rights of the matter were so patent.[2]

In the following month the Pope gave a judicial and face-saving summing up of the exchanges to date, and awarded the verdict to Wolsey. Charles de Hautbois, Bishop of Tournai, freely yielded the see. It had been given to Louis Guillard, who had deserted his charge. Wolsey, Bishop elect of Lincoln, had then been appointed administrator for life. His translation to York cast some doubt on the validity of the appointment, so the latter had been confirmed. Later the Pope had learned that Guillard had been in peaceful possession of the see when Henry captured Tournai; and he therefore revoked Wolsey's appointment. Henry and Wolsey had appealed against this decision. Guillard had never done homage, and Henry was anxious that someone should be appointed who was not hostile. Otherwise sedition might be raised in the city, with disastrous results.

[1] *LP* ii, 3045.   [2] Ibid.

The Pope considered that it was not for the good of the Church that Louis should retain the see when he was not acceptable to Henry; and he reconfirmed the appointment of Wolsey, making it clear that this was not done as a result of Henry's petition, but in the light of his own mature deliberation. Further, the reinstatement of Wolsey held good only if Guillard failed to appear in Tournai to do homage to Henry within forty days after notices announcing the Pope's ruling had been affixed to the church doors in the diocese. It is interesting to speculate what would have happened to Guillard if he had ventured to come to Tournai; but he did not, and Wolsey was 'restored, replaced, and fully reinstated' as administrator of the diocese.[1]

Although the Pope's decree seemed to make Wolsey the final victor, the dispute was still in progress in the middle of 1518, by which time it was clear that the English occupation would not last for ever. Sampson seems to have conceded defeat as early as July 1517, for he dropped the style 'Bishop elect'. He reported that the Dean of Tournai had suggested to the 'French Bishop' and his father that Wolsey might be able to provide an alternative see, but the pair were 'very estrange and nothing agreeable'. Sampson went on to say that the French elect that was, was once again going to try to enter as Bishop in all the main towns, i.e. in the diocese outside Tournai and the Tournaisis. There was even some talk that he would try to take possession of part of the King's dominion, which could be very dangerous. If he did come upon the King's ground, Sampson assured Wolsey that he would 'not fail to look upon him'.[2]

Sampson suggested that if it were not for the fact that the King's honour and Wolsey's were at stake it would be better to drop the pretence that Wolsey was Bishop. Even within the *bailliage* it was necessary to invoke the aid of the Governor to collect the revenues. A little money had been collected, however, and he inquired whether he should pay it over to the Governor, leaving it to Wolsey to claim an equivalent amount in England. The money collected in Tournai was mostly 'very ill pence', and it would pay Wolsey to make a claim in London, where he would be paid in good money.[3] Sampson also asked

[1] SC 7/26(37); Hocquet (a), xlvii; Rymer, pp. 584–5; *LP* ii, 3140.
[2] SP 1/15, ff. 202–202 b; *LP* ii, 3438.   [3] Ibid.

permission to come to London to see to his own affairs; and his request was granted. With his return to England the unequal struggle for the bishopric for all practical purposes ended.[1]

In the course of 1518 it became clear that Henry was at last prepared to allow Tournai to return to France—at a price. Although Wolsey had made virtually nothing out of the bishopric, it was still a potential source of revenue for him, and it was in his interest that England should retain the town as long as possible, whatever the national interest might be. Francis was well aware of this, and saw that it would be necessary to buy Wolsey's support for the restoration of the city. He therefore offered him a pension in lieu of the revenues of the see. Even a small pension regularly paid was worth more than substantial revenues which could not be collected.

In fact the pension offered was very generous—12,000 *livres tournois* for life.[2] It was worth about £1,300 a year, and compared very favourably with the revenues Wolsey would have derived from the bishopric had there been no opposition from the Bishop elect. Moreover, whereas the income from the bishopric had to be painfully collected through agents, who no doubt helped themselves to more than their permitted share, the proposed pension would be regularly paid every half year without any deductions. So long as England and France remained at peace it was a gilt-edged security, and worth infinitely more than Wolsey's highly-speculative investment in the bishopric, which had paid no dividend in five years. It is impossible to say with certainty to what extent Francis's offer of a pension brought the two countries nearer together. There were other reasons why Wolsey favoured a *rapprochement*. But it can be said with certainty that there was no limit to Wolsey's appetite for wealth, and that at the least the pension must have had some slight effect on his judgement as to how England's interests would best be served.

The Bishop elect's long vigil on the threshold of his diocese ended on Saturday 12 February 1519. On that day he entered the city with a small entourage; and on Sunday morning he went to the Cathedral, where he was enthroned in the presence of de Coligny, who had been commissioned by Francis to receive Tournai from Henry's representatives, Louis de Proisy,

---

[1] SP 1/16, f. 20; *LP* ii, 3674.   [2] Rymer, p. 610; *LP* ii, 4354.

who had returned to his office of *Bailli* after an interval of six years, and many other notabilities. He then sang High Mass, and afterwards returned to his palace, where he entertained the leading citizens to a solemn feast. He also gave some money to each of the 36 *collèges des bannières*, so that they could arrange their own celebrations. The problem of divided loyalty, which may have troubled some of the citizens during Guillard's exile, was ended.[1]

[1] Hocquet (a), lvi.

VII · JUSTICE: THE COURT SOVEREIGN

UNDER the French regime the Governor of Tournai was as a rule also *Bailli*, the head of the judicial system. This was certainly true of the first English Governor, Sir Edward Poynings, although his commission neither as Governor nor as *Bailli* survives. It seems likely that he was authorized by the King in general terms to exercise the functions that had belonged to Louis de Proisy, who held the offices at the time of the siege, although he was absent from the city. There had been no time to evolve detailed procedures to replace the system of appeals to Paris, where the final appellate jurisdiction had lain, and the simplest course was to empower Poynings to do everything that his predecessor had done, to provide a breathing space in which new arrangements might be made.

The royal court over which the *Bailli* presided dealt with matters affecting the state, for example, cases arising from transactions under the royal seal, forgery, *lèse-majesté*, premeditated acts of aggression by armed bands, attempts against the King, his family, or his officers, and so on. The *Bailli* also heard appeals from the city courts, where the *prévôts* and *jurés* judged criminal causes, and were empowered to impose sentence of death, loss of limb, temporary or permanent banishment, and imprisonment. Their sentence could be appealed through the *Bailli* to the *Cour de Parlement* in Paris. Judgement in civil causes was reserved to the *échevins*, who could inflict only fines. Cases concerning the trade guilds were handled by the deans and sub-deans. There were also two religious courts, dealing with offences against the canon law—heresy, sacrilege, magic, sorcery, blasphemy, crimes in sacred places, for example; but the *Bailli* was not directly interested in these, as the line of appeal was through the Archbishop's court to Rome.

The *Bailli* was supported by a *procureur* representing the King, an advocate who acted as his spokesman, and six sergeants responsible for carrying out judicial decisions. There were also two royal scriveners, who authenticated contracts and other

civil documents deposited with them, and a keeper of the royal
seal.[1] It seems that under English rule the judicial establishment was carried on on much the same lines. The first 'seal
royal' was a Tournaisien appointed by Sir Edward Poynings.
He was replaced in July 1515 by a yeoman of the guard,
Roger Hacheman, who was nominated by Henry and given
'the place and office *sigilli nostri regalis*' for life, his appointment
being made retrospective to the date of the King's entry into
Tournai.[2] By September 1516, however, the keeper of the
royal seal was a Tournaisien lawyer, Jean de la Saulch, who
was probably better qualified for the office than a soldier;
and at this time the scriveners were also Tournaisiens, Jean de
Clement and Antoine Joseph.[3]

When Mountjoy succeeded Poynings as Governor he received
a formal commission as *Bailli Garde de Justice*. This commands
him to maintain the King's rights in Tournai, to summon the
prévôts and *échevins* as may be necessary, to dispense justice to all
who seek it, to appoint the customary judicial officers, and
generally to act as a good and loyal *Bailli*, in return for which he
will receive all the profits and emoluments which his predecessor, Sir Edward Poynings, had enjoyed. He took the oath in the
King's presence on 20 January 1515. The letters patent which
announce the appointment also commanded all officials and the
people of Tournai to allow him to enjoy his rights as *Bailli*, and
to obey him as they would the King himself. Moneys due to the
bailliage are to be paid to him at the accustomed dates.[4]

It has been shown above[5] how the transfer of Tournai's
allegiance from the French to the English Crown was effected
with little administrative upheaval, largely because of the
relatively independent status of the city. Tournai was just as

---

[1] Hocquet (b), pp. 69 ff.   [2] C 76/197, m. 6; *LP* ii, 714.
[3] PRO 31/8/144, f. 261.
[4] C 76/196, m. 6; Rymer, p. 387; *LP* i, 2617(22). The dating of this document
is puzzling. It is given as 20 January 1514 in *LP*. This follows the French Roll,
where the date is clearly 20 January 1514, and in which the contiguous
membranes are equally clearly 5 H. VIII; but the correct date must be 20
January 6 H. VIII, i.e. 1515. The supporting evidence is: (a) Sir Edward
Poynings was in office as Governor and *Bailli* throughout 1514; (b) the letters
patent appointing Mountjoy as Governor are dated 20 January 1515; and (c) his
commission as *Bailli* refers to his appointment as Governor.
[5] See Ch. II.

much part of the kingdom of France as the other *bailliages* and *sénéchaussées* that recognized Louis XII as their sovereign, but for many centuries she had played a considerable part in shaping her own affairs. Her isolation in an enclave deep in the Low Countries fostered a spirit of self-sufficiency among the citizens. Moreover, the city had a major rôle in the commerce of the region she supplied with her manufactures—cloth, carpets, and tapestry in particular—and her economic prosperity had made possible, and no doubt had also encouraged, an independent attitude of mind.

This attitude was revealed by both the wealthier classes and the common people in the weeks before the city was forced to surrender in 1513. The former were anxious to come to a financial settlement with the enemy under which they would be left in peace, and which certainly would have been deemed treasonable by their sovereign; and the latter boasted that they were quite capable of looking after themselves against the English (in spite of the fact that they were civilians without the benefit of a professional garrison), even when it was plain that no help would be forthcoming from the French army. But if the city was for most purposes a self-contained and self-managing entity, in the field of justice at least she had important links with Paris.

At this time France had about fifty *bailliages* and *sénéchaussées*, territorial districts for the administration of justice, each headed by a *Bailli* or *Sénéchal*. (The term *bailliage* was used in the north and east, *sénéchaussée* in the south and west, but the procedures in the two types of district were broadly the same.) In common with the other *bailliages*, the district of Tournai, Tournaisis, Mortagne, and St. Amand, to give it its full title, had its royal *Bailli* to preside over the principal court. It was, however, open to any citizen dissatisfied with a judgment given against him in the *Bailli's* court to appeal to the supreme court of France, the *Grande Chambre* of the *Parlement de Paris*. This was a court of first instance for certain important causes, and for certain causes involving important people, but it also functioned as the final court of appeal for the *bailliages* and *sénéchaussées* in both civil and criminal causes.[1]

---

[1] There were some matters that could not be taken to the supreme court, however. For example, civil disputes in respect of sums of 21 *livres tournois* or less (Aubert, p. 278).

It was inevitable that in a commercial community there should be a good deal of litigation in progress at any given moment. The manufacturers and merchants of Tournai could afford the luxury of court proceedings, including appeals to the supreme court. Further, all their dealings with the English make it abundantly clear that they had a highly-developed sense of their rights, and that they were always prepared to fight for them to the last ditch. Thus, when the capture and occupation of the city severed the link with the *Parlement de Paris*, the appeal system was suddenly frozen and a good many cases were halted at various stages. Those whose business interests were affected found themselves in a state of great uncertainty.

This prevailed for the first four months of the occupation, and it was one of the more important items that Tournai's representatives raised with the English government during the session of Parliament that ran from 23 January to 4 March 1514.[1] We can only speculate how this and the other matters the members from Tournai took up with their new masters were actually handled. They may have been discussed at meetings with the King and his councillors. At the beginning of 1514 Henry was still savouring his glorious campaign, as he imagined it, and was no doubt willing to show himself 'gracious lord' towards his new subjects, who had made the difficult journey from Tournai in the depths of winter. Indeed, he was fulsomely ingratiating in his early dealings with the captured city; and in spite of his natural disinclination for all but the most important business he must have felt obliged to meet the Tournaisiens and listen to what they had to say.

However the matter was handled, the outcome was two decisions, which were given effect in letters patent before the end of the parliamentary session. The first enabled the appeal cases in the pipeline to flow again; and the second sought to provide machinery for the future consideration of appeals which under the old regime would have found their way to the *Parlement de Paris*.

The first of these two instruments,[2] which were drafted in French for the benefit of the King's new subjects, starts by

---

[1] See Ch. II.
[2] C 82/401 $\frac{5}{422}$; PRO 31/8/144, f. 239; Hocquet (a), xxix; *Ordonnances*, p. 287; *LP* i, 2676(2), 2684(108).

reciting how those deputed by the councils and commonalty of Tournai to attend Parliament have drawn attention to the fact that the *Bailli's* court and the subordinate courts are awaiting decisions of the *Cour de Parlement* on a number of cases. Further, those decisions received from the *Cour de Parlement* just before the city was captured have not yet been implemented, since the courts of the *bailliage* are in some doubt as to whether they may properly enroll and execute them without the special leave and commandment of their new sovereign. He for his part most earnestly desires his loyal subjects to have justice, undelayed by these peculiar circumstances. He therefore commands that the *Bailli, prévôts, jurés, échevins*, and all other judges who have in hand a lawsuit which has been decided by the *Parlement de Paris* to proceed as if the decision has been given by Henry's own judges, and to see that it is executed according to 'its form and tenor'.

There was one proviso, however. The *Bailli* through whom these appeals had found their way to Paris no longer held office, but had been replaced by Sir Edward Poynings. The new Governor had no previous knowledge of the cases in question, and it was therefore specially provided that the judgements of the *Cour de Parlement* should be referred to him for his consideration and approval before the local court enrolled and implemented them. Poynings was put in the picture about an important part of his new responsibilities, and given the chance of modifying any judgement that seemed to be undesirable in the light of the new circumstances of Tournai.

This measure solved the immediate problem of the outstanding appeal cases; but it was still necessary to set up machinery to replace the *Parlement de Paris* as the supreme court of appeal. This was done by letters patent[1] of the same date (26 February 1514), which refer to Henry's desire 'to recover and return to our obedience our kingdom of France, which is our true patrimony and heritage, for a long time by force and violence occupied by our enemies', and to his success in bringing Thérouanne and Tournai into the fold. As a result, these cities can no longer take their appeals to 'our supreme *Cour de Parlement* at Paris', which court is now disobedient and in rebellion.

---

[1] C 82/401 $\frac{5}{421}$; PRO 31/8/144, f. 237; Hocquet (a), xxx; *Ordonnances*, p. 288; *LP* i, 2684(107).

The King, however, earnestly desires that justice should be available for each and every one, and has therefore ordained that five notable men, learned in the law, shall have full authority to hear and determine all causes and matters that went to the *Parlement de Paris* before the surrender of Tournai. The new court—the 'court sovereign'—is to sit in Tournai, where the five judges are required to reside, but its jurisdiction extends to Thérouanne and, in anticipation, to any other places in his kingdom of France which Henry may recover. (The inclusion of Thérouanne was no more than window-dressing, for after its capture the town had been virtually blown off the map in an orgy of demolition personally supervised by Henry and Maximilian; and in any case the shattered ruins had immediately been abandoned to France.) The intention seems to have been to reproduce in miniature the *Cour de Parlement*— very much in miniature, since the *Parlement de Paris* was organized to handle appeals from many districts, of which Tournai was only one. Provision is made for the appointment of a *greffier* or clerk of court, who is apparently to concern himself with both civil and criminal cases, although in the *Parlement de Paris* there was a *greffier civil*, the senior clerk of court,[1] a *greffier criminel*, and thirdly a *greffier des présentations*, who determined the order in which cases would be heard. There are also to be two *huissiers* to carry out the duties of sheriff's officer, compared with twelve or fourteen such officers in the *Parlement de Paris*.

The court will hold its assizes once a month on a convenient day, and is empowered to do everything that the *Cour de Parlement* formerly did. Those wishing to avail themselves of the facilities it offers are required to pay the same fees as had been customary in Paris. Finally, the King has ordered that a seal bearing his arms shall be provided for the use of the court.

Provision had now been made for the implementation of judicial decisions outstanding from the *Parlement de Paris*, and for the establishment of a court to replace the *Parlement*. It seems that matters rested there for a very long time. Nearly a year later—on 12 February 1515—Mountjoy reported to the King

---

[1] '. . . la principale de ses fonctions consistait à veiller à la mise au rôle, à la rédaction et à la transcription des lettres, actes, pièces de procédure, arrêts, à garder les minutes, les documents des procès' (Aubert, p. 235).

that he had discussed proposals for the stipends of the judges of the 'court sovereign' with the municipal authorities, and that they had thought them very good. With their usual caution, however, they had pointed out that the annual elections were due in a week's time, and suggested that a matter of such importance should be cleared with the newly elected councils.[1] About the same time 'the court sovereign and the commissioners' (presumably the judges) was one of the items in a list which Lancaster Herald was sent to discuss with the King's Council.[2]

Five months later nothing had happened. The Earl of Worcester told the *Chefs de la Loi* that the King wanted to save the citizens the trouble of crossing the Channel in search of justice, and that he still hoped that a supreme court would be established in Tournai.[3] He invited the *Chefs* to consider this, and perhaps to suggest the names of men to act as judges and to advise as to their salaries and so on. Worcester may have felt that the municipal authorities' reluctance to make progress was due to their continuing loyalty to France. They might be reluctant to set up machinery in the city that implied that the link with Paris was finally broken. He reminded them that there was now firm peace between England and France and that Francis had totally renounced all his claims to Tournai. The *Chefs* dutifully noted what the Earl said, and appointed some of their number to consider the points raised and provide satisfactory answers.[4]

Apparently the Tournaisiens had no useful suggestions, for a month later Worcester and his fellow commissioners told the King that doctors of law 'for the court of resort' would have to be found in England. It was going to be difficult to get suitable men locally, and in any case the King's English subjects would serve him faithfully and at a lower cost than natives of Tournai. (This suggests that the *Chefs de la Loi* had proposed an exorbitant rate for the job.) It was of course desirable that any Englishmen chosen should be proficient in French.[5] Before coming to this conclusion, Worcester may have tried to recruit

---

[1] Cal. E I, f. 43 b; *LP* ii, 148.   [2] SP 1/10, 51; *LP* ii, App. 3.
[3] 'une court souveraine en laquelle on porroit avoir toutes provisions comme on feroit en sa court souveraine'.
[4] Hocquet (a), xxxviii.   [5] Cal. E I, f. 63 b; *LP* ii, 148.

judges further afield in the principal cities of the Low Countries, for there is an item in the treasurer's accounts allowing Jean le Sellier 40*d.* a day for 'riding about the King's business for the court sovereign'.[1] Nevertheless, in spite of the lack of support from those whom the court was intended to help, it seems to have been established, at least in embryo, in the course of 1515. The first president of the court sovereign was probably Mountjoy; but it is difficult to be certain. Under the former regime the *Bailli* was head of the judicial system in the city and presided over the royal court; and, since the court sovereign was established to replace the *Cour de Parlement* in Paris, it was logical that the English *Bailli*, who was already the apex of the judicial system, should also preside over the new court. This appointment is not referred to, however, in Mountjoy's commission as *Bailli*, in spite of the fact that the King's decision to establish the court of five judges had been announced twelve months earlier. The only surviving copy of his commission to act as president of the court is undated, but is placed among documents of 1516 in the Cottonian manuscripts;[2] whereas a similar commission to Sir Richard Jerningham is dated 1 October 1515 in the French Roll.[3]

The two commissions are broadly on the same lines and follow the letters patent establishing the court.[4] They recite how civil and criminal cases had formerly been appealed from the judges of the city and the *bailliage* to the *Cour de Parlement*, which can no longer conveniently be done. Since the occupation began, the only alternative for citizens seeking to appeal from the judgements of the local courts has been to make the long journey to England, braving the great perils of the sea and incurring considerable expense. Henry, however, having the best interests of his subjects at heart, as befits a great prince, and being anxious that all should have justice, has appointed a court of four men skilled in the law, over which William Blount, Lord Mountjoy, will preside. An advocate, procurator, clerk, and two ushers will be provided.

The rules of the court are then described. Although in the two

---

[1] SP 1/12, f. 169; *LP* ii, 1514. [2] Cal. E I, ff. 120–1; *LP* ii, 2737.
[3] C 76/196, m. 21; Rymer, pp. 519–20; *LP* ii, 979.
[4] C 76/197, m. 21; Rymer, p. 519; *LP* ii, 979 (Jerningham); Cal. E I, ff. 120–1 (Mountjoy).

commissions Mountjoy and Jerningham are clearly described as president, it is stipulated that the senior of the four professional lawyers 'shall preside', which suggests that the Governor was merely a figurehead and that the substantive decisions belonged to the lawyers. It is envisaged that some of the four chosen judges may also be judges in one of the lower courts; and there is no objection so long as they do not preside 'lest the appeal should seem to be made from the same to the same'. The court is given very wide jurisdiction. It has full authority to hear civil, criminal, and mixed cases, 'however grave and serious', and to examine witnesses and receive new proofs—that is to say it was not simply charged with the duty of considering the verdict of the subordinate court, but could retry a case.

If the judges ruled that an appeal failed, the case was sent back to the lower court, so that the original decision might be carried out. The appeal court did, however, have its own powers 'to correct and punish the guilty according to the nature of their crime, either with imprisonment, corporal or capital punishment'. There was no appeal against its decisions, which were to have all the force that those of the *Cour de Parlement* had had; and the court was authorized to grant the same remedies, and to charge the fees for this service that had been customary in Paris. It was left to the judges to decide where and when they would sit, choosing a day 'as most fitting for the purpose'.

The order in which Mountjoy and Jerningham were appointed is of interest, as it may reflect the importance which the King and Wolsey attached to the court sovereign. If Mountjoy was the first president, and was replaced after only a few months by Jerningham, who was at this time no more than treasurer, it suggests that the status accorded to the court had diminished; but if the appointments were made the other way round the reverse may be true.

Although their two commissions are substantially the same, there are differences in the drafting which may be significant. Mountjoy's speaks of 'our' city of Paris, 'our' court there, and 'our' Chancery in Paris, echoing the language of the letters patent setting up the court of five judges, which includes 'our' kingdom of France, 'our' supreme *Cour de Parlement*. Jerningham's, however, studiously eschews the possessive pronoun. It might therefore be guessed that Mountjoy was appointed at a time when relations between England and France were strained, and Henry was still clinging to the fiction that the capture of Tournai was the beginning of a series of campaigns to recover to England the whole of the French kingdom. In each case, however, the preamble refers to the kingdom of France 'which belongs to us by hereditary right', and it may be that the elimination of the possessive pronouns (if Jerningham's commission came second) was the work of the draftsman rather than the policy-maker.

The only other significant difference between the two commissions is that Mountjoy was authorized to appoint the four other judges (which was reasonable, since he was the King's deputy in Tournai), whereas the King kept in his own hands the right to appoint Jerningham's four colleagues. It may be asked why the Governor should give way to the treasurer as head of the court sovereign, if this is indeed what happened. The explanation probably is that Mountjoy found his duties very burdensome, and was only too glad to unload on his subordinates as much as he could. The management of the garrison was a heavy job which the French governors had not been concerned with—because there was no garrison under the French regime. Nor did their judicial functions include running a court in substitution for the *Cour de Parlement*.

Although the original intention had been to set up the appeal court in Tournai, the King seems to have changed his mind in the course of 1515. In a dispatch of May in the following year Mountjoy refers to the fact that 'your Grace is minded and determined to have your court sovereign in your Chancery within your realm of England like as in time past it was at Paris'. He does not want to question a royal decision, but considers that it is his duty to draw Henry's attention to the fact that this proposal will be 'noyous unto your subjects here both for the journey by sea and land and also for fault of language when they come there'. He adds that the difficulties are so great that even when a man has a very good case he will rather let it go by default than take the trouble of lodging an appeal in London.

Mountjoy also says that 'it should be contrary to your Grace's grant made unto them by Act of Parliament'. This is strange, as he must be referring to the only Act relating to the affairs of Tournai, which was passed in 1514; and this is not concerned with the replacement of the appellate jurisdiction of the *Cour de Parlement*.[1] It is true, however, that one of the provisions of this statute enabled a merchant with a claim against someone in England to have the case heard in Tournai, and the Governor was therefore right in suggesting that one of the objectives of English policy in this field had been to make the long and arduous journey to England unnecessary.[2]

Apparently the King was unmoved by Mountjoy's plea. A delegation came from Tournai at the beginning of 1517 to discuss, among other matters, the arrangements for the court sovereign, and presumably to argue that it should be located in the city. They were given a testy reply, for it is recorded: 'There needeth none other advertising but the good pleasure of the King our sovereign lord and his Council for of long time past they (the citizens) have been sufficiently instruct and advertised as touching the effect to have a sovereign court.' This is amplified in a marginal note which says 'the resort to be had to the King's Chancery in England';[3] and it looks as if Henry, who had become increasingly angry at the intransigent attitude of his new subjects, had decided to harden his heart. If they wanted to have the right of appeal to a higher court, they must pay the price of having to come to England. All the fine words in the commission to the presidents of the court sovereign, about the King's anxiety to save the citizens great expense and trouble, and the many and great perils of the sea, were conveniently forgotten.

This is confirmed by the report of the delegation when they returned home in April 1517. The *prévôts* and *jurés* asked to hear first of all what was going to happen about appeals from their jurisdiction, a matter in which they had a strong professional interest, and which was also of interest to the citizens as a whole. The formal answer was that the King, ever anxious to show good will towards his loyal subjects of Tournai, and to treat them as if they were Englishmen, had decreed that for the good of justice appeals should be heard in the Chancery in England; and that appellants would henceforth have to take

---

[1] 5 Henry VIII, c. 1.   [2] Cal. E I, f. 101; *LP* ii, 1894.
[3] SP 1/14, f. 238; Cal. E I, f. 132; *LP* ii, 2858.

their cases to the Chancellor, wherever he happened to be.[1] Although the record of the discussion is quite dispassionate (it could hardly be otherwise, as the Governor had access to the city's papers and would have been quick to act upon any hint of dissatisfaction with English policy), the decision to hold the court in England must inevitably have been severely criticized within the four walls of the municipal council chamber.[2]

The King asked the four councils to send particulars of the procedures formerly used in lodging appeals in Paris, so that similar arrangements might be adopted in England; and however much they may have deprecated his gross breach of faith they hastened to comply with his request. There was, however, no ready-made description of the procedures, and in order to get the facts clear it was necessary to examine a number of the city's lawyers and businessmen who had been particularly concerned with the appeal system. The main features that emerged were summarized and sent to London for the information of the Council in July 1517.[3]

It had been necessary for the appellant to lodge his appeal as soon as judgement was given against him in the lower court, either in person or through his attorney. The case then came before the *Cour de Parlement* within the next three months. If the appellant did not appear in Paris on the due date he lost his case and was fined sixty *livres* into the bargain. He had no further right of appeal and the original judgement against him was proceeded with. If the lower court had found against him in his absence, and in the absence of his representative, and it was therefore impossible for him to lodge an appeal there and then, he could still petition the King for special permission to appeal.

[1] Hocquet (a), xlvi.

[2] Miss Marjorie Blatcher has suggested that the decision to hear appeals in England may have resulted from Wolsey's growing influence, although he did not become Chancellor until December 1515. If appeals were to be taken to England, it would have to be to the Court of Chancery, since the Court of King's Bench (which had the oversight of 'insufficiency' and 'error' in lower courts in England) was not designed to receive appeals of the type intended to come from Tournai. This view is consistent with Wolsey's desire to involve himself in all legal matters, and with his disregard for legal niceties. There is no doubt that the court sovereign should have been left in Tournai, on the ground that it would have been more convenient for the Tournaisiens and that it would have made for better legal decisions.

[3] E 30/810; Rymer, pp. 593–5; *LP* ii, 3458.

The four councils provided a model instruction which the French King had been accustomed to use in these circumstances. It is addressed to the senior usher of the *Parlement*, and recites how so-and-so has appealed to the King and Council from a judgement against him by the *prévôts* and *jurés*. The King orders the *prévôts* and *jurés* to appear before his *Cour de Parlement*, which will be held in his Chancery, to defend their judgement. The parties in the case are also to appear, and they are forbidden under severe penalties to do anything in the meantime that might prejudice the true course of justice.

If the party successful in the lower court had a good reason for wanting the appeal to be heard at an early date, he could make an application to the King. If it was granted, letters were sent to the principal usher, explaining that long delay in hearing the appeal might damage the interests of the successful party, and ordering him to see that the appeal was taken at a suitable earlier date. If the case in the lower court had been considered on the basis of written submissions (*'par escript'*), it should be determined on the same basis in the appeal court. Equally, if the evidence had been oral, the parties should be instructed again to offer oral evidence in the *Parlement*. Finally, the hearing should be completed in a single day.

At the end of their memorandum the four councils set out the scale of charges which had applied for the use of the Chancery seal, the services provided by the clerk of the court, and so on.

Although we have a good deal of information about the attempt to establish an appeal court, first in Tournai and then in England, very little has survived about the practical administration of justice. The members of the garrison were subject to what is now called military law; but they were also subject to the ordinary law of the land. Minor breaches of discipline that could not be dealt with by a man's captain went to the marshal and under-marshal, who no doubt took good care to keep the Governor well informed about their proceedings. More serious offences came before the Governor and his council;[1] and quite

---

[1] As early as November 1513 Henry wrote to the citizens, telling them that if they had any grievance—presumably after exhausting the possibilities of the existing local courts—they should take it to the Governor, who had his strict orders to see that justice was done (Hocquet (a), xxvii; *LP* ii, 2450).

often it was deemed necessary to have the sentences they pronounced confirmed by King and Council in London. The municipal courts continued to function in the usual way, except that the absence of a readily accessible court of appeal made their responsibilities much heavier. Litigants knew that it might be impracticable to appeal from the judgement handed down by the local court, so long as the court sovereign was not fully operational, and they must have insisted on having their cases argued with greater strength than they would normally have required of their lawyers.

The records afford occasional glimpses of the course of justice, especially when the case involved one of the neighbouring towns. In 1515, for example, Mountjoy had to negotiate the extradition of a citizen of Courtrai, who was alleged to have committed murder, and who took refuge in one of the villages of the Tournaisis. The authorities in Courtrai sent men to bring the offender back, whereupon Mountjoy demanded that he should be returned to Tournai 'for saving of the King's right and the Bishop's'. The council in Courtrai admitted that they had been in the wrong, and 'according to good justice' sent the man back to the place where they had recaptured him. What happened to the accused thereafter is not clear, but the logical next step would have been for Courtrai to make formal application for his return, and for Mountjoy to agree, saving the King's right.[1]

Shortly after this episode three members of the Tournai garrison were in a tavern within the jurisdiction of Courtrai, where there were a good many people 'of the country' and also a number of Henry's subjects. A brawl started, in which two young men from the Tournaisis were killed. The three members of the garrison were undoubtedly responsible, and Mountjoy had no hesitation in ordering their arrest. But since the crime had been committed in Courtrai, and the accused men had been arrested there, the law of Flanders required that the Governor should return them to the scene of the crime 'for saving of their prince's right'—the converse of the earlier case.

The matter was debated by the Governor's council, which accepted that the request from the Courtrai authorities was reasonable. Mountjoy therefore wrote to them undertaking to

[1] SP 1/11, f. 87; *LP* ii, 918.

surrender the prisoners at an agreed time; and he instructed Richard Hansard, the under-marshal, to escort the men to Courtrai. Hansard, however, who probably had no intention of allowing his fellows to be brought to justice, 'handled that matter so slackly and negligently' that the men escaped, first into sanctuary and then right out of Tournai. The Governor was deeply distressed at this development, and confessed to Wolsey that it was the most shameful thing that had happened to him since he first entered the King's service. It suggested that he was incompetent; and it might have serious political repercussions if it was believed in Flanders that the English were conniving at the escape of men wanted in the Low Countries. 'And forasmuch as the matter concerneth the King's honour and toucheth my poor honesty so near I had much liever the matter were examined before my Lords of the Council, and that he may be sent for rather to make his answer there than afore me.'

Hansard argued in his defence before the Governor that the three prisoners had been taken from him by force, but Mountjoy was satisfied that the evidence did not support this. After the men escaped, both those who were on guard duty and the soldiers passing the time of day in the streets stood idly by, and indeed threatened any who made a move to recapture them. Mountjoy said that if Hansard was summoned before the Council in England he could send witnesses, who would describe exactly what had happened; and he begged that if he was found guilty, 'he shall be so punished . . . that it may be well known in the parts of Flanders, in whom the fault is'. It was probably only the fact that Hansard was Wolsey's man that had saved him from being handed over to Courtrai in the place of the prisoners he had allowed to escape. (Strictly speaking, he was liable to the penalty which the prisoners would have suffered had they been found guilty.) Mountjoy concluded by saying that he wished that Hansard had deserved the many favours he had bestowed on him—out of deference to Wolsey— since he became Governor.

In the event, Hansard was not summoned before the Council, although he may have received a gentle reprimand from Wolsey. He remained in office, and the hostility between him and the Governor, which dated from the time when Mountjoy tried to block his appointment as under-marshal, continued unabated. In the following year, on one of the many occasions when the Governor referred to his wish to be freed from his office, the attitude of Hansard was a factor contributing to his unhappiness. He said to Wolsey: 'I find Hansard the under marshal high minded towards me, and not using himself to me after the best manner.' He had put up with his insubordination only because of Wolsey's interest in the man.[1]

Mountjoy also found himself adjudicating as *Bailli* in disputes between the town authorities and the religious bodies in Tournai. On one occasion a yeoman of the guard accused of homicide found sanctuary in a room between the kitchen and the refectory in the Augustinian monastery, where he was arrested. The prior protested to the Governor at this violation of sanctuary, to which the *procureur général* of the town replied that the room in question was not technically sacrosanct. Mountjoy ruled that the yeoman should be returned to the monastery, where he would be placed in a chapel which was above suspicion as a place of sanctuary. This would be without prejudice to the status of the room where the offender had been arrested, which would be the subject of a further enquiry. The implication was that if it was ultimately decided that the room was not sacrosanct the municipal authorities could have their way with the man; but if it was, he could remain in the chapel and take his chance of escaping from there.[2]

[1] SP 1/12, f. 161; *LP* ii, 1510.   [2] PRO 31/8/144, f. 261.

VIII · RELATIONS WITH FRANCE

THE possibility of an attack by the French was in the mind of the Governor and his council all through the occupation, although the danger was never very real. The rout of the French forces at the Battle of the Spurs, and the loss of Tournai, were dishonourable episodes in the history of France which had become talking-points throughout Europe; and it was presumed in the garrison that sooner or later the French would try to square the account. However, there was virtually no danger of attack in the first months of the occupation. The French army was in a state of disarray and Louis XII was a tired old man. Moreover, to get at Tournai the French would have to go through the Emperor's territory, and while there were no physical barriers to stop them, it did mean that they would have to take on not only the English in Tournai but also any forces that Maximilian put into the field, as he was required to do by his treaty with Henry.

As soon as Henry had returned to England rumours spread that the French were going to make a determined attempt to recover the town. There was a report that the citizens had sent a priest to the King of France, beseeching him to recapture the city, on the ground that it had been betrayed by a handful of the leading merchants in spite of the loyalty of the ordinary citizens—which was not very far from the truth. None of them wanted to remain in Tournai under English rule, and they would abandon their homes and willingly face death if French sovereignty could not be restored.[1] It was also rumoured that the French army was actually bound for Tournai;[2] but no serious threat to the city materialized.

Henry planned to resume active hostilities against France some time before 1 June 1514.[3] In the earlier part of the year military preparations were made in England, on the assumption that a new and even more splendid assault would be launched across the Channel, supported by an attack from the south through the agency of Ferdinand of Spain. News of the

---

[1] *VC* ii, 352.   [2] *VC* ii, 348.   [3] See above, p. 30.

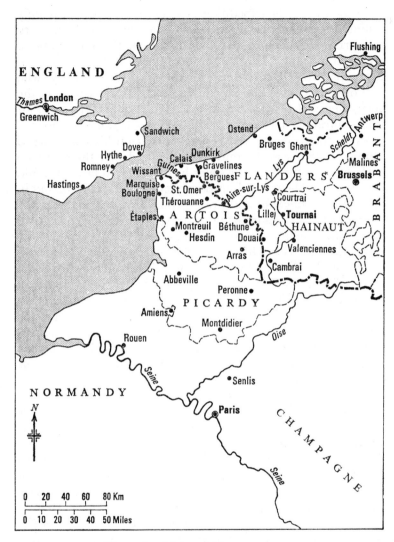

Tournai and her neighbours, 1513–19

preparations inevitably reached France, and it was said that the
aging Louis XII was so terrified at the prospect of Henry's
leading a second expedition against him that no one dared
mention England in his presence.[1]

[1] *MC* 684.

In the event, the expedition of 1514 never sailed. The only military action against France was a landing near Cherbourg in reprisal for a French attack on Brighton. The Pope came to terms with France. Ferdinand opted out of the league against her, thus letting Henry down for the third time. Wolsey, who had organized the 1513 expedition, and was well aware of the staggering cost of war, began to favour a policy of peace, for financial rather than moral reasons. Henry had had his hour of glory in the field and was content to rest on his self-awarded laurels. In any case he must have realized that there was no certainty that the beginner's luck he had enjoyed in 1513 would be repeated. The whole European picture had changed, and in August 1514 England and France concluded a peace treaty.

One of the clauses in the peace treaty provided that England and France should continue in undisputed possession of the territories which each held at the date of the treaty. This meant, of course, that England now occupied Tournai with the formal assent of Louis XII; and the Governor took the opportunity of reminding the citizens that they still owed their loyalty to Henry. Some members of his council attended a meeting of the four councils to make the position clear, and received satisfactory assurances. If any citizens had not taken the oath they would be punished; and for good measure the city as a whole would take the oath again.[1]

This did not mean, however, that the English forces in Tournai could relax their vigilance. In the sixteenth century alliances were not sacred, even while they lasted; and the general post that had just taken place showed that they did not last long. If the chance came, Francis, who had succeeded Louis at the beginning of 1515, and who was young and ambitious, would not hesitate to snatch back Tournai. The new King's desire to recover the city was apparent when Henry's treaty with Louis was being renegotiated. The Duke of Suffolk, who was ambassador in Paris, reported that Francis was prepared to confirm the earlier treaty as it stood, but had suggested that Tournai should be restored on such terms 'as might most stand with your honour and profit'.[2] Spinelly, also writing to the King, said that in Brussels there was 'a great speaking of the diminishing of the garrison at Tournai'. The King's faithful

---

[1] Hocquet (a), xxxvi; *LP* i, 3458.   [2] Cal. D VI, f. 169; *LP* ii, 82.

friends in the Low Countries thought it unwise. Henry should have waited until he was absolutely certain that there was no danger from France.[1]

In March of the same year, when the new treaty was still under discussion, Francis considered that there was every possibility that England would attack *him*; but he believed that Henry had no hope of success. If he came with a small force he would be beaten. If he brought a large army he would waste enormous sums of money and achieve nothing. Francis himself thought that he was now on such good terms with the Low Countries that he could regain Tournai whenever he chose.[2] The Duke of Suffolk reported that it was hoped in Paris that when the two young Kings met (which in fact did not happen until 1520 at the Field of Cloth of Gold) some suitable arrangement might be worked out for the return of the city.[3]

Now was the time for Henry to clear out of Tournai without loss of face and to the great benefit of England's finances; but he could not yet bring himself to surrender the memento of his glorious campaign. He thus burdened the Exchequer with huge and unprofitable expenditure; and he committed his troops in Tournai to four more uneasy years, in which the possibility of a surprise attack by the French was never long out of the minds of the Governor and his council.

It very soon became evident that the peace treaty was not taken seriously, either by the garrison, or by the government in the Low Countries, for whom the absence of the French influence in Tournai had some significance. Immediately after the treaty had been signed, Spinelly told the King that it was considered that the city was bound to be attacked. He had been talking with 'a great personage' well disposed towards England, who was convinced 'by many appearances, that your city of Tournai standeth in great danger of the Frenchmen, notwithstanding your new treaty made with them'.[4]

Shortly afterwards the authorities in the Low Countries suggested to Spinelly that Henry was finding the cost of Tournai so heavy that he had it in mind to hand the city back, which they would deprecate. They were sure that the French must make an attempt to recover it, because their honour was at

---

[1] Galba B III, f. 314 b; *LP* ii, 70.
[2] *VC* ii, 592.
[3] Cal. E I, f. 124; *LP* ii, 132.
[4] SP 1/10, f. 125 b; *LP* ii, 303.

stake, and they thought that so long as the city remained in English hands it gave Henry an incentive to make further attacks on them. Moreover, if the French could recapture the city it would give them 'a perpetual bridle for Flanders'. A proposal that Gravelines and Dunkirk should be given in exchange for Tournai had been mooted. As these towns were on the Channel coast they could be maintained more cheaply by England, but there was no guarantee that their inhabitants would welcome English sovereignty any more than the Tournaisiens had done.[1]

The danger that the French might attack Tournai was enhanced by the presence on the Continent of Richard de la Pole, whose brother Edmund had been pretender to the throne of England, and had been executed by Henry as a precautionary measure before the 1513 expedition sailed. He could be used to provide an air of respectability, if indeed that was necessary, to a French enterprise against Tournai; and in any case he was recognized by Louis XII as the rightful king of England.[2] De la Pole—'the White Rose'—was regarded as a potential source of danger all through the occupation.

It was decided right away that so far as de la Pole was concerned attack was the best form of defence. If he could be removed from the scene a possible threat to Henry's survival as king would be eliminated. The Governor and council in Tournai and Henry's ambassadors in the Low Countries assiduously applied their minds to the problem of how to dispose of the traitor and renegade (as they regarded him). It was not easy, however; for de la Pole, who was living at Metz in Lorraine (an imperial city, as it happened),[3] was well guarded and was careful not to stray too far afield. He was aware that an English hand-gunner might try to pick him off from behind a convenient hedge.

Early in 1515 the former Governor, Sir Edward Poynings, now ambassador in the Low Countries, was in touch with a man (not named in the correspondence) who was said to be prepared

---

[1] Galba B III, f. 266; *LP* ii, 536.
[2] Scarisbrick, p. 32. Richard de la Pole fought with the French army at Pavia in 1525, where he was among the many who lost their lives (ibid. p. 135).
[3] *LP* ii, 2183.

to assassinate de la Pole. Poynings wrote to Henry from The Hague in June, reminding the King that he had several times asked what was to be done about the traitor, and enquiring if he now agreed that 'the enterprise' should go ahead. If the answer was yes, what line should be taken with the party who had volunteered for the job?[1] He kept in close touch on this subject with the Earl of Worcester, who was in Tournai and who elaborated what they had in mind in a letter to Wolsey a month later. He said that Poynings knew of a man who would take the matter in hand; but if for any reason this came to naught Worcester himself had someone who would do the job just as well.[2]

It was not only the danger that de la Pole might lead an attack on Tournai, or provide the justification for it, that worried the Governor and his council. Although de la Pole was many miles away his mere presence on the Continent had a disturbing effect on the garrison. If any of the troops contemplated desertion and hesitated to return to England, because of the danger of capture on the Channel crossing, they could console themselves with the thought that they might instead offer their services to the White Rose. There is no evidence that large numbers of them did this, but during Mountjoy's first troubled weeks as Governor some former members of the garrison planned to join de la Pole and tried to get serving soldiers to go with them.[3] Mountjoy played down the episode. He told Wolsey that he had 'had some business with certain simple persons out of wages, which were purposed to have gone to Richard de la Pole, as they have confessed'; but he had not considered the matter important enough to report to London at the time. He was now proceeding to have the men punished according to their deserts.[4]

In August Worcester told Wolsey that the man who had volunteered to Poynings to do away with de la Pole had recently visited Tournai to discuss his proposals; and he had promised to go to Metz to see if the White Rose was still there. He hoped to return to Tournai very soon and it might then be possible to come to some firm arrangement. Someone else—perhaps the second string Worcester had referred to earlier—had offered to

[1] Galba B III, f. 277; *LP* ii, 609.   [2] SP 1/11, f. 23; *LP* ii, 742.
[3] SP 1/10, f. 148; *LP* ii, 325.   [4] SP 1/10, f. 150; *LP* ii, 326.

'take the matter in hand and to deliver him me in this town, or to make an end of the matter'; and he was keeping this man in Tournai 'with fair words' until he had heard how Poynings' volunteer had fared. He had himself sent a spy to get definite news of de la Pole's whereabouts, and to find out 'by whose help he is succoured and founden'. It was rumoured that he was being looked after by the Duke of Lorraine at the expense of the French King.[1]

So far there had been little more than a great deal of fine talk about disposing of de la Pole; but in November the talk became more practical. John Russell and Thubianville, captains in the Tournai garrison, were sent to the town of St. Nicholas in Lorraine to get in touch with the most promising assassin, Perceval de Matte, and to tie him down to some positive proposal. They brought back a detailed account of what he had in mind—and how much he wanted to be paid.

De Matte, whose home was in Burgundy, about a hundred miles from Metz, said he would have to make a study of de la Pole's habits, for example to find out at what time he usually went into the fields to course hares or to watch his horses exercise. It was known that he ventured forth only when it was fine and it might therefore be necessary to wait for suitable weather. So he must not be hurried. De la Pole was as a rule accompanied by one or two of the local nobility and six to eight servants, and for this reason de Matte considered that if he was to organize a successful ambush he must have the support of a few foot soldiers. He told Russell and Thubianville that he had an understanding with the commander of the cavalry in Metz, and if there was a hue and cry after the White Rose had been dispatched, the pursuers would be led on a false scent to give de Matte plenty of time to make his escape.

The two captains, who seem to have been favourably impressed by the businesslike attitude of de Matte, promised to meet him again when they had discussed his proposition with the Governor and council of Tournai. He for his part went off to Burgundy to hire some confederates, having undertaken to wait at his home for a month for final instructions from the English.

The price asked for doing the job was staggering. In the first place de Matte wanted a down payment of 3,000 gold crowns

[1] Galba B V, f. 332; *LP* ii, 809.

for expenses. If the attempt failed, he expected for himself a pension of 200 crowns a year for life, for which security was to be provided in Calais, and pensions of 50 crowns a year for his confederates. If it succeeded, his pension was to be 400 crowns, and his chief assistant was to have like provision. Before he committed himself he wanted an absolute guarantee that his terms would be observed; and he seems also to have proposed (although the manuscript is badly mutilated at this point and it is difficult to make sense of it) that the Earl of Worcester's seal should be deposited with him to ensure that the English kept their part of the bargain. Finally, he feared that his honour might be at risk if he, a Burgundian with no political justification, assassinated an Englishman; and he therefore asked that he should formally be declared to be a servant of the English King.

Russell and Thubianville simply noted the price, since they were not authorized to haggle with de Matte; but it must have astonished them. On a conservative estimate—assuming that the assassin's team were not all in their dotage—the enterprise, if successful, would have cost Henry at least 16,000 gold crowns, or about £4,000, a good deal more than the fee paid to the headsman who removed Edmund de la Pole from the English political scene.

Their presence aroused some suspicion. On All Saints' Day, when they were at Pont à Mousson not far from Nancy, the Grand Commander of the Hospital of St. Anthony demanded to know who they were and what their business was. They had a ready explanation. They were two gentlemen on a pilgrimage to St. Nicholas. This satisfied the Grand Commander, who sent them a present of wine and invited them to supper. After supper he became expansive, and told them that there was an English Prince living in Metz for whom he was very sorry. He had been instrumental in getting him various pensions, in which he had been promised a half share. Russell and Thubianville, no doubt grateful for this windfall information about the subject of their mission, asked why the King of France troubled to maintain this Englishman. They were told that it enabled him to get early warning of any invasion attempt by Henry of England.[1]

---

[1] Cal. D VIII, ff. 34–6; Ellis, 3rd Ser. i, pp. 202–12; *LP* ii, 1163.

Nothing came of de Matte's costly and elaborate proposition; and it is conceivable that, even if the price had been right and the enterprise certain of success, Henry and his Councillors would have thought twice about giving it their blessing. Francis may have regarded de la Pole as a useful source of information about England's intentions, on the assumption that the White Rose's friends in England would keep him posted about the course of political events there; but this process could work equally well the other way round. De la Pole was in close touch with the French Court, and it might be possible through him to glean some idea of what Francis's intentions were, not only with regard to England, but for Europe as a whole. In short, the White Rose may have been worth more to Henry alive than dead.[1]

Indeed, this seems to be the only rational explanation why de la Pole was allowed to survive. So long as he was out of England he posed no real problem, although he might have been a force to reckon with had France succeeded at some stage in landing an army on English soil; but on the Continent he could do no harm, except perhaps to the morale of the unruly element of the Tournai garrison. Had he been living in the heart of Paris there would have been little chance of killing him; but he was living the life of a gentleman in the free town of Metz, often disporting himself in the surrounding country-side without seriously worrying about his personal safety.

Further, and this is significant, he was frequently visited by two paid agents of the King of England—Hans Nagel and Peter Alamire—whom he seems to have received as trusted friends.[2] Surely either of these two could have contrived his end a dozen times over, with no more equipment than a sharp dagger and a swift horse to speed them back to the safety of Tournai. Nagel at least seems to have had the makings of a double agent, for he himself admitted that his dealings with de la Pole at one time

---

[1] Nevertheless, in December 1515 Worcester was still pressing Wolsey for a decision 'as touching the matter of R. de la Pole'. He had had no indication as to what he should say to the gentleman who was prepared to undertake the enterprise. He had promised to give him an answer, one way or the other, within a month which was due to expire on 12 December. If only the King would say what he wanted done, his command would be executed with diligence (Cal. D VII, f. 50; *LP* ii, App. 16).

[2] *LP* ii, *passim*.

had been directed against England, which necessitated a pardon from Henry;[1] but wherever their true loyalty lay—and it probably belonged to the side that paid the highest price—it should not have been too difficult for Henry to arrange the elimination of the White Rose, had he really considered it to be vital. Of the pair of spies Spinelly said 'these two be as brethren for Hans doth nothing in that behalf without Alamire's counsel, by whose means we know as much as Hans knoweth of Richard's purposes'. He added that if Nagel was allowed into England 'he shall study to work treason . . . and also for lack of him we shall know nothing of Richard's enterprises'.[2] This strengthens the idea that the spies were being used to watch de la Pole rather than to try to kill him.

This idea is also supported by the steady stream of information about him that came through Alamire (who signed his communications with the musical symbols 'la', 'mi', 're') and Nagel to the English ambassador in the Low Countries for onward transmission to London. Alamire and Nagel, however, were by no means the only agents employed to watch de la Pole. In June 1516 Spinelly arranged with Jacques Hesbek, a servant of the Master of the Posts in Luxembourg, to go to Metz to make a report on the postal services between de la Pole and Paris, and if possible to intercept some of the letters;[3] and in the following year this man was still supplying information. He reported in April that Richard had just come back from France well arrayed, and with a chain of gold 'mightily good'.[4]

In May 1516 a budget from France contained a highly circumstantial account of a meeting between Francis and de la Pole, who had been summoned from Metz to Lyon. The two were riding on the White Rose's horse, when the King, who was seated behind, said: 'I know that the King of England is my utter enemy, intending to destroy and deprive me from my state in Italy, sending his right great sums of money to the Emperor and retaining the Swisses in his aid for that intent; wherefore glad would I be to serve him with like favours.' Francis added that he accepted that de la Pole had a good title to the English throne, and that as soon as he had made peace

[1] *LP* ii, 1478.   [2] SP 1/12, f. 139; *LP* ii, 1479.
[3] Galba B IV, f. 102; *LP* ii, 2081.   [4] Galba B V, f. 188 b; *LP* ii, 3108.

with the Emperor he would give the White Rose both men and money to enable him to obtain his rights in England.[1]

It is difficult to take this account of a bizarre summit meeting seriously. How, for example, did the reporter overhear the precise words murmured by the King into the ear of the pretender as they jogged along? Why did Francis choose this uncomfortable moment to discuss an affair of such importance? No doubt much of the other information that flowed from Metz about de la Pole's movements and intentions was equally suspect. The fact remains, however, that so long as he lived he provided a point of contact with French political thinking which the English government seem to have considered to be worth preserving, in spite of the fact that he was also a focal point to which the disgruntled soldiers of Tournai might be attracted. De la Pole continued to be a key factor all through the occupation. One of Sir Richard Jerningham's first acts as Governor at the beginning of 1517 was to send 'espials into divers parts and in especial to the town of Metz in Lorraine'. The spy sent to Metz was a man-of-arms, a native of the town, and Jerningham was confident that if anyone could find out de la Pole's secrets, it was he.[2]

However much Louis in 1514, and Francis in 1515, may have wanted to bring the return of Tournai within the scope of their peace talks with England, Henry would not agree. In spite of the intolerable financial burden he was determined to cling to his conquest, and that was that. But towards the end of 1515 even the King was beginning to see reason. When Sir Richard Wingfield was sent on a mission to Paris the future of Tournai was one of a number of questions he was briefed to raise. He was instructed to let it slip as casually as possible that the Earl of Worcester had just gone to Tournai to put in hand the building of a new citadel, the strengthening of the existing fortifications, and the establishment of the court sovereign. 'If it be politically handled it is thought the French King and his Council shall be driven and in a manner enforced, to make some manner overture or offer for the recovering thereof without further delay.' If the French were already aware of the purpose of Worcester's

---

[1] Cal. D VI, f. 351; *LP* ii, 1973.   [2] SP 1/14, f. 261; *LP* ii, 2926.

visit to Tournai (which seemed highly probable), Wingfield was to confirm the reports they had received.

It was hoped that Francis would conclude that, if he did not make an immediate bid for Tournai, the city's defences would be made so strong that he would never be able to recover it by force. If he looked like taking the bait, Wingfield was authorized to help matters along by saying 'as of himself' that even stronger fortifications were planned. He was to observe carefully 'every device, overture, or answer' made by Francis and to keep Henry fully informed about his reactions.[1]

Apparently Francis was not taken in by the ambassador's gambit, for he continued to hope that Henry would return the city of his own accord, or at least as a result of prompting by Wolsey. He undertook in a memorandum about this time to ensure that Wolsey would have the full possession of the bishopric of Tournai, and, seeking to exonerate himself from any blame for causing trouble in the diocese, claimed that he did not even know that the Bishop elect had been in Flanders.[2] His optimism about the fate of the city seems to have been shared by people in the Low Countries generally. There is at least one indication that the odds on his getting back Tournai were more than two to one in his favour. Worcester, who seems to have thought the point important enough to report to Henry, said that a certain merchant had wagered two to one (in horses) that Tournai would be in Francis's hands before New Year's Day; but the odds were not attractive enough to produce any takers.[3]

Mountjoy may have felt that the odds were about right, for he was in a constant state of apprehension about the danger of attack. No doubt he was wise to be on the alert, but it needed only a small movement of troops in northern France to convince him that the worst was about to happen. In October 1515 a report that 'certain assemblies of the Frenchmen' were marching on Tournai caused him to send all over the region 'divers and sundry folk one after another to bring me report'. These spies confirmed that musters had been taken, which implied that some enterprise was afoot; but their accounts of the intended destination of the troops varied—they seemed to be going

[1] Cal. D VI, f. 245; *LP* ii, 827.   [2] Cal. D VI, ff. 274-8; *LP* ii, 828.
[3] Cal. D VI, ff. 198-9; *LP* ii, 856.

everywhere except to Tournai—and as it turned out they were disbanded before they attempted anything. Although this scare came to nothing, it made the citizens stock up with food, something that Mountjoy had failed to persuade them to do in the six months of his governorship.[1]

The English ambassadors in the Low Countries were also on the lookout for French designs against Tournai. Even more than their successors in later times they could not afford to be taken unawares, if they wished to continue to enjoy their sovereign's favour. They therefore tended in self-defence to report anything that looked like a hostile move on the part of France. Dr. William Knight told Wolsey in January 1516 that he had heard through 'one that is much privy unto the French purposes' that as soon as Francis was satisfied that he had nothing to fear from the Swiss, he would turn on Tournai. He added that many of those who had been banished from the city had congregated in Paris and were eagerly awaiting the day when they would return home.[2] A week later he reported that the barber of the Abbot of St. Martin's at Tournai was saying that for some weeks a band of German mercenaries had been expected to attack the town. Many of the inhabitants were therefore going to the French ambassador in Brussels, in the hope that before long they would be able to make a triumphal return to their city. People on the borders of Luxembourg had been ordered to bring their goods and chattels into the walled cities, so that they might be safe during the troubled times that were likely to follow.[3]

At the beginning of February, Knight, who was in Brussels, believed that the danger had passed,[4] but his fellow ambassador Sir Thomas Spinelly thought that Francis might still use the Germans to attack Tournai, the recovery of which he was sure was 'of a great reputation and profit at this present season' to the French. Mountjoy must therefore see that the city's defences were in good order. Spinelly wanted to send a spy among the German troops 'to learn their secrets', but he was short of money and could not raise enough to hire anybody.[5]

Jerningham gave Wolsey his own assessment of the situation.

---

[1] Cal. E I, f. 72; *LP* ii, 988.
[2] SP 1/12, f. 85; *LP* ii, 1414.
[3] SP 1/12, f. 114; *LP* ii, 1434.
[4] SP 1/12, f. 137; *LP* ii, 1478.
[5] SP 1/12, f. 152; *LP* ii, 1496.

When the two had last met, Wolsey had commanded him to write privately from time to time, for he well knew how much his own position at the centre depended on a reliable intelligence service, and he liked to have as many sources of information as possible. Jerningham's understanding was that there were 4,000 Germans about two days' journey from Tournai—a fact which he said had made the garrison more than usually conscientious about carrying out guard duties. There were also in the neighbourhood 200 French men-of-arms under the command of Antoine de Créquy and the Duke of Vendôme, who were supposed to be en route for Scotland; but Jerningham reminded Wolsey that the French were skilful deceivers. It was quite usual for them to spread a rumour that they were going to do one thing and then to do something quite different. The Governor had therefore sent spies to the German mercenaries' camp and to the French men-of-arms.[1] Mountjoy wrote to Henry at this time with much the same account, except that for good measure he put the Germans' strength at 5,000.[2]

The threat passed and the Governor and his council breathed freely again; but they maintained their efforts to keep themselves well informed about the movement of French troops and of the French King, who would probably lead any major attack on the city. They might theoretically be at peace with their near neighbours, but they well knew that these could not be trusted. In the spring of 1516 Mountjoy was worried because so little had been heard of Francis. It was rumoured that he was dead, or 'not in the best of wit'; and to find out the truth the Governor sent a spy to Lyon, where the King was supposed to be.

The spy spent Easter week there and established that Francis was very much alive. The King took part in an Easter procession, barefoot and wearing a silver tinsel gown, 'to pray for victory against the Emperor'; and he several times went for pleasure trips on the Saône, 'with his young noblemen casting oranges out of one boat into another and using many other pastimes'. This spy also brought back news of the French garrisons between Tournai and Lyon. Lack of pay, which was more than a year overdue, had driven the soldiers from the garrison towns, and they were all living in the surrounding

---

[1] SP 1/12, f. 156; *LP* ii, 1498.   [2] Cal. E I, f. 78 b; *LP* ii, 1509.

villages, 'eating and pillaging' the villagers out of house and home.[1]

In May 1516 Mountjoy was informed through his espionage system, which seems to have worked efficiently, that a messenger was coming to Tournai from the French King with letters directed to the Dean and Chapter of the Cathedral, at which he confessed himself to be 'somewhat a-marvelled'. He arranged for the messenger to be intercepted, but it proved to be un-necessary, since in the event the man came straight to the Governor's residence. He said that he was a messenger from the University of Paris, and that he had been asked by one of the French King's messengers to deliver a letter to the Bishop of Tournai or his vicar. Mountjoy sent this letter on to Henry, pointing out that although the subject-matter was innocuous (it was concerned with processions and sermons to be made for the peace between Francis, Henry, and Charles, and because the French Queen was with child, and was probably a circular letter which an official had absent-mindedly sent to Tournai), he considered it to be offensive, because it was addressed by Francis to the Bishop of Tournai 'as to his councillor and sub-ject'. Mountjoy half suspected that the messenger had come straight to him only because he had got wind of the fact that he would be arrested if he tried to deliver to the Dean and Chap-ter; and he told Henry that if the man had tried to deliver the letter direct he would have had him punished for his presump-tion in bringing such a communication to Tournai, where his master the French King had no standing whatsoever.[2]

The suspicion that Francis was up to some mischief grew during the summer of 1516. It was reported that he was craftily attempting to recover the city through a number of former citizens who had refused to take the oath of loyalty to Henry.[3] That the French King 'intended an enterprise' was repeated by Mountjoy in June.[4] A month later the council in Tournai wrote to Henry that 'a man of this town', who had shown him-self to be a faithful and true subject, had informed them 'that the French King is clearly determined to come into these parts with as great a puissance right shortly as ever he had in Italy

[1] Cal. E I, f. 95; LP ii, 1837.   [2] Cal. E I, f. 99; LP ii, 1855.
[3] Cal. D VI, ff. 351–2; LP ii, 1973.
[4] Vesp. F XIII (ii), f. 244; LP ii, 1995.

for the reduction of the Duchy of Milan'. It was not certain whether the King intended simply to attack Tournai, or whether he proposed to overrun the Low Countries as well, but on the whole it seemed that Tournai was likely to be his sole objective.[1]

The information had reached the council's informant through a kinsman of his no longer resident in the city. This kinsman had allowed him to read letters from Guillaume Bonnivet, the Lord Admiral of France, about the French government's plans for Tournai, never for a moment suspecting that he would be guilty of such a breach of faith as to pass on the contents of the letters to the English. The council considered that if the town was attacked by Francis the man who had received the letters from Bonnivet 'would be one of the chief aiders'. He was in very good favour with the French, who had offered him a pension. He had turned it down, however, on the ground that it would show him to be closely associated with the French, and perhaps lead the Governor to confiscate his possessions in Tournai.

The council were also informed at this time by a servant of the financier Leonardo Frescobaldi, who had been in France to collect money for his master, that he had learned in Abbeville that a member of Francis's Council had urged the King 'to put in execution the enterprise of Tournai' as soon as possible. The citadel was still unfinished, but if the attack was deferred much longer the new defences would be completed and the garrison's power to resist much increased. 'The King answered that he would shortly, and in time, remember it; and thereupon he drank to the lord's good luck.' In reporting this to Henry, Jerningham said that if Francis attacked the town they would be able to withstand him, with God's help. They had no problems about their defence, 'saving for fault of gunners'. These were most necessary in time of siege, as the King well knew. Jerningham and his council reckoned that because of the 'great compass and circuit' of the town they needed between 200 and 300 gunners until the citadel was ready.[2]

As the autumn approached, without any positive sign that the French were going to launch an attack, the Governor and council began to relax; but the cumulative effect of reports

---

[1] Cal. D VI, ff. 303–4; *LP* ii, 2131.   [2] Ibid.

about French troop movements suddenly led the King and Council to conclude that a French attempt against the city was in fact imminent. Wolsey wrote to Mountjoy in August, saying that Henry had been warned by Sir Richard Wingfield, Governor of Calais, Sir Thomas Spinelly, and 'sundry espies' that 'the Frenchmen be about an enterprise against Tournai.' It was understood that all their preparations were made, and that Francis was in a position to launch the attack whenever he chose. Mountjoy was therefore ordered to see that the city was 'well and substantially furnished, and such things to be foreseen and put in a readiness as shall be requisite for the surety and defence thereof if anything should be attempted'. He was also to send out spies 'for attaining of the very truth and surety of their intent and purpose'; and to send the reports, as they came in, post-haste to London.

In reply, the Governor was at pains to point out that he and his colleagues had kept the King fully informed about rumours of French troop movements. They too had heard from Sir Richard Wingfield, and both before and after receiving his report they had sent out spies 'to know what assemblies were made and the cause thereof'. They had come to the conclusion that there was nothing to be feared; and that a possible explanation of the recent musters was simply that Francis had been putting on a display of force for the benefit of the ambassadors of Ferdinand of Aragon. Wolsey might rest assured that Mountjoy would get ample warning of even the slightest threat to the city, through his friends in the surrounding territories and the spies at his disposal. Nevertheless, he asked that he should be kept informed about any reports of French intentions that reached London; and he, for his part, promised to keep Henry fully posted. He also suggested that he could learn a good deal more about 'their privities and their enterprisings' if he was enabled to bribe one or two of the French King's advisers.[1]

Any hope that Mountjoy's uncharacteristically firm line with Henry would dispose of their fears about a French attack must have been dispelled by a dispatch from Dr. Cuthbert Tunstall, ambassador to Charles, written in September. He told Henry that a canon of Lille who held a benefice in Tournai had been

[1] Cal. E I, f. 115; Strype, pp. 14–16 (contains some inaccuracies); *LP* ii, 2353.

drinking 'long together' with a certain treasurer,[1] who seemed to be well informed about the intentions of the French forces. The canon regarded himself as one of Henry's subjects, and thought it was his duty to tell the ambassador that great preparations were being made in France against Tournai, and that numbers of exiled burgesses of the city were co-operating. Tunstall added that if the French did 'advance their malicious purposes' he believed that Charles would come to the defence of the city.[2] There seems to be no doubt that Henry took seriously the threat of an attack, for he let it be known to the Venetian ambassador in London about this time that he was on the point of leading an army across the Channel. Giustiniani, however, was much too experienced to be taken in, and reported to his masters in Venice that the story of the proposed invasion was a fiction, which he was supposed to transmit to the Signory in the hope that they would pass it on to Francis, who would desist from his proposed attack on Tournai, believing that England was about to take the initiative.[3]

Apprehension in London mounted in the early months of 1517, and Giustiniani came to the conclusion that the danger of war was greater than his earlier dispatch suggested. He reported to the Signory that the King's Council was meeting much more frequently than usual, 'as if all their enemies were upon them', because of the possibility that the French, who were now at peace with Italy and Spain and had nothing to fear from the Emperor or the Swiss, would mount an attack on Tournai or Calais. England was well prepared for war. Some years ago there had been a census of able-bodied men, and a large army could be raised at short notice.[4] The ambassador accurately assessed the position of the English government, for three weeks later Henry told Jerningham that reports had come in that France was gathering an army and fitting out warships, probably to attack Calais, Guines, or Tournai. He must therefore see to it that the town's defences were in good order, 'looking to the munitions, putting our ordnance in a readiness, and bestowing the same in places most behoveful for the defence

---

[1] The manuscript is so mutilated at this point that it is impossible to tell where the treasurer came from.
[2] Galba B IV, f. 182; *LP* ii, 2358.   [3] *VC* ii, 774.
[4] *VC* ii, 855.

of our said city'. Stocks of food were to be built up, and once again spies were to be sent 'to all quarters for knowledge of the certainty, not sparing for any costs or charges to be sustained in making of the said espials, whereof we shall see you sufficiently answered and recompensed'. The spies' reports were to be sent to London immediately.[1]

Shortly after this Jerningham submitted a comprehensive situation report to Henry. He confirmed that there had been a strong rumour that Francis was going to attack Calais or Tournai. The French King had 1,400 German mercenaries in a village on the borders of Champagne, and 6,000 at another village. The captains of these troops were understood to be discussing their plans with the French leaders. Jerningham also mentioned concentrations of French troops totalling about 4,000 men; and he told Henry that he was rushing this news to him, so that he would not be blamed for 'late and dull advertisements'. He added that he had planted spies among both the French and German troops, and, as the chances of an attack on Tournai seemed very great, he had put all things in readiness for the defence of the town.

In the same dispatch Jerningham revealed how easy it was to be caught out in the welter of espionage and counter-espionage. Jean Gourdin, one of his agents, who had been sent to Thérouanne to see what progress the French had made in rebuilding the fortifications razed by Henry in 1513, brought in a report about a spy named Beaughienville. Gourdin had chanced to be in a stable when Beaughienville's nephew came in and had a long confabulation with a young Scot while he saddled his horse in the next stall, unaware that he was overheard. At the end of it the nephew handed over a packet of letters to be delivered to Francis's mother, which was enough to confirm Gourdin's suspicions that uncle and nephew were up to no good. He provided a detailed description of the clothes worn by Beaughienville and his servant on their trips to England, so that the authorities there would be able to keep an eye on them on their next visit, and arrest them if it seemed desirable.[2]

Jerningham, no doubt delighted to have an opportunity of showing Henry that his ear was close to the ground, immediately passed all this information on to London. This Beaugh-

[1] SP 1/15, f. 68; *LP* ii, App. 32.   [2] Cal. D VI, f. 283; *LP* ii, 3084.

ienville, a highly suspect gentleman of Picardy, 'of middle size, with a slender leg', made frequent trips to England disguised as a merchant. He usually wore a coat of English cloth, cut in the English style, a grey fustian doublet pleated 'at mid arm' and quilted with red thread. His hose were white, and his mount a roan with four white feet. His servant wore a grey coat, and had one hose red, the other black.[1] Captain Thubianville, in whose company Gourdin had served, told Sir Edward Poynings that if Henry wanted to have Beaughienville captured he would be delighted to do the job, and deliver him secretly to Fort Risban in Calais.[2]

What neither Jerningham nor Thubianville realized was that, although Beaughienville undoubtedly was a spy, he was hired by Wolsey to spy for England. In January 1517 he was in touch with the Governor of Calais, Sir Richard Wingfield, through the agency of someone who is described simply as 'the priest', and tried to impress on him that a French attack on Tournai was imminent.[3] He also complained to Wolsey that he was inadequately paid for his services.[4] What is not explained satisfactorily is why his nephew should have been carrying letters to the French Queen Mother. This suggests that he may have been a double agent, and that Jerningham's suspicions were well founded. But whatever he was up to, he gave satisfaction so far as Wolsey was concerned, for the pension of 100 crowns a year which he was paid was continued at least to the summer of 1518.[5] If he *was* a double agent, his English employers considered that he gave good value for that part of his activity which was devoted to their service.

In 1517 the political climate was beginning to change. Francis, and the expatriate Tournaisiens, still wanted the city to be returned to France, but on the whole more peaceful methods began to be favoured. Charles de Créquy, Dean of Tournai, was one who used his influence to try to bring England and France together again. He had several conversations with Richard Sampson, the gist of which was that it would be in the mutual interest of the two countries to be genuinely at peace; and, although the Dean did not openly bring Tournai into his

[1] Cal. E I, f. 142; *LP* ii, 3097.
[2] Cal. E I, f. 141; *LP* ii, 3091.
[3] Cal. E I, f. 123; *LP* ii, 2761.
[4] Cal. D VI, f. 280; *LP* ii, 2745.
[5] SP 1/17, ff. 46–9; *LP* ii, 4406.

calculations, he must have realized that possession of the city would have to be part of any bargain. He said that all he needed was an hour with the King and Wolsey. Sampson replied that these were matters of supreme importance which he could not possibly raise with Wolsey; but in fact he reported the conversations very fully, so that the King could take the chance of using de Créquy's influence if it seemed likely to be profitable.[1]

There was still a great deal of mutual suspicion, however. In January 1518 Wolsey told the Governor that the French were amassing troops, ostensibly for an expedition against the Turks, but actually that they might be used against Tournai. He must therefore send out spies 'for attaining of the perfect knowledge of the preparations, minds and intent of the said Frenchmen'.[2] Next month Jerningham was still sensitive about the future. On hearing that David Cochrane, a Scot who was one of the King of Denmark's heralds, was in Antwerp with letters 'of great charge' from his master to Francis, he sent John Russell (who had been used against de la Pole) to intercept the letters, so that Henry might be 'advertised of many great secrets'.[3]

Russell succeeded in capturing Cochrane, but the servant who was carrying the letters escaped into a wood. The herald seems to have taken a light-hearted view of an incident which was both alarming and a gross breach of diplomatic immunity, assuming that they were wasting their time. His dispatches were of no interest to Henry. They dealt, for example, with requests from the King of Denmark to Francis for galleys to be used against the Swedes, that he should intercede with the King of Scotland on behalf of two Scottish knights who had been banished for murder, and so on. To prove that he spoke the truth, Cochrane arranged for his servant to bring the letters and allowed Jerningham and his colleagues to read them.

Jerningham's suspicions were not allayed, even though it turned out that the herald had at one time been a loyal servant of Henry VII. The King of Denmark had 12,000 troops under arms, and there was no certainty that they were going to be used against Sweden. He told Henry that he had arranged for Cochrane to deliver the letters to the French King as planned;

[1] SP 1/15, f. 83; *LP* ii, 3121.   [2] SP 1/16, f. 123; *LP* ii, 3907.
[3] Cal. E I, ff. 183–6; *LP* ii, 3978.

and that if he discovered 'anything that should be prejudicial to your highness he will advertise me—so that it touch not the King his master'. Jerningham gave the man a suitable reward, and held out the promise of further rewards if he provided useful information about the secrets of the French King. There is no evidence that David Cochrane earned his further rewards; but a spy in Wolsey's pay at the French Court brought news to Tournai in May 1518 which, if it was true, suggested that Cochrane may have been playing a double game. Wolsey's agent, Henry Crossene, claimed that Francis, Christian II of Denmark, Richard de la Pole, and the Duke of Albany 'be all in one confederation'. The supposed plan was that de la Pole should mount an invasion of England from Denmark, his troops being mainly *Landsknechte*. The Duke of Albany was to sail for Scotland from Brittany and to attack England from the north. The Duc de Vendôme was to lay siege to Tournai. All these enterprises were to take place simultaneously, so that Henry's forces would be divided. In reporting this, Jerningham said bitterly that, if it was all true, Wolsey and the Council might have cause to regret that they had not paid more attention 'to our oft writings for the advancement of such works as should have been most necessary for the surety of this the King's citadel'.[1]

Wolsey's agent was probably drawing on his imagination, or perhaps reporting the gossip of the French Court as hard fact, so that he might earn his keep, for the great three-way assault on England never materialized. Some months earlier Wolsey had come to the conclusion that England must arrive at a real understanding with France, even if it meant abandoning Tournai. The city was costing far too much, and it was not providing him with the income he was entitled to expect as its Bishop. Although it was not until October 1518 that the treaty was signed which bound England and France, and later the rest of Europe, into a new alliance, Étienne Poncher, Bishop of Paris, and Pierre de la Guiche came to London in November 1517 as Francis's ambassadors, to discuss terms for the return of Tournai.[2] The assiduous Giustiniani was able to report that Henry seemed likely to agree to the restoration on certain conditions. He thought that the business was for all practical

---

[1] Strype, pp. 16–19; *LP* ii, 4201. [2] *LP* ii, 3788.

purposes settled, although it still depended on the King of France.[1]

At least one of the King's advisers was unhappy about the future, however. The Bishop of Winchester, Richard Fox, was worried by tales of troop concentrations in Normandy. Although he decided that they were not aimed against England, he nevertheless felt impelled to warn Wolsey about the state of the south-coast defences: 'and my lord if the said war be intended against the King's grace and his realm, as I trust it be not, the Isle of Wight and Portsmouth be full feeble for defence or resistance, and the rather because our manner is never to prepare for the war till our enemies be light at our doors.'[2] More than five years were to elapse, however, before England and France were whole-heartedly at war again.

[1] *VC* ii, 992. [2] SP 1/16, f. 145; *LP* ii, 3952.

IX · RESTORATION

THE first real chance for Louis XII to regain Tournai came in the middle of 1514, when Henry was offering him peace and the hand of his sister Mary in marriage. Louis's ambassadors were briefed to say that Tournai was not a very important matter (no doubt to keep Henry from getting inflated ideas about the price he was prepared to pay for it), but, nevertheless, that if the city was not returned he would not agree to the marriage. Henry would have to guarantee to hand it over as soon as the marriage had taken place.[1] This proved to be the most difficult point in the negotiation. After everything else was settled the fate of Tournai still hung in the balance.[2] In the end Henry won. Louis took Mary as his wife; Henry kept Tournai; and England and France were at peace from 7 August 1514.[3]

Tournai inevitably came up again when Francis I succeeded Louis XII on 1 January 1515, and the peace treaty with England had to be renegotiated. Francis suggested hopefully that there might be 'honourable restitution' of the city, and offered to pay a substantial sum for it. He pointed out to the Duke of Suffolk, who was leading the English embassy to Paris, that the place was a great burden to England and that if peace was firmly established there was little advantage in retaining it. Suffolk replied that the best course would be first to renew the peace treaty, and to discuss the question of Tournai later. His reason, as he told the King's Council, was that, if the restoration of the city was provided for in the treaty, the rumour would spread in France that Henry had to buy peace by surrendering it, and this would not do. Far better to have a separate and secret agreement to restore the city, which would be announced when in due course the two kings met.[4]

Wolsey wanted Tournai to return to France, but only if England got some tangible compensation. Nicholas West, one of the English ambassadors, refers to 'your matter of Tournai'

---

[1] *LP* i, 2957.   [2] *VC* ii, 454.
[3] Rymer, p. 413; *LP* i, 3129.   [4] Cal. D VI, f. 214; *LP* ii, 175.

in a letter to him,[1] and later Suffolk followed Wolsey's instructions to inquire 'as of himself' what territory Francis would give in exchange. He suggested the county of Guines; but Francis claimed that this would raise 'a great clamour'. The people of the county were the best Frenchmen in France. Suffolk replied that to give up Tournai would cause no less a clamour in England.[2] A few days later the French King was boasting to the Venetian ambassador that he could recapture the city whenever he chose.[3]

About the same time the ever-cautious Spinelly was suspicious of Francis's intentions. He told Henry that he was constantly urging Mountjoy to keep 'good and sure watch' in Tournai, and that it was generally felt in the Low Countries that the King would be well advised to look to the defences there 'at least till such time as it were plainly known how your highness standeth with the Frenchmen'.[4] At the beginning of April Tournai was still being haggled over. The French Chancellor said it had no value for Henry, and he could not understand why he wanted to keep it. The English ambassadors replied that everything could be settled to the satisfaction of the French when Henry and Francis met. This, said the Chancellor, was what they had been told when the earlier treaty was signed: to which Suffolk replied that if Louis XII had not died Henry would have offered to return Tournai.[5]

At the end of the day Tournai was left out of the account. There was no reference to the city in the renegotiated treaty.[6] Henry had missed his second chance of ridding himself of a huge liability.

Another chance of reaching a settlement came in August 1515, when Sir Richard Wingfield was sent on an embassy to Paris. The line to be taken in his meeting with the French King is spelled out with great precision in a twelve-page document signed by Henry.[7] This sets out the matters on which he must stick rigidly to his brief, and those on which he may rely on his discretion as the discussion proceeds. He is first to express Henry's gratitude for the consolation and comfort afforded to

---

[1] SP 1/10, f. 62; *LP* ii, 177.   [2] Cal. D VI, f. 176; *LP* ii, 231.
[3] *LP* ii, 267.   [4] SP 1/10, ff. 104–5; *LP* ii, 291.
[5] Cal. D VI, f. 222; *LP* ii, 304.
[6] Cal. D VI, f. 261; Rymer, p. 476; *LP* ii, 301.
[7] Cal. D VI, ff. 240–245 b; *LP* ii, 827.

his sister Mary, recently widowed by the death of Louis XII; and then to say that Henry reciprocates Francis's wish that they should meet face to face. At this point the ambassador must be careful to 'pause and stop', allowing the French King to make the running about the time and place of the proposed meeting. He is to do no more than 'mark well such answers as he shall make upon the same'; and to leave Francis in no doubt that he cannot commit his royal master. Thereafter, using all the 'wisdom, policy and sober persuasions' at his command, he is to raise a number of general matters.

Finally, in dealing with the possibility of restoring Tournai, the document carefully prescribes the line the ambassador is to follow; but on this topic he is ordered to give Francis the impression that the ideas put forward are his and his alone. Henry is about to embark on a costly building programme in Tournai, and surely it must have occurred to some of the English Council that this may be the right moment to get rid of a heavy liability before it becomes totally crippling. He must add, however, that there are reasons for going slow. Wolsey has not yet made a reasonable profit out of the bishopric, and indeed his claim to it is not clearly established. If the city goes back to France while Louis Guillard has at least an equal right to the diocese, Wolsey must abandon all hope of adding the revenues of Tournai to his already substantial income. Further, it will weaken Henry's bargaining position if Francis is given the impression that he is seriously thinking of abandoning Tournai.

As Wingfield was Governor of Calais it was natural that he should know of Henry's plan to build an impregnable fortress in Tournai. He was instructed to let slip casual references to the plan, in the hope that Francis and his Council would conclude that unless they made an immediate offer for the city it would become so strong that they could never recapture it. If, however, it appeared that Francis already knew what was afoot (which was likely, as there were many 'good Frenchmen' in Tournai), Wingfield was to confirm the reports, still giving the impression that he spoke without Henry's authority. It was hoped that these tactics would induce Francis to take the initiative and make a generous offer for the return of the city. He did not take the bait, however, and it was not until 1517 that the possibility of restoring the city was again discussed. In

16—E.O.T.

that year there was a series of diplomatic exchanges, in which Henry took a personal interest,[1] and which cleared the way for formal negotiations that began in London in September 1518. It was agreed in principle that Tournai should be restored; that a marriage should be contracted between the Dauphin and Henry's daughter Mary; and that the meeting between Henry and Francis which had first been mooted in 1515 should now take place.[2] It was also agreed that Wolsey should surrender his claim to the bishopric of Tournai in return for a substantial pension from the French King.[3]

On Monday 30 August the Admiral of France, Guillaume Bonnivet, left for England,[4] armed with commissions from Francis to treat with Henry for a mutual defence pact, for a marriage between the Princess Mary and the Dauphin (aged two years and a few months respectively), for the restoration of Tournai, the Abbey of St. Amand, and the castle of Mortagne, and for a meeting between Henry and Francis.[5] Bonnivet's embassy caused a great stir in France, for it was thought to be the most splendid that had ever left the country. An anonymous correspondent in France said that the ambassadors were accompanied by thirty gentlemen, fifty archers, and companies of wrestlers, musicians, and tennis players. This individual, who was surprised that Tournai was to be given up for only 400,000 crowns, also said that there was talk that the English would also surrender Calais and Guines, but he thought that they would hardly be such fools as to do that.[6]

Many had high hopes that the negotiations would lead to a lasting peace; but at least Sir Richard Jerningham had serious misgivings. He told Wolsey that he had heard that Henry and Francis planned a marriage between Mary and the Dauphin (it may seem strange that he had not been informed officially, but it had been decided to keep the proposals as secret as possible), and, if this was true, it was likely in his opinion that

---

[1] e.g., Richard Pacey refers to 'the article devised by the King himself [i.e. Henry] touching the restitution of Tournai into the French King's hands' (SP 1/16, f. 316; *LP* ii, 4275).

[2] *VC* ii, 1047, 1048, 1055.   [3] Rymer, p. 610; *LP* ii, 4354.

[4] Cal. D VII, f. 27; *LP* ii, 4405.

[5] Rymer, pp. 611, 614, 616, 618; *LP* ii, 4351.

[6] Cal. D VI, f. 25; *LP* ii, 4356.

England would find the Burgundians just as difficult as the French had been in the past, for the marriage would be far from popular with them.[1] Spinelly, writing from Zaragoza, echoed Jerningham's fears. Influential men in the Low Countries had made representations to Charles that he should prevent Tournai from falling into the hands of the French, which would be a great disaster. They had suggested that a levy should be imposed on his territories 'beyond the sea' to purchase the city. The Bishop of Burgos and other leading members of the Spanish Council considered that Charles should spare no effort to get his hands on the city before Francis.[2]

William Knight was equally unhappy. If the Emperor died, which was quite likely as he was an old man, and if France took over Tournai, it would inevitably mean that that country would 'usurp' the Low Countries. On the other hand, if he did not die, Knight thought that he would lend his support to the traitor Richard de la Pole.[3] A week later he reported that the people of the Low Countries were in great fear, for they believed that the return of Tournai to France would lead to war.[4] Margaret of Savoy confirmed that there was great dissatisfaction about the proposal to restore the city, and said that the French would break any agreement they made with England whenever it suited them.[5]

However, in spite of the gloomy forebodings of Spinelly and Knight, the negotiations went ahead according to plan. Sebastian Giustiniani, the Venetian ambassador in London, regularly reported developments to the Doge. Nicholas de Neufville, who had earlier come to England to prepare the groundwork for the French mission, returned to London towards the end of August; and it was understood that the ambassadors would follow a few days later. At the same time Giustiniani grumbled that Wolsey was being very secretive about the terms of the proposed treaty.[6] Sir William Sandys was ordered to provide ships at Calais—enough to carry at least 500 horses, which was said to be the minimum number the French ambassadors would have in their train. In fact, the Bishop of Paris, Étienne Poncher, sailed from Boulogne on 25 August,[7]

[1] SP 1/17, f. 23; LP ii, 4364.   [2] Vesp. C I, f. 187; LP ii, 4384.
[3] SP 1/17, ff. 65–6; LP ii, 4447.   [4] Galba, B VI, f. 74; LP ii, 4460.
[5] Galba B VI, f. 76; LP ii, 4492.   [6] Giust, ii 208; LP, ii, 4392.
[7] SP 1/17, f. 36; LP ii, 4396.

and landed at Sandwich. It had been intended that the whole
of the French party should enter London together, which meant
that the Bishop would have to mark time in Sandwich, where he
found his quarters uncomfortable, but Wolsey told him to come
on by himself, as he would be better looked after in London.[1]

The Bishop may have been enticed to London by Wolsey in
advance of the main embassy in the hope that it might be
possible to wring concessions from him while he was still on his
own. His arrival by himself on the evening of 1 September
puzzled the ever-watchful Giustiniani, who feared that an
alliance between England and France might have unpleasant
implications for Venice. As soon as he heard of Poncher's
arrival he went to Wolsey's palace to find out what was afoot.
He was told that the Cardinal had already got down to business
with the Bishop, and, according to his report to the Signory,
high words—which he may have overheard as he waited for the
meeting to break up—passed between Wolsey and the Frenchman. After the meeting he got hold of Richard Pacey, who did
not tell him much. Wolsey refused to see him, as did the Bishop
of Paris;[2] but a few days later the Bishop relented. 'Like all
French ambassadors he acted with much reserve', but at least he
confirmed that Tournai was to be surrendered on terms that
quite satisfied the English. During the whole of the negotiations,
however, Wolsey refused to grant Giustiniani an audience,
claiming on one occasion to be indisposed;[3] but the Venetian
hoped to see Henry, and make it plain to him that peace
between England and France would not be very agreeable to
the Signory.[4]

He managed to arrange an audience with Henry, but it was
not much help, as the King 'was going out on pleasure'. Henry
made no bones about the fact that diplomatic calls took second
place to hunting or dancing or whatever form of pleasure was
the order of the day. Giustiniani tried his luck with Sir Thomas
More, who had just been made a member of the King's Council,
but he claimed that he knew nothing. He said that the whole
business of the negotiation had been conducted by Wolsey
singlehanded, and even Henry did not know what was going on.
The ambassador was eventually allowed to see Wolsey, who

---

[1] SP 1/17, f. 39; *LP* ii, 4401.   [2] *VC* ii, 1067.
[3] *VC* ii, 1071.   [4] *VC* ii, 1070.

seemed to him to be unwell (perhaps his earlier indisposition was not diplomatic), and he hastened to take his leave; but Wolsey called him back to tell him that France and England proposed to include Venice in their alliance. Poncher later confirmed this, and added that Wolsey drove a very hard bargain. There were still some difficulties to be ironed out, which would be tackled after the arrival of Bonnivet, the leader of the mission, who had been held up by bad weather.[1]

The French ambassadors, including the Bishop of Paris, who by this time had been in London for three weeks, made their formal entry on 23 September. The embassy was led by Bonnivet, and included Francis de Rochechouart, Seigneur de Campodenario, Nicholas de Neufville, Seigneur de Villeroi, and a huge number of followers. Giustiniani records that such a display had never before been seen in England, or perhaps anywhere in the world.[2] Edward Hall puts the numbers at eighty or more noblemen and young gallants of the Court of France, accompanied by a great multitude of rascals and pedlars and jewellers, who brought over 'hats and caps and divers merchandise uncustomed, all under the colour of the trussery[3] of the ambassadors'. The total number he put at 1,200, which was considered to be far too many for an embassy.[4]

The ambassadors' train, which included 600 horses, seventy mules, and seven baggage wagons, was met by a large company of English nobles and gentlemen at Blackheath, and escorted in triumph to London.[5] The news of the splendour of the French invasion had of course come to the ears of the King's Council, and they could not be outdone. The High Admiral, the Earl of Surrey, was appointed to meet the visitors, and no doubt to put on a display that would uphold the honour of England. Hall's description of the occasion, although it was committed to paper long after the event, is probably near the truth. According to him, Surrey,

in a coat of rich tissue cut on cloth of silver, on a great courser richly trapped, and a great whistle of gold, set with stones and pearl hanging at a great and massy chain baldrick-wise, accompanied with 160 gentlemen richly apparelled, on goodly horses came to Blackheath and there amiably received the ambassadors of France.

[1] *VC* ii, 1072. [2] *VC* ii, 1074. [3] 'Baggage' (*O.E.D.*).
[4] Hall, p. 593. [5] *VC*, 1074.

The young gallants of France had coats garded with one colour cut in ten or twelve parts very richly to behold; and so all the Englishmen accoupled themselves with the Frenchmen lovingly together, and so rode to London. After the two Admirals followed 24 of the French King's guard, which accompanied 24 of the King's guard. And after them a great number of archers, to the number of 400, and in this order they passed through the city to the Taylors' Hall and there the chief ambassadors were lodged, and the remnant in merchants' houses about.[1]

The hard bargaining that the Bishop of Paris had complained about continued after the arrival of the whole mission, one of the main points of difficulty being the bond of friendship between France and Scotland, which England wanted to weaken as far as possible. The ambassadors daily met the English representatives at Greenwich, while the gentlemen in their party passed the time dancing in the Queen's chamber with the ladies of the English Court. The merchants who had smuggled their wares in the ambassadors' baggage displayed them for sale in the Taylors' Hall, making it 'like to the pound of a mart'. This evoked many fruitless protests from English merchants, who could not compete with the duty-free prices of the French.[2]

Henry formally received the embassy at Greenwich on 26 September. The Venetian ambassador's secretary, Nicolo Sagudino, has left an account of the occasion. The King sat at the end of the hall, more splendidly dressed than Sagudino had ever seen him before, facing more than 400 of his lords, knights, and gentlemen, wearing silk and cloth of gold. On the right hand of the King sat Cardinal Wolsey and Cardinal Campeggio, and behind the principal English courtiers crowded the French gentlemen who had accompanied the embassy. The ambassadors were presented to the King, who embraced them lovingly, and they then took their places in front of him to listen to a Latin oration from the Bishop of Paris. The Bishop of Ely replied, and the public part of the function was over. Henry, Wolsey, and the ambassadors withdrew into a private apartment for supper.[3]

Agreement was finally reached at the beginning of October, subject to one or two matters left to be settled in Paris when Francis ratified the treaties agreed in London between his

[1] Hall, pp. 593–4.   [2] Hall, p. 594.   [3] Hall, p. 594; *VC* ii, 1085.

ambassadors and Henry. On Sunday 3 October Wolsey proclaimed in St. Paul's Cathedral the successful outcome of weeks
of negotiation, and celebrated mass 'with unusual splendour'.
He was enthroned on a dais 'raised six steps from the ground'
next to the altar. Near him was the papal legate, Cardinal
Campeggio, also on a dais, but only three steps high; and there
were twelve Bishops and six Abbots all in bejewelled mitres.
The principal chapel and the choir were hung with gold brocade embroidered with the royal arms, and Henry sat in a
special pew covered with cloth of gold. While high mass was
being sung, two low masses were said before the King at a small
altar, with a cross of solid gold, and gold and silver-gilt orna-
ments.

When mass was over Wolsey and Campeggio gave their
benediction to the congregation, and then to the King and the
ambassadors; and after Richard Pacey, the King's Secretary,
had made 'a good and sufficiently long oration' Henry and the
ambassadors approached the high altar to swear perpetual
peace between France and England. Henry's magnificent attire
must have made a deep impression on the onlookers. It is
described in detail by an anonymous writer whose account is
preserved in the archives of Mantua. He wore a robe of crimson
satin lined with brocade, and a tunic of purple velvet peppered
with pearls and precious stones—rubies, sapphires, turquoises,
and diamonds of the first water. Round his neck was a collar
studded with the finest garnets, as big as walnuts.[1]

The way was now clear to launch the celebrations which such
a momentous occasion demanded. Immediately after the ceremony in St. Paul's Cathedral the whole company adjourned to
the Bishop of London's palace, where they were entertained to
midday dinner by the King. In the evening, presumably after
a suitable interval, they moved on to Wolsey's own palace,
where 'a most sumptuous supper' was served in a banqueting-
hall so full of gold and silver that Giustiniani, whose dispatches
provide the most comprehensive record of these events,[2] and

[1] *VC* ii, 1088.
[2] This is an example of the principle that at this time events tended to be less
well recorded in the capital where they occurred than in the other capitals of
Europe, and which has its parallel in the relatively poor documentation of an
expedition led by the King in person as compared with one led by his lieutenant
(see above, p. 27).

who was, of course, one of the guests, said that you might have
fancied yourself to be in the tower of Crœsus.[1]

After supper the minstrels came in 'richly disguised', followed
by three gentlemen in long gowns of crimson satin, carrying
golden cups filled with angels and royals, dice, and playing
cards. 'These gentlemen offered to play at mumchance[2] and
when they had played the length of the first board, then the
minstrels blew up.'[3] Twelve masked couples appeared, all
dressed alike; and after they had entertained the company with
their dancing they put off their masks, to reveal that the leading
couple were Henry himself and his sister Mary, the dowager
Queen of France. When the mummery was over, 'the Admiral
and lords of France heartily thanked the King that it pleased
him to visit them with such disport, and then the King and his
company were banqueted and had high cheer, and then they
all departed every man to his lodgings.'[4]

The various treaties were signed on 4 October, and on the
following day were held the espousals of the Princess Mary and
the Dauphin, whose future marriage was an integral part of the
over-all agreement (although the chronicler Hall claims that
the marriage proposal was merely a pretence, to enable the
French to recover Tournai more easily).[5] The Bishop of
London, Dr. Cuthbert Tunstall, delivered an oration, and the
French ambassadors asked the consent of the King and Queen
to the marriage contract, which was duly given. Wolsey then
placed a small ring with a large diamond on the first joint of
the Princess's finger, and Bonnivet, who stood proxy for the
Dauphin, moved it over the second joint. According to one
observer, the child, who was dressed in cloth of gold covered
with jewels, with a black velvet cap, and who seems to have
only partly understood what was going on, afforded some light
relief by enquiring of the French ambassador: 'Are you the
Dauphin of France? If you are, I wish to give you a kiss.'
Finally, the marriage contract was signed on the high altar.[6]

On Thursday 7 October jousts were held in which Henry

---

[1] *VC* ii, 1085.

[2] A dicing game in which the chances are complicated by a number of arbitrary
rules.

[3] Hall, p. 595.   [4] Hall, p. 595; *VC* ii, 1085.   [5] Hall, p. 594.

[6] *VC* ii, 1085, 1088.

shivered eight lances. Bonnivet rewarded this performance with the gift of a fine horse. In the evening came the final banquet, which exceeded in splendour all the other entertainments. The table was in the form of an enormous horseshoe, at the head of which sat Henry, with Catherine on his right and his sister Mary on his left. On Catherine's right came Wolsey, a duchess, Bonnivet, a lady, the Spanish ambassador, another lady, the Venetian ambassador, and so on in descending order of precedence. The other wing was balanced by Cardinal Campeggio on Mary's left, the Bishop of Paris, another of the French ambassadors, the Danish ambassador and so on, each man paired with a lady of the English Court. The unknown Italian correspondent who has already been quoted[1] was impressed by the magnificence of the plate and drinking vessels. He records that 'on the buffet were 82 vases of pure gold of various sorts, the smallest being the size of a tall glass, one foot high, and amongst them were four drinking cups two feet high, and four similar flasks, and two salt cellars, which were not used for the service of the table, though all the guests drank out of gold, and the silver vessels were innumerable.'[2] On the other hand, the English chronicler Hall is more concerned with what the company ate: 'a banquet of two hundred and sixty dishes; and after that a voidee[3] of spices with sixty spice plates of silver and gilt, as great as men with ease might bear'.[4]

After supper the whole company, except the Queen, who was pregnant and wished to rest, went into the great hall, where a masque was performed. It had been specially written for the occasion, and opened with the appearance of a man on a winged horse who explained that his steed was Pegasus. He had flown to the whole world to announce the peace and the proposed marriage of Mary to the Dauphin; and the whole world was singing about these great events. He, however, was not much of a singer himself, and he therefore invited two twelve-year-old children to deputize for him, which they did with great success. Then a curtain was drawn back to reveal a magnificent stage set—a castle standing upon a rock, in which was a cave contain-

[1] See above, p. 235.   [2] *VC* ii, 1088.
[3] 'A collation consisting of wine accompanied by spices, comfits, or the like, partaken of before retiring to rest or the departure of guests' (*O.E.D.*).
[4] Hall, p. 595.

ing nine beautiful maidens, like radiant goddesses. Outside the cave sat nine youths, and the minstrels played off stage.

On the rock grew five trees, an olive, a rose, a fir, a pome-granate, and (presumably invented for the occasion) a lily. Between the olive and the rose sat a little girl about three years old (Princess Mary was nearing her third birthday). She was dressed as a queen, and had a representation of a dolphin in her lap. (At this time 'Dauphin' was commonly spelt 'Dolphin' in England.) Pegasus's rider provided a commentary for the benefit of the spectators. The rock was the rock of peace. The olive tree was given to the Pope because it signified peace; the fir to the Emperor, as it was the tallest and strongest; the lily to the King of France, since being beautiful and odoriferous, it was well suited to him; the pomegranate was round and golden, and therefore appropriate for the King of Spain, who was lord well nigh of the whole globe, and very wealthy; and the rose went to the King of England, because it was his emblem, and being beautiful, of a fine colour, and exquisitely scented, it was rightfully his. All these potentates rejoiced at the new peace, as did the whole world.

This, however, was instantly disputed by a Turk who had been hovering in the wings ever since the beginning of the mask. He was in the world, and he did not rejoice at an alliance directed against him. He produced fifteen armed men, who fought a tournament against fifteen representing the allies, and when it was over (it may be assumed that the allies won, although the chronicler does not say so) the youths and maidens gave a display of dancing to the music of lutes and other instruments.

The end of the mask was the signal for yet another banquet. 'One hundred courses of eatables, made neither of meat, nor of eggs, nor of cheese, nor of fish, though how made would be long to narrate, were served. These dishes were put on table before the King and after His Majesty and the grandees had partaken of them, there was a scramble for the rest,' and for comfits which Henry threw among the Frenchmen. At the end of the evening the King distributed silver drinking cups to his guests, and presented the robe he was wearing—it was of stiff gold brocade, lined with ermine—to Bonnivet; and so the final entertainment came to an end. Before the French ambassadors left London, however, further gifts were showered upon them. Bonnivet received plate worth 3,000 crowns, and three horses; the Bishop of Paris and the other ambassadors also received generous quantities of plate; the gentlemen in waiting had plate and apparel worth 500 crowns each; and the other gentlemen of the embassy had 4,000 crowns to divide between them. Finally, the ambassadors were given a fine suit of armour to take back to their royal master.[1]

Some idea of the administrative effort occasioned by the decision to return Tournai to France may be gathered from an enumeration of the instruments needed to make it effective. In the first place there is the commission authorizing the Duke of Norfolk, Treasurer and Marshal of England, the Bishop of Durham, Keeper of the Privy Seal, the Earl of Worcester, Lord Chamberlain, and the Bishop of Ely to treat with the French ambassadors about the surrender of the city, the Abbey of St. Amand, and the castle of Mortagne. This was issued on 1 October,[2] although the discussions with the ambassadors had been in progress for some days before this. Then comes the treaty itself, signed on 4 October, of which the French counterpart survives,[3] and Henry's oath sworn 'sur le canon de la messe et Sainctes Evangilles par nous prestement touchées que nous entretiendrons et ferons entretenir inviolablement le traicte de la délivrance de Tournai', which pledged him to observe the terms of the treaty.[4] This completed the first round of documents.

It was, of course, still necessary to obtain and record Francis's agreement to the terms of the treaty as accepted by his ambassadors. A commission was therefore issued on 9 November to Worcester, the Bishop of Ely, Thomas Docwra, Prior of St. John's, and Sir Nicholas Vaux, captain of Guines, to enable them to take Francis's oath that he would observe the articles signed in London;[5] Worcester and his colleagues were also provided with a form of receipt for the 50,000 crowns which Francis was to pay for the return of the city;[6] and the Governor

---

[1] This account is based on Giustiniani (*VC* ii, 1089); the anonymous Italian (*VC* ii, 1088); and Hall, p. 595.
[2] C 82/476 $\frac{10}{104}$; *LP* ii, 4467.
[3] Rymer, p. 642; *LP* ii, 4476.
[4] PRO 31/8/137, f. 110; *LP* ii, 4476.
[5] C 82/467 $\frac{10}{135}$; *LP* ii, 4654, 1 (v).
[6] C 82/467 $\frac{10}{135}$; *LP* ii, 4654, 1 (vi).

of Calais, Sir Richard Wingfield, Sir William Sandys, his treasurer, and others were authorized to receive this money.[1] Next in the chain of instruments is a commission to Worcester and his colleagues to hand over Tournai, St. Amand, and Mortagne on the payment of the sum agreed;[2] and a writ to the Governor, Sir Richard Jerningham, to allow the French to take possession.[3]

The decision to restore Tournai was, of course, only one element in a much wider complex of agreements, which included the general treaty of peace, the contract of marriage between Mary and the Dauphin, the proposal that Henry and Francis should meet face to face, and that the French King should bind himself to stop attacks by Frenchmen on English shipping in the Channel. All these matters gave rise to as many instruments as did the Tournai agreement, necessitating many thousands of words of careful drafting.

The Tournai treaty is itself linked with the general peace treaty and the marriage contract. Friendship between England and France is to be strengthened by the marriage of Henry's daughter Mary to the Dauphin of France; and on account of the marriage and to remove all suspicion between the two sovereigns it is agreed that Tournai shall be handed over to France. The terms of the agreement are then set out in detail. Within forty days of the ratification of the treaty Henry or his deputy will hand over Tournai, the Tournaisis, Mortagne, and St. Amand in return for 600,000 gold crowns; of this, the first 50,000 will be paid the day the French take over the city, and the balance thereafter every six months, on 1 May and 1 November, at the rate of 25,000 francs (in gold crowns) until the whole sum is liquidated. Francis agrees to bind himself by letters patent to make these payments, and also to appear before a judge and two notaries to promise to make payment in the manner specified, under pain of excommunication if he defaults. He is also to require the notaries to draw up a public instrument confirming that this has been done, which is to be handed to the representatives of the King of England.

It is further agreed that the cost of any damage suffered by the French Crown or by the citizens of Tournai, as a result of

---

[1] C 82/467 $\frac{19}{135}$; *LP* ii, 4654, 1 (vii).   [2] C 82/468 $\frac{10}{138}$; *LP* ii, 4654, 6 (i).
[3] C 82/468 $\frac{19}{138}$; *LP* ii, 4654, 6 (ii).

the English occupation, shall be written off. The citizens will enjoy the privileges which they had before the English took over, and Francis will forgive them any penalties they may have incurred by swearing allegiance to Henry—provisions for which the Tournaisiens later expressed their gratitude to the English King. One of the clauses in the treaty presents something of a mystery. It says that Francis shall be responsible for paying Henry the unpaid balance of the 50,000 gold crowns that the Tournaisiens promised to pay Henry when they capitulated in 1513; but this was received by Sir Robert Dymock in 1516,[1] and the reference in the treaty is to the unpaid balance of the annual tribute the city agreed to pay for ten years, over and above the tribute they had been accustomed to pay the French Crown.

Henry is allowed to remove all gunpowder, cannon, fire-arms, cannon-balls of stone, iron, and lead, offensive and defensive weapons, victuals, and military supplies generally. Francis will make available the men, horses, and carts needed to transport these stores, but at Henry's expense.

The other main provision of the treaty is that Francis is required to provide as many hostages as Henry deems necessary as a guarantee that he will abide by the treaty. These must be noblemen, who will remain in England until the terms of the treaty are finally fulfilled, which was, of course, a long way in the future, since the agreement to return Tournai was linked with the marriage contract, which, given the tender age of the betrothed couple, could not be fulfilled for many years. If any of the hostages should die within the material period he is to be replaced no later than one month after the fact has been notified to the French King; and it is open to Francis to replace any hostage at any time with one of equal status. The loose drafting of this clause—there is no indication as to how many hostages is a reasonable number—caused trouble during the final stages of the negotiation in Paris.

We are indebted to the assiduous reporting of Sebastian Giustiniani, the Venetian ambassador in London, for much of the surviving information about the French embassy to London. We are equally indebted to his brother Antonio, the Venetian

[1] E 36/256, p. 383; *LP* ii, p. 1512.

ambassador in Paris, for the background of the final stages of
the negotiations in Paris in December. He wrote to the Signory
from Chartres on 13 November to say that, except for Bonnivet,
the French ambassadors were home again. According to Francis
they had brought good news which would be announced later.
The Court was shortly going to Paris to receive 'with great
honour' an embassy from England.[1]

About the same time the official news of their impending
change of sovereign was broken to the citizens of Tournai. Sir
Richard Jerningham summoned the *Chefs de la Loi* on Thursday
18 November to tell them that he had received letters from the
King, setting out the details of his alliance with France and the
proposed marriage of the Dauphin and Mary, 'par lequel
traittié ceste ville seroit en briefz jours remist es mains dudit
Roy de France'. Two days later this welcome news was passed
on to a meeting of the four councils.[2]

The ambassadors appointed by Henry to finish off the negotiations in Paris—the Earl of Worcester, Nicholas West, Bishop
of Ely, Sir Thomas Docwra, and Sir Nicholas Vaux—were an
experienced team, and Worcester in particular knew English
Tournai and its problems as well as anybody. They sent a
stream of reports back to Henry and Wolsey, which give a full
picture of their journey to Paris and the course of the final
negotiations there.

Their first dispatch, from Calais on 21 November, shows how
difficult travel was in the sixteenth century, even when the
travellers had all the resources of the government behind them.
The weather at first seems to have been not too bad for the time
of year. The ambassadors reached Dover on Saturday 13
November, and next day crossed to Calais without incident
(except that the Bishop of Ely was more seasick than he had
ever been before),[3] having left at Dover most of their retinue,
horses, baggage, and carriages. The transports made a second
crossing with more of their belongings, and then returned to
Dover, hoping to complete the operation within a day or two.
'Howbeit, by force of tempests which came out of the south-east
some of them [i.e. the ships] were perished and drowned, some
broken, and the residue sore hurt.' Not one of the transports

---

[1] *VC* ii, 1113.   [2] Hocquet (a), 1.
[3] SP 1/17, ff. 184–5; *LP* ii, 4582.

was left seaworthy. They were repaired and recaulked with great speed under the direction of the mayor of Dover, but it was not until 23 November that six ships were fit to sail again, and on that day they carried over another instalment of horses and baggage. This still left many servants and more than 140 horses in Dover, and the ambassadors had to wait a few days longer for them to catch up. Worcester told Wolsey that they found the delay very distressing, as it meant that they were unable to 'accomplish the King's high pleasure and command-ment with such diligence as we would'.[1]

The embassy left Calais for Boulogne on Saturday 27 November, exactly two weeks after sailing from Dover. The Governor of Boulogne, de la Fayette, had warned them in advance that it was not possible to put up such a huge number 'in clean houses without danger', so it was arranged that Sir Nicholas Vaux should take some of the gentlemen via Guines direct to Montreuil, where they would all rendezvous on 29 November. Worcester hoped that with luck they would get to the outskirts of Paris on Saturday 4 December, 'albeit the ways be very deep and foul', making three weeks for the whole journey.[2]

They were met half a mile outside Boulogne by de la Fayette, who, after a cordial welcome, escorted them to their lodgings 'with a great triumph and shooting of guns'. Next day he feasted them in the castle, and said that they could have the gates opened at any hour of the day or night—a privilege which they were hardly likely to want to use. Some of the King's harbingers had been sent from Paris to show the embassy the quickest route, but they had to make a detour right at the start. The causeway leading from the town in the direction of Montreuil was impassable, and they had to take a boat over the harbour to find a road that could safely be used.[3]

They reached Montreuil on 29 November, in the middle of the afternoon, after a journey of about twelve hours. On the way they met a dispatch rider with an urgent message from Francis for de la Fayette, who was accompanying them. Dor-val, who was to look after them in Amiens, could not get there before Thursday 2 December, and the King wanted everything

---

[1] Cal. D VII, f. 37; *LP* ii, 4594.   [2] Cal. D VII, f. 39; *LP* ii, 4613.
[3] Cal. D VII, f. 39 b; *LP* ii, 4613.

to be just right before the Englishmen arrived in the town. Would de la Fayette therefore ensure that they did not reach Amiens before Friday 3 December, to give Dorval plenty of time to organize things? Worcester reluctantly agreed, consoling himself with the thought that Tuesday was St. Andrew's Day, when it would in any case be appropriate to rest; but he was already worried by their slow progress. He bitterly regretted his decision, for the lodgings provided in Montreuil were 'very evil', and he and his fellows could not wait to leave them.[1]

It is hardly surprising that the embassy found Montreuil intolerable, for it was a small town, incapable of playing host to several hundred men and horses—the latter being just as difficult to provide for as human beings. No doubt, after argument with de la Fayette, who was under strict instructions to delay them, they insisted on moving on to Abbeville on 1 December. Here they were met by the Bishop of Amiens (with apologies for the absence of his father, who normally would have received them, but he was old and feeble), the Governor of the castle with his retinue, mounted on great horses, and the mayor and burgesses. The latter presented them with three puncheons of wine (about three hundred gallons); and later the Bishop invited them and the gentlemen in their train to his father's house. They were received in the gallery by the old man, who had 'no more use of reason than a child', and then sat down to a 'right great supper with abundance of all delicacies in these parts'.[2]

The Bishop of Amiens also had been briefed to delay the ambassadors. He suggested that they should mark time in Abbeville, again on the ground that it would take at least a day to get everything ready in Amiens. Dorval was bringing so many noblemen with him that the town would be filled to overflowing. It would have to be divided in two, half for the English and half for the French. By now Worcester was becoming very impatient at the delays, but the Bishop was adamant. The whole of Thursday must be spent in Abbeville. The embassy was allowed to move forward again at eight o'clock on the morning of Friday 3 December, and reached Amiens at two in the afternoon.

They searched high and low for Dorval, who was supposed

---

[1] Cal. D VII, f. 41; *LP* ii, 4617.   [2] Cal. D VII, f. 43; *LP* ii, 4638.

to be so busily engaged finding them quarters; but he was nowhere to be found. Nor was there any sign of the mayor and burgesses, who also had been expected to meet them; and Worcester complained that 'it was a great season ere we saw or spake with any of them'. When the civic dignitaries put in an appearance they apologized and said that they had not expected their visitors to arrive so early in the day. Worcester, however, discovered that the truth of the matter was that Dorval had gone off hawking on the other side of the town, and the citizens had decided that protocol precluded them from greeting the ambassadors before the King's representative had done so. 'Fearing that they would be blamed by the King their master' for failing to meet the Englishmen with due ceremony, they were especially generous with their gifts—carp, pike, trout, barbels, crayfish, and eels, together with 400 gallons of wine to wash them down.

It must have dawned on Worcester and his colleagues by this time that Francis had an ulterior motive in delaying their progress. The mayor and burgesses probably confirmed their suspicions when they came to them and said that they had been greatly at fault in not receiving their distinguished guests with due ceremonial. They must be allowed to make amends by putting on a great dinner for them on the following day. Worcester replied that, much as he and his fellow ambassadors would like to accept the invitation, they must reluctantly decline. They had been so long on their journey, 'by reason of sea and otherwise', that they must tarry no longer. He told Wolsey that to make it difficult for the citizens to press their invitation 'we feigned that we had received letters from the King's highness and your grace wherein ye not only marvelled that we tarried so long by the way but also gave us straight commandment diligently to speed us to the French King, and not to make our abode in any place one whole day.' Unfortunately, feeling perhaps that he must not lay down the law in France, he added: 'Without it were the pleasure and express commandment of the French King.'

He thus played into Dorval's hands. The Frenchman promptly said it *was* Francis's pleasure that the ambassadors should tarry. The King needed time to organize the appropriate festivities in Paris. His own ambassadors had given him such glowing accounts of 'the great cheer and entertaining' they had enjoyed in London that he feared that French hospitality might appear to be second to English. 'And so,' Worcester sadly told Wolsey, 'we are in a manner forced to tarry here.' The three separate banquets which were provided, there being no dining-hall in the town big enough to take the whole embassy at one sitting, were poor compensation for yet another delay.

On Sunday 5 December they were allowed to escape from the hospitality of Amiens; and because the towns that still lay between them and Paris were so small they had to divide their forces. Worcester and the Bishop of Ely took half the English party to Breteuil-sur-Noye. Docwra and Sir Nicholas Vaux took the rest to Montdidier, while the French company 'went another way betwixt both', probably through Ailly-sur-Noye. The plan was for all three parties to meet on Tuesday 7 December at Senlis, about twenty-five miles from Paris. The news had come through, however, that Francis now wanted the ambassadors to delay their arrival until Sunday 11 December, ostensibly because the Court could not be assembled before then. In telling Wolsey about this new delay Worcester added that it was known that the King 'had gone a-hunting ten or twelve leagues beyond Paris'. The real reason for the delaying tactics employed by the French is not clear, but they occasioned some comment at the time. Writing to the Signory on 6 December, Antonio Giustiniani said that Francis had left Paris 'until after the entry of the English ambassadors' because the King of England had been absent from London when *his* ambassadors arrived there.[1]

The three parties duly reassembled in Senlis on the appointed day. The citizens were ready with a gift of fish and wine—only two hundred gallons, perhaps because a small town could afford no more. As soon as the French contingent arrived, Dorval hastened to inform Worcester that Francis wanted them to remain in Senlis all next day because it was Our Lady's Day, on which it was not convenient for noblemen to travel. On Thursday they would go on to St. Denis. On Friday they would formally enter Paris and, with luck, would have their first audience with Francis on Saturday.[2]

---

[1] *VC* ii, 1125.   [2] Cal. D VII, ff. 46–46 b; *LP* ii, 4638.

Worcester ended his dispatch with a plea that was almost common form. He said that since leaving England 'we never had one letter from the King's highness nor from your grace, which is to us a great discomfort'; and he begged Wolsey to send answers to questions put to him in earlier dispatches. The Bishop of Ely added a postscript, reporting that the gentlemen in their retinue were comporting themselves 'soberly and sub-stantially' as Wolsey had ordered; and he had no doubt that they would continue to do so to the King's honour. They had been generally praised for their appearance and excellent manners; and in Senlis an Observant Friar had gone so far as to preach a sermon demanding that all the noblemen of France should follow the good example set by the ambassadors' train.[1]

The embassy reached St. Denis on Thursday 9 December and next day were entertained to dinner by the Abbot of St. Denis. Afterwards—about one o'clock in the afternoon—they set off for Paris, accompanied by Dorval and a hundred gentlemen of Francis's household. They were met in the outskirts of the city by the *prévôt* and burgesses, who gave them a hearty welcome; and as they rode to their lodgings 'there were divers gentlemen that met us masked of which some rode amongst us and some met us in divers places standing still and beholding us until we were past them.' For reasons he does not explain, Worcester concluded that Francis himself was one of the masked men who subjected them to this strange scrutiny. He told Henry that their retinue marched in splendid order and that it would have gladdened his heart to see them. The French for their part said that they had never seen such a brilliant embassy in Paris, although the Venetian ambassador commented that there was some surprise at the small number of horses in the ambassadors' train—fewer than two hundred.[2]

When all the Englishmen were settled in their lodgings, where the King had provided wine 'according to every man's degree' and the citizens had sent hippocras and comfits, Bonnivet and de Villeroi called on Worcester to welcome the ambassadors in the King's name; and it was arranged that their first meeting with Francis should take place on Sunday 12 December, twenty-nine days after they had left England.[3]

[1] Cal. D VII, f. 49 b; *LP* ii, 4639. [2] *VC* ii, 1126.
[3] Cal. D VII, ff. 51-51 b; *LP* ii, 4652.

The talks began on Sunday 12 December, when Francis formally received the English ambassadors, first in the presence of the whole Court, and then privately, when he made a long speech about 'the singular love and mind' which Henry bore to him and which he heartily reciprocated. From now on he would regard himself and his subjects as Englishmen, and Henry and *his* subjects as Frenchmen; and to prove that he was in earnest he would set about learning English. Although the alliance now established between the two countries was strong, he believed that when he and Henry had their long-awaited meeting it would become so much stronger 'that no pen can write it'. After much more on these lines from both sides the ambassadors withdrew, it having been agreed that they would get down to business on the following day.

The two main outstanding matters were the action that Francis was prepared to take against French pirates who were attacking English shipping, and the number and quality of the hostages, without whom none of the series of treaties would become finally effective. The piracies were taken first. The Englishmen made it plain that unless they stopped forthwith and unless there was compensation for damage already suffered, their instructions were to proceed no further. The French delegation replied that Francis regretted the activities of the pirates, and had sent commissioners to Normandy, Brittany, and Gascony to ascertain the facts; but they had not yet had time to report. (When they were in Boulogne, the English ambassadors had been assured by the Governor there that Francis was 'sore troubled and greatly displeased' at the piracies, and that they were now being investigated on the spot.[1]) The French team pointed out, however, that they had just heard from Normandy that three or four French ships had been attacked by Englishmen. After a good deal of plain speaking, in the middle of which the French delegation withdrew to study the piracy treaty in detail, it was agreed that both countries were doing all that was expected of them.[2]

The hostages presented more difficulty. It was possible to pretend that the piracy problem was settled, but there could be no pretence about the hostages. A number of bodies, as yet unspecified, had to be physically in London before Tournai was

---

[1] Cal. D VII, f. 39 b; *LP* ii, 4613. [2] Cal. D VII, f. 54; *LP* ii, 4652.

handed over, and that was that. To speed things up the English ambassadors asked for the names of the men to be offered, together with a statement of their qualities, parentage, and income. Ideally all would be 'elder brethren and inheritors of good value'. The French pointed out that the number had never been agreed in London, and suggested four, to which it was replied that Henry might settle for four if they were important enough.[1]

Three days later Worcester reported to Wolsey that they were still having trouble over the hostages. The French were adamant that they would provide no more than four. No higher number had been mentioned in the earlier negotiations. Further, they claimed that it had been understood that they would not openly be known as hostages, but simply as servants of Queen Catherine. Now that it had been noised abroad in Paris that Francis was indeed committed to give hostages, 'certain princes and noblemen be in very great displeasure therewith'. The English ambassadors pointed out that the treaty clearly said that the agreed number was 'such as the King [i.e. Henry] shall be contented with'—which could be any number; and if there had been a leakage about the fact that there were to be hostages, the French themselves were to blame.

Worcester went on to say that they had now received the names of six men, with 'their values and other qualities', from whom Henry would have to choose four. He feared that the King would find them of too low a value, but they were the best that the French would offer. Bonnivet was most anxious that they should be accepted without further argument. He had given his personal assurance that, although they looked unimportant on paper, Francis would be as loth to see them harmed as he would the greatest prince in the land. More important, at least in the eyes of Bonnivet and his colleagues on the embassy to London, who had landed Francis in this mess, was the fact that if the matter was not settled quickly and unobtrusively there might be a political storm that would 'put them out of favour and authority'. Worcester confirmed that there might be trouble, and invited Wolsey to ponder the matter 'according to your high wisdom, and with as hasty expedition as may stand

---

[1] Cal. D VII, ff. 53–54 b; *LP* ii, 4652.

with your pleasure to send us the King's determinate mind and
resolution in this behalf'.[1]

The Bishop of Ely wrote to Wolsey on the same day. His
letter shows that he was acting within the English embassy as
Wolsey's personal ambassador, and is evidence (if more is
needed) of the dominant position that Wolsey held in English
affairs at this time. West had gone to Court with the other
English ambassadors to deliver Henry's letters to the Queen,
and while he was there Francis asked to see him alone. He took
the opportunity of handing over letters from Wolsey to the
King, which had been entrusted to him rather than to the
leader of the mission; and also of saying how profoundly grateful Wolsey was that Francis should have such trust in him. He
for his part had conceived in his mind and heart such a love and
favour towards Francis that henceforth he would be glad to do
him all the pleasure and service he might—saving always his
duty to Henry. The Bishop added that Wolsey had staked his
life, honour, and goods on satisfactory restitution being made
for the depredations of the French pirates; to which Francis
replied that Wolsey had equally engaged his own honour, and
that he would see to it that both were saved.

He further undertook 'that he would enterprise no great
matter' in future without first seeking Wolsey's advice, and
generally gave the impression that he regarded the Englishman
as being one of his own leading councillors. When this satisfactory position had been established, West handed over Wolsey's
formal resignation from the bishopric of Tournai, making it
clear that although he had incurred great expense in purchasing
bulls to support his claim to the see, and in resisting the
machinations of the Bishop elect, he sought nothing in return—
that is nothing more than the pension which he had already
been awarded by Francis. West reported, however, that there
was a general feeling that Wolsey ought to have 'a marvellous
great gift' as a New Year present. He had been consulted as to
what form it should take; and while he said that he had no idea
what Wolsey would want most, he suggested that 'goodly plate
or some other rich jewels' would not come amiss.

It came to Francis's notice at this point, perhaps as a result of
a judicious reminder by West, that the first instalment of

[1] Cal. D VII, ff. 58–9; *LP* ii, 4663.

Wolsey's pension, which was in effect part of the purchase price the French King was paying for Tournai, and which had become due on 1 November, was still unpaid. Francis was furious at the omission, for he realized how important Wolsey was to his cause. Bonnivet, the Bishop of Paris, and the Treasurer of France were all ordered to make West accept the money, but he refused, having no authority from Wolsey. He advised the Frenchmen to 'take some sure means' to make the payment quickly, whereupon they decided to put the transaction 'in a banker's hands'. West, alarmed lest this might mean a loss on the exchange, hastened to warn Wolsey to look out for this when payment was made in London.

A passage at the end of West's letter throws light on Wolsey's standing, at least in his eyes. He explains that they 'have sent two great letters at this time of one tenor', one addressed to the King and the other to Wolsey. This was necessary because of a difference of opinion between him and Worcester, who wanted to send a detailed account of their negotiations to the King, and no more than a brief letter to Wolsey, saying that they had written fully to Henry. West said he was quite sure that Henry would simply pass the dispatch on to Wolsey, being too lazy to read it, but Worcester still insisted that they must write to the King. They compromised by 'doubling' the dispatch and sending the full version to both Henry and Wolsey.[1]

It was not until 14 January that the ambassadors were able to report to Henry that the matter of the hostages had been settled in principle; but it was still necessary to get the four chosen men to England, if the letter of the treaty was to be observed. Until this was done there could be no question of handing over Tournai.[2] In fact, the hostages turned up unexpectedly in Calais on 22 January; and as Calais was English soil, this was good enough for the purposes of the treaty. The four men—de Morette, de Montmorency, de Moy, and de Monpesat—were highly indignant that the authorities in Calais had not been told precisely when they were coming. The Earl of Worcester was waiting at Péronne to hear that they were safely in English hands, before he went to hand over Tournai; and they therefore asked Sir William Sandys, who

[1] Cal. DV II, ff. 60-2; *LP* ii, 4664. [2] Cal. D VII, f. 83; *LP* iii, 23.

received them, that 'the very time and hour' of their arrival
should be notified to Worcester forthwith. This was duly done.
The last obstacle to the surrender of the city was removed.[1]

The differences of opinion during the final stages of the
negotiations did not mar the entertainments, which Francis had
planned with avowed intention of eclipsing Henry's performance in this field.[2] The first ceremonial occasion was in Notre
Dame Cathedral on 14 December, when Francis swore to
adhere to the peace treaty, and signed the oath in the presence
of two notaries, as he was bound to do.[3] Afterwards the congregation adjourned to dinner in the Bishop of Paris's palace,
'where a royal feast with abundance of all delicacies and all
manner melody according to the honour of so great a prince'
was provided. Two days later the betrothal ceremony was performed in the chapel of the *Tournelles*, and again there was
feasting afterwards.[4]

The principal entertainment was the dinner in honour of the
English ambassadors held on 22 December. According to one
estimate, it cost Francis upwards of 450,000 crowns, or three-
quarters of the sum he had agreed to pay Henry for Tournai.
Several accounts have survived, mostly by Italians living in
Paris; and taken together they provide a detailed picture of one
of the great social functions of Francis's reign.

Francis had chosen for the occasion the great courtyard of the
Bastille, which was big enough to hold the huge company. It
was approached by a long broad street, arched over with
branches of boxwood and laurel, and adorned with the
armorial bearings of the King and his leading nobles. The
splendour of the courtyard was heightened by the contrast
between its vastness and the narrow passage which led the
crowds of guests in from the street. They found themselves in a
miniature universe, ablaze with light. The sky was bright blue

---

[1] SP 1/18, f. 14; *LP* iii, 37. Service as a hostage was not only potentially dangerous, it could be very costly. Francis wrote to Henry at the end of 1519 to tell
him that the four hostages, who were supposed to remain in England for 14 years,
had missed valuable offers of marriage. He thought it right that they should now
be exchanged for others (Rymer, p. 732; *LP* ii, 4687; *LP* iii, 532).

[2] Cal. D VII, f. 91.   [3] Rymer, p. 661; *LP* ii, 4649.

[4] Cal. D VII, ff. 55–55 b; *LP* ii, 4652, 4655; *VC* ii, 1129. (Antonio Giustiniani
wrongly dates these two ceremonies 13 and 15 December.)

linen powdered with stars and golden fleurs-de-lis. The twelve signs of the zodiac were round the horizon, and from the dome of the sky hung golden balls representing the planets, and twelve chandeliers each with twelve torches. Round the walls of the improvised banqueting-hall, which were hung with cloth of gold, were innumerable sconces each holding its flaming torch; and three galleries, richly decorated with tapestry had been erected one above the other round the courtyard for the ladies. Although the guests did not see it as they emerged from the gloom into this brilliant scene, the whole courtyard was covered over with waxed sail-cloth to keep off the rain. It might have been worth while risking an open-air function in the summer, but hardly in the middle of December.

At one end of the courtyard, which was floored with wooden planks covered with drugget, was a raised platform for the King and his principal guests, of whom the most important were four Cardinals and the English ambassadors. The platform was surmounted by a canopy of intertwined evergreens from which hung oranges and three golden lilies. A smaller canopy of cloth of gold was suspended over the King's chair, which itself was covered with cloth of gold, and in large tubs round the platform there were trees festooned with apples, pears, and oranges. Two long tables for the retinue of the English ambassadors and Francis's French guests stretched across the courtyard at right angles to the high table; and in each of the four corners were cupboards displaying many rich vessels of gold and silver—a regular feature of the sixteenth-century banquet.

The evening began with dancing. Then, after water had been brought for the King to wash his hands, they sat down to supper, Francis having his sister the Duchess of Alençon next to him. (The Queen watched the proceedings from one of the galleries overlooking the high table.) While the guests were being seated the minstrels struck up 'in the Italian fashion', and the entry of the viands on large dishes, 'some of which emitted fire and flames', was announced by a procession of eight trumpeters, the archers of the King's guard, five heralds, and the eight seneschals in ordinary of the household. The Lord Steward, wearing cloth of gold trimmed with sable, brought up the rear. The high-table guests were served from gold dishes by twenty-four pages, and the others were looked after by 200 archers.

As soon as the feast, which lasted four hours, was over, the tables were removed to make space for dancing, and those who did not want to dance went into the galleries to watch. Several companies of maskers performed, 'all pompous with new liveries of cloth of gold and silver'; and then, when all had had their fill of dancing—about two hours after midnight—a collation of sugar-plums and other confections was brought in by the ladies, some of whom were dressed in the Italian fashion 'in damask, satin, and velvet of several sorts, with gold embroidery representing foliage, fruit, fish and other fanciful things slashed about their apparel', and some in the French fashion, wearing cloth of gold and silver. At length the company broke up and exchanged the brilliance and warmth and make-believe of the improvised banqueting-hall for the cold and dark reality of the December night.[1]

Mortagne, which was part and parcel of the territory of Tournai, although some miles to the south-east of the city, was in the possession of Antoine de Ligne, Count of Faulconberg. There is some doubt as to how the place came into his hands. According to Philibert Naturelli, *prévôt* of Utrecht, Henry had awarded the Castle of Mortagne to the Duke of Suffolk, for services rendered on the 1513 campaign.[2] Suffolk, perhaps being better aware than his sovereign of the disadvantages of owning property in a foreign country, accepted the gift with gratitude, and then got Henry's permission to sell the Castle. His buyer was de Ligne, and, according to Naturelli, he paid 1,000 crowns for the property. Henry gave his blessing to the transaction, for de Ligne had also served in the 1513 campaign, and at least at this time enjoyed Henry's favour. It was understood, however, that the place should be open to the English King at all times.[3]

De Ligne was a difficult man, ambitious but irresponsible. His letters reflect his unstable character. In November 1514 he complained to Henry that enemies had slandered him to the

[1] *VC* ii, 1128, 1132, 1133, 1134.

[2] A note of 'conditions agreed upon between the King of England and the Count of Faulconberg to serve in his wars' is in Vit. B XX, ff. 90–91b.

[3] Le Glay, ii, p. 179; *LP* ii, 4678.

English ambassadors in France;[1] and in the same year he was involved in litigation over payment for wagons he had used in the 1513 campaign.[2] A year later he was badgering Wolsey both direct and through Mountjoy.[3]

When the fate of Tournai was under discussion in 1515 the Governor said that whatever happened to the city Henry must take over Mortagne, which could be had 'for reasonable money'. Apparently he was under the impression that de Ligne owned it. He suggested that the Earl of Worcester should meet the Count to discuss the matter.[4] Worcester shared Mountjoy's view. He told Henry that if he was minded to keep Tournai it was essential to take Mortagne back into his own hands (showing that he at least was aware that de Ligne held the Castle at Henry's pleasure). Worcester pointed out that if the man in possession of Mortagne was hostile to Tournai, as de Ligne was supposed to be, he could interrupt its food supply, and damage it in other ways.[5]

In 1516 Mountjoy was still urging that something must be done about de Ligne. There was a rumour that he had been offered a command in the Spanish army, and the Governor thought that if it was true it would make it easier to get him out of Mortagne.[6] This time his advice was acted on. An embassy which included Sir Edward Poynings was commanded to 'practise for the restitution of the Castle and Lordship of Mortagne'. According to Mountjoy, de Ligne would be happy to return the Castle, were he reasonably compensated. He had spent a good deal of money in improving the fortifications, but he was content to leave compensation for this expenditure to Henry's generosity. Mountjoy's letter to the King is badly burned, but he seems to be saying that the heirs of 'the old Lord of Mortagne' had a claim on the Castle. It would pay Henry to let this claim succeed, and then offer to buy the Castle at a low price. This suggests that he was still under the impression that

---

[1] SP 1/9, f. 189; *LP* i, 3474.   [2] Cal. E I, f. 35; *LP* ii, 3279.
[3] SP 1/12, f. 17; *LP* ii, 1295.   [4] Cal. E I, f. 65; *LP* ii, 825.
[5] Cal. D VI, f. 198 b; *LP* ii, 856. Sir Richard Whethill made the same point in a letter to Wolsey in 1516. Most of Tournai's food and other goods came by water, past the Castle of Mortagne, and it would be easy enough for de Ligne to intercept it if he thought that the garrison was not strong enough to retaliate (SP 1/13, f. 266; *LP* ii, 2260).
[6] SP 1/13, f. 38; *LP* ii, 1622.

Henry had no legal claim to Mortagne. Mountjoy also reported that the King of Spain was highly displeased at the rumour that de Ligne had been given a Spanish military post, which seems to have been invented by the Count himself.[1] However, nothing happened. De Ligne still remained in control of the Castle.

In July 1518, when there was much speculation about the future of Tournai, de Ligne began to feel uneasy about his position. He owed allegiance to Louis XII when he joined forces with Henry in 1513, and he saw that if Tournai returned to France he would be in trouble. It would help to have Wolsey on his side, so he presented him with a fine mule.[2] The English ambassadors were well aware that de Ligne hoped to hold on to his little empire, even after losing the protection of the English garrison in Tournai. While they were still in Calais they wrote to Wolsey that they had learned from Meautis, the King's French secretary, that Sir Edward Poynings had a copy of the patent assigning Mortagne to de Ligne, which reserved the right for the King to put as many soldiers into the Castle as he pleased. Worcester himself was satisfied that de Ligne had to hand the place back whenever he was required to do so; and he asked that Wolsey should send a copy of the patent if he could find it, so that they would be armed against de Ligne, 'for as we here say, he is very obstinate'.[3]

The French, who had a good intelligence service, knew that the Count was going to cause trouble. While the English embassy was making its way to Paris, Dorval reminded Worcester that Henry was bound to hand over Mortagne along with Tournai. There were strong rumours that de Ligne had no intention of giving up the place. If so, would Henry take it by force? Worcester replied diplomatically that there was no reason to believe that there would be any trouble. De Ligne would do whatever Henry told him to do. That was all very well, replied Dorval, but he nevertheless wanted Worcester to know that, if a force had to be sent from Tournai to capture Mortagne, Francis would be glad to supplement it. He had already taken the precaution of sending troops to the frontier, where they would stand by ready for all eventualities. Worcester

---

[1] Cal. E I, f. 101; *LP* ii, 1894.   [2] SP 1/17, f. 99; *LP* ii, 4328.
[3] Cal. D VII, f. 38 b; *LP* ii, 4594.

RESTORATION 257

said that Francis might rest assured that Henry would do whatever was necessary. Dorval said that this made him 'right well
content'.[1]

Worcester, however, was far from content, and he asked
Wolsey for urgent advice. Henry was in honour bound to hand
over Mortagne, and, even if it meant dipping into his own
pocket, he must do it without any help from France. Wolsey
knew the French well enough to realize what 'great bruit and
boast' they would make of it if Henry failed to carry out his
undertaking. 'Wherefore in our poor minds it were both good
and honourable that the King's promise were performed without their help, if so conveniently may be done.'[2] He had been
informed by Jerningham a few days earlier that de Ligne had
no intention of giving up the Castle willingly, and that he had
about 100 workmen strengthening it.[3]

Soon after they reached Paris, Wolsey told the ambassadors
that Henry had written to de Ligne, ordering him to hand over
Mortagne. Worcester replied that, if he refused to obey, they
would need instructions 'for the forcible removing of him by
power . . . to his great displeasure and utter undoing'. Once
again he stressed that it would have to be done without any help
from the French, because Henry's honour was at stake. There
was a more practical reason. If the French were called in to help
Henry to recover his own possession, they expected to be paid,
which was quite reasonable. Thus the peaceful eviction of de
Ligne would protect both Henry's honour and his purse.[4]

All the time the English ambassadors were in Paris the problem of Mortagne remained unsolved. De Ligne seemed to have
every intention of fighting to the last ditch to defend his little
empire. He was boasting, with singular optimism, that both the
Emperor (Henry's ally) and the military leader Robert de la
Marck (Francis's subject) would rally to his cause, bringing
with them 40,000 men—a figure which, if he actually used it,
shows how unbalanced he must have been. According to the
prévôt of Utrecht, if de Ligne did not listen to reason, the French
were prepared to lend Henry some companies of light cavalry,
which would be stationed in St. Amand and the vicinity
of Mortagne, to support any action that the English were

[1] Cal. D VII, f. 48 b; *LP* ii, 4639. [2] Ibid.
[3] Cal. D VII, f. 42; *LP* ii, 4617. [4] Cal. D VII, f. 57; *LP* ii, 4663.

compelled to take. He added that if fighting did break out it could mean great danger to the general peace.[1]

In January there was still no sign that de Ligne was coming to heel. A draft dispatch to the English ambassadors referred to the fact that 'the peaceable deliverance of the said Castle without business or contradiction' seemed to be most unlikely, although the handing-over of Tournai and its associated territories was now imminent. The King was therefore sending Worcester two letters addressed to de Ligne, 'one concerned in courteous manner with credence to you committed and the other containing sharp clauses'. If de Ligne continued to be obstinate, in spite of the 'courteous' approach of the ambassadors, they were to change their tune and hand him the second letter.[2]

When they delivered the polite letter they were to say Henry was astonished that the Count had not obeyed his request to come to England. Indeed, he had done no more than send an obscure temporizing letter. The King was committed to hand Mortagne over to France 'upon right urgent and honourable causes and conditions', but, in view of de Ligne's good service in the 1513 expedition and the fact that he held the Castle by gift from the King,[3] Henry 'will not see him excluded from the same but only by honourable kind and loving means', which could be discussed if de Ligne came to London, which he would have to do very quickly.[4]

However, if the Count continued to be stubborn, the ambassadors were to remind him of his written undertaking to restore the Castle on demand, and to point out that any compensation would be *ex gratia*. If this had no effect, Worcester was to say 'as of himself' that it would be madness for a tiny magnate to challenge the might of France and the Empire— England was carefully left out of it. He would inevitably lose and suffer the direct consequences. If this seemingly personal and friendly plea failed to move the Count, the ambassadors were to produce the 'sharp letter', and solemnly declare that Henry's honour was at stake. He would have to do everything

---

[1] Le Glay, ii, p. 179; *LP* ii, 4678.   [2] Cal. D VII, f. 86; *LP* iii, 41.

[3] This does not necessarily mean that the place was not first given to the Duke of Suffolk.

[4] Cal. D VII, f. 86; *LP* iii, 41.

in his power to throw de Ligne out. The French King had agreed to send troops to Mortagne to join with a force from Tournai.[1]

By this time de Ligne was beginning to see reason, partly because Margaret of Savoy had tried to make him abandon his impossible position. He offered to hand the place over to her, on condition that she should see that he was compensated, both for the Castle and the money he had spent in fortifying it; and she accepted the offer. She explained to Worcester that all she wanted was to avoid bloodshed on her borders, and she hoped that Henry would understand her motives. Worcester replied through Jean de Hesdin, one of her councillors who had brought the message, that he had no authority to bargain about the surrender of Mortagne; and that Clarenceux King of Arms was already on the way to deliver the King's letters to de Ligne. However, if Margaret would hand the Castle over to them, they would gladly receive it, and the question of compensation would be discussed later. De Hesdin said that this would not do. Margaret wanted to wait until she had heard from Henry himself. De Hesdin had a personal interest in the transaction, for he had visited Mortagne two or three times with a retinue of 100 men ostensibly in Henry's service, which had cost him 800 florins; but he was told that he too would have to wait until Henry's pleasure was known.[2]

De Ligne, having thus committed his affairs to Margaret, marched out of Mortagne with his retainers and artillery, and made for his other stronghold at Bailleul in Hainaut. Here he received Henry's 'peremptory letter'. He wrote to the Governor of Tournai, saying that it was more severe than he deserved, but, in view of the threats made against him, and his desire not to break the peace just concluded, he had decided to throw his hand in. He had given the place to Margaret, and he left it to Henry to decide what compensation he deserved.[3]

The Count realized that he had been playing with fire, for he discreetly kept out of the way during the final stages of the transaction. The formal instrument through which he gave up

[1] Cal. D VII, f. 86 b; *LP* ii, 41.

[2] SP 1/18, ff. 26 b–27; *LP* iii, 58; SP 1/16, f. 125; *LP* ii, 3911. (The latter document is shown under the wrong year—1518—both in the volume of manuscripts and in the *LP*.)

[3] SP 1/18, f. 26; *LP* iii, 58; Cal. D VII, f. 85; *LP* iii, 52.

possession of the place—'the town, Castle, lands, and Seigneury of Mortagne'—was completed on 8 February, and still assigned the property to de Hesdin. The Count regretted that he could not see to the hand-over in person, partly because he was seriously ill, and partly because he was engaged in very important business elsewhere.[1]

Nevertheless, he was well enough and had leisure enough to write to Henry on the same day. He understood that the King was very angry with him for having delivered Mortagne to Margaret; but of course he would not have dreamed of doing this had she not made it perfectly clear that it was Henry's intention that he should do so, in order that she might pass the place on to him. Indeed, this was the impression that Henry's letters had given. Finally, the rumours that he had intended to hand the Castle direct to the French, in return for payment, were of course completely without foundation.[2]

The final act in this miniature drama came when the English ambassadors informed Wolsey on 11 February that they had received the town and Castle of Mortagne from de Ligne by the hands of de Hesdin, and duly surrendered them to de Coligny, the French King's commissioner.[3]

Worcester and his colleagues set out from Péronne on the last stage of their journey to Tournai on 27 January. It was only about fifty miles away, but they wanted to have plenty of time to make the necessary preparations for handing over the city. They also wanted to make sure that the English troops were in good order, so that they would march out 'to the King's honour' when the hand-over took place. It would be humiliating to lead

---

[1] Rymer, p. 693; Hocquet (a), lii; LP iii, 66: 'Et pour ce que nous ne povons estre de notre personne à faire la dite rendition et debvoirs en ce pertinens tout à cause d'aulcunes grandes maladies, comme aultres noz grans et urgens affaires à nous presentement survenus.'

[2] Galba B V, f. 375; LP ii, 3930. (This document is wrongly placed in 1518 in LP.)

[3] Rymer, p. 694; LP iii, 71: Cal. D VII, f. 93; LP iii, 72. It was not long before de Ligne realized that he had made a mistake in trying to retain Mortagne. He wrote to Henry in April, offering his services and apologizing for not coming to England as he had been ordered to do. He had been unable to make the journey, for reasons which he had already explained to the King (LP iii, 201). He asked Wolsey to help him in July, when he said that he regretted losing the King's favour, but not the Castle (Cal. D VII, f. 147; LP iii, 387).

ill-disciplined companies in full view of the critical eyes of some of the leading soldiers in France. The ambassadors reckoned that it would take them five or six days to put everything in readiness.[1]

Before they left Péronne they met Gaspard de Coligny, Marquis de Châtillon, who had been commissioned by Francis to receive Tournai on his behalf, and suggested that the French should pay right away the 50,000 francs that were due on the surrender of the town. This would make it easier to issue the garrison's final pay, and their conduct money. Indeed, if the 50,000 were paid in advance, Worcester said 'we would have voided all the soldiers out of the town the same day that they (the French) should have entered; and moreover we offered them that I, the King's Chamberlain, my Lord of St. John's and Master Vaux would tarry still with them as pledges.' The French commissioners refused to co-operate, however. They pointed out that the treaty required them to pay up only when the town was theirs, and they would not be moved. The Englishmen explained that all they had wanted to do was to pay the garrison in French crowns, 'to spare some of the King's nobles'; but they did not press this balance-of-payments point. Although the two sets of commissioners ostensibly parted good friends after this meeting, it seems that the acrimony which marked the transfer of the city dated from this time. Worcester said that the English side would, of course, stick to their part of the bargain. They would proceed forthwith to Tournai, to be ready to hand over the city; but he reminded the Frenchmen that there was no question of doing this until the French hostages were safely in English hands.[2]

The English party arrived in Tournai on 30 January, and at once wrote to Robert Fowler in Calais, asking him to send money for the soldiers' wages and conduct money. They hoped that the King would approve of this arrangement, which at least meant that the 50,000 francs due from the French could now be remitted intact to London. Further they claimed that it had the advantage that 'the King's honour should therein be saved, that his garrison should be paid without the Frenchmen's money', a point which had apparently not weighed heavily with them when they asked de Coligny for payment in advance

[1] SP 1/18, f. 25; *LP* iii, 58.   [2] Ibid.

for the specific purpose of paying the garrison. It also meant that the soldiers could be paid off sooner, and the King would thus save five or six days' wages. Many of them were in debt, and the commissioners thought that it would be unfortunate if the French arrived before they had had a chance of settling with their creditors. Worcester hoped that Henry and Wolsey would agree that they had done the right thing 'for the King's honour and profit' in arranging for money to come from Calais.[1]

The day after the English ambassadors arrived in Tournai they met the four councils and the Dean and Chapter in accordance with the King's instructions—meetings which protocol required to be repeated with the French commissioners. The citizens said that they were deeply grateful to Henry because he 'had so well remembered them and provided for their wealth and surety' in his treaty with Francis. They would be glad to do anything that the King or his commissioners asked of them. Worcester, who had suffered at their hands as much as anybody, was not deceived by this sudden change of heart. The fact remained, he sadly reported, that 'we cannot perceive but they be gladder to return French than to continue English'.

The ambassadors carried letters from Henry addressed to all members of the garrison—the Governor, officers, all the King's servants, and the soldiers. These were duly read out and Worcester was able to assure the King that everyone was 'right well contented thereof'. All were ready and willing to return home and do whatever the King commanded, 'like good and true subjects'.[2] The chronicler Hall, writing a good many years later, gives a less happy account of the soldiers' reaction, and he may well have been right. Worcester was hardly likely to enlarge in his reports to the King on any dissatisfaction that manifested itself during the take-over period.

Under the treaty Henry was allowed to remove the cannon, gunpowder, and cannon-balls from the city, and Worcester and his colleagues considered it important that these things should be 'trussed and shipped' before the French arrived. It was no easy matter to transport heavy guns overland at the best of times, and virtually impossible in the winter; but the river Scheldt flowed through the middle of Tournai, and it was possible to carry the guns and ammunition by water all the way

---

[1] SP 1/18, f. 25 b; *LP* iii, 58.   [2] SP 1/18, ff. 27 b–28; *LP* iii, 58.

to Calais, where it was to be taken over by the master of the ordnance there. Worcester reported on 4 February that 'the guns and ironwork and all that is worth carrying is shipped'; but the wooden gun-carriages and the old wooden gun-wheels had been left behind.[1]

Francis's commissioner, de Coligny, arrived in the neighbourhood of Tournai on 8 February, accompanied by a retinue of 300 nobles and captains, and took up his residence in the house of Jean Grenier, a mile or two from the city. The *Chefs de la Loi* at once came to welcome him, bringing with them a gift of the best Beaune and Rhenish wine that they had been able to lay their hands on. (When they received Henry six and a half years earlier he had to be content with Beaune, and there is no suggestion that they tried to find the best for him.) De Coligny followed Henry's example by restoring their citizenship to all banished men who entered the city with him, or who sought permission to enter within three days of his arrival. He was also required to leave undisturbed the privileges the citizens had enjoyed under English rule, and any ecclesiastical appointments made by Henry or Wolsey.[2]

There was to be some trouble, however, before the English troops marched out of Tournai and the French troops marched in. The last cannon were safely got away on 8 February at crack of dawn, and shortly afterwards the Bishop of Ely and Robert Fowler rode out to receive from de Coligny the 50,000 francs which Francis had contracted to pay before he was allowed to take possession of the city. De Coligny said that he was authorized to hand the money over only after his troops were inside the city walls, and in spite of the Bishop's protests set about putting his men in marching formation. The Bishop indignantly reported to Wolsey that

he caused his trumpets to be blown and displayed both his own banners and the Duke of Vendôme's, M. Piennes', Captain Bayard's and others with their wiffelers banners for conduct of the footmen. And set forth all his artillery and his company on array like as he should have joined battle; and there were shouts made with '*Vive le roi de France!*' And in the same manner M. de Châtillon was in full purpose to have entered into Tournai. The which sight and manner nothing liked me. Wherefore I showed him that it should not stand

[1] SP 1/18, f. 28 b; *LP* iii, 58.   [2] Hocquet (a), lv.

with the King my master's honour to suffer any man to enter into
any town of his in such manner of wise like a conqueror. And that
this town should be delivered to the French King upon covenants of
marriage and upon certain conditions. Wherefore I prayed him to
roll up his banners and not to sound his trumpets at his entry.

De Coligny answered pointedly that he knew rather better how
to enter a town than did the Bishop; and he proposed to make
his entry exactly as he thought fit.

The Bishop insisted that it was quite out of order to seek to
approach the town in warlike fashion, and asked that the French
should stand by until he had had a chance of consulting the
Earl of Worcester. Worcester agreed with the line West had
taken, and sent Clarenceux King of Arms to the French headquarters to demand 'that in no wise he should enter with
sound of trumpets, nor with his banners displayed'. De Coligny,
being well aware that so long as the English troops were inside
the city he had to do what he was told, accepted the inevitable;
and in due course he approached the gates in silence and without flaunting a single banner. The 50,000 francs were paid over
outside the wall, a receipt given, and the keys of the town
handed over. Only then were the French infantry and artillery
allowed to march in, headed by de Coligny, with Worcester on
his right hand to underline the fact that Tournai was being
handed over to France by agreement. At the entrance to the
citadel they were met by the Governor, Sir Richard Jerningham, with a retinue of 100 men, and the keys of the citadel were
also handed over.[1]

To the citizens it must have seemed that the clock had been
put back six and a half years. Once again they owed allegiance
to the French Crown; once again their *Bailli* was Louis de
Proisy, who had held the office in 1513, and had escaped when
the city surrendered to Henry; once again their Bishop was
Louis Guillard, who had been appointed in 1513, and had
striven so valiantly to take up his office, or at least the fruits of
his office, during the whole of the occupation, and who now had
a clear field to make what he wanted of the see. The *Chefs de la
Loi* and the four councils, who had done their best to show
loyalty to Henry and his Governor, could now breathe freely
again, and show whole-hearted allegiance to the man whom all

---

[1] Cal. D VII, ff. 94–5; *LP* iii, 74.

along they must have regarded as their true sovereign. The renegade Jean le Sellier—perhaps the only man who would have considered putting back the clock as a personal disaster— had died two years earlier, and therefore presented no problem either to the municipal authorities or to the English government, although it is likely that he would have been given sanctuary in England.

X · CONCLUSION

WHATEVER Henry may have thought his objectives were when he crossed the Channel to France at the end of June 1513, he cannot have numbered the capture of Tournai among them. Although the expedition was carefully prepared, largely by Wolsey, there is no record of any real attempt to plan the campaign in advance. The usual practice in the sixteenth century was for the commander-in-chief to put himself into the hands of the Almighty, both before a campaign began and before he committed his troops to battle. It would have been presumptuous for the council of war to sit down in England and evolve anything like a detailed plan of campaign. Not only was there no guarantee that providence would afford the general support needed for the success of such a plan, but there were also practical problems, more the responsibility of the council of war, which could not be foreseen months, or even weeks, ahead. The huge agglomeration of ill-assorted companies that made up the sixteenth-century army struggled across the countryside no faster and no more purposefully than a prehistoric monster. Where and when it met the equally ponderous forces of the enemy was largely a matter of chance. Worcester's journey from Calais to Paris at the end of 1518, which should have taken perhaps three days, took three weeks. How much more difficult, therefore, for an army to determine in advance its destination, how long it would take to get there, and what it would attempt to achieve when it arrived.

It was the Emperor, however, rather than providence that led Henry to the walls of Tournai, no doubt in the hope that if the city were taken it would be added to his dominions. Henry may almost be forgiven for embarking on the 1513 campaign. The other monarchs of Europe had more reason for standing up to Louis than he, for he was protected by the English Channel, but it was arguable that someone had to stop French aggression, and he may have been right in taking a hand in the game. Even an aimless campaign in Northern France would demand the attention of a substantial number of Louis' troops.

In any event, the young English King was burning to distinguish himself on the field of battle and any outlet for his military ambition was welcome. His adventure was at worst an excusable gamble from the moment that he landed in Calais to the moment when the Tournaisiens threw in their hand and opened their gates to the besieging forces.

At that point the gamble ceased. The decision to leave a large English force in the city, almost certainly in spite of objections by Maximilian, must have been very largely Henry's, although it was no doubt discussed with his leading advisers, including Wolsey. It was taken in the calm atmosphere of the council chamber, and all who contributed to the discussion must have realized what a costly undertaking the King was embarking on. No record of the discussion has survived, but it seems inevitable that responsibility for the decision must belong mainly to Henry and his Almoner. It is difficult to apportion the blame between them. Did the King think that Tournai was the beginning of a new English empire on the continent of Europe, or perhaps that it was a strong point from which he could exercise a new influence on the European political scene? Did Wolsey share his master's illusions? Or did he encourage them in the knowledge that an English Tournai meant a bishopric for him? The truth probably is that they were equally responsible for the decision to occupy the city, surely one of the most costly of Henry's reign.

At least one authority is quite satisfied that Henry's decision was taken after careful deliberation and in the light of reasoned objections by his principal advisers. Rapin-Thoyras tells us that the King assembled his council of war to consider whether he would be wise to retain possession of Tournai. It was strongly argued that because of its isolation and great distance from Calais it would be very difficult to keep hold of it. However, the King had his way. This was an astonishing decision, especially in view of what had happened at Thérouanne. That heavily-fortified town had been starved into submission, and in spite of the fact that it fell into Henry's hands with its fortifications virtually intact—they were so strong that the English guns made little impression on them even after weeks of siege—he ordered it to be razed. It could have been occupied much more cheaply than Tournai, and although it was well inside the boundaries of France it could probably have been maintained much more easily than Tournai, because of its proximity to Calais. Why, then, did Henry destroy Thérouanne, when it seemed to be an outpost of Calais, and go to the trouble of retaining Tournai, which was anything but a natural outpost?

Rapin's answer is quite simple. It was Wolsey who was responsible for the different fate of the two places. Thérouanne had nothing to offer him, but the bishopric of Tournai was a tempting morsel which caught his eye. It was certainly for this reason that the English kept Tournai; and perhaps it was also for this reason that the siege was undertaken in the first place. Wolsey, according to Rapin, was able to get Henry and his Councillors to do just what he wanted.[1] It seems likely, however, that there is a good deal of hindsight in this judgement, and that it is unfair to Wolsey. It was probably Maximilian who persuaded Henry to destroy Thérouanne; and it was almost certainly Maximilian who led Henry to Tournai. At some stage, probably after the English troops had entered the city, Wolsey must have realized that the occupation might hold something for him. It was most unlikely that the Bishop elect would take the oath of loyalty to Henry. The see would fall vacant, and Wolsey would fall heir to it. It was Maximilian's cunning, however, rather than Wolsey's ambition that made all this possible.

It is perhaps pointless to consider seriously whether Tournai was intended to be a colony or an integral part of Henry's realm. The whole episode of the capture and occupation of the city was a mistake, and it may be flattering the King to suggest that he ever pondered deeply the status of his new territory. Certainly at the outset it seems as if Tournai was intended to become part of England. The presence of representatives from the city at the Parliament of 1514 indicates that at that stage something like full integration was in the King's mind. This is confirmed by the reciprocal trading rights which were legislated for in that Parliament, and by the proposal to use the Court of Chancery as the city's appeal court. Indeed, the status which Tournai had formerly had in relation to France—that is to say that it was part of the French King's dominions, although

---

[1] Rapin, p. 70.

isolated from them—was for all practical purposes duplicated, with England taking the place of France.

The promise of the early months was not fulfilled, however. The great distance from London meant that the city had if anything to be even more independent than it had been under French rule. It also meant that on those occasions when policy matters had to be discussed with London it took a very long time to get a decision. The process of seeking guidance from England, which in practice meant from Henry and Wolsey, if not simply from Wolsey himself, was further bedevilled by the municipal authorities' practice of sending delegations of the leading citizens to discuss matters in London which should have been settled on the spot, or at least referred home by the Governor. Much of the communication between London and the municipal authorities would never have taken place if there had been any goodwill on the part of the city. The four councils, however, regarded the Governor not as their highest authority, but rather as the representative of a foreign power who had to be bargained with. If his decisions were unpalatable they assumed the right to appeal to London.

The three-cornered dialogue, between the citizens, the Governor, and the King's Council made life very difficult for the Governor. Indeed, it was almost impossible for him to govern. As soon as they found themselves in trouble the citizens appealed to London. Henry himself was probably largely responsible for their attitude, for at the beginning of the occupation his policy of conciliation was interpreted as a policy of weakness by the municipal authorities, and they were so emboldened that it was very difficult to get their co-operation in any matter if it did not suit their own purposes. Towards the end of the occupation Henry began to see that he had been wrong in treating the citizens leniently, and although his increasing irritation at their attitude emerges clearly from the documents it was too late to discipline them. Had the Governors been encouraged to take a hard line right from the start things might have been very different; but once the initial mistake had been made it was virtually impossible to retrieve the position.

The self-righteousness of the municipal authorities on which Richard Sampson commented unfavourably to Wolsey—it was

shameful that they should be so unco-operative towards a
sovereign 'that hath been so gracious unto them that all the
world speaketh of his singular goodness'[1]—was reflected in the
religious sphere. The Dean and Chapter were in an even more
awkward position than the civic leaders. The latter might or
might not have been guilty of treason when they surrendered to
Henry, but at least their guilt or comparative innocence
remained the same all through the occupation. Not so with the
religious leaders. Their penultimate higher authority was the
Pope, not Francis I or Louis XII; but their chain of command
was turned upside down at regular intervals, depending on
whether the Pope recognized Wolsey or Guillard as their
Bishop. This must have put great strain on their loyalty, but
they were a very self-composed group, and were no doubt well
able to adjust their consciences to the needs of the moment.

They were no less skilled in the rules of debate than their lay
brethren in the four councils, as the Earl of Worcester found to
his cost in 1515. He had brought with him certain instructions
for them from the King, and after he had expounded what was
required of them, they said that they would be delighted to
'perform the same to their power, for so their minds is to do,
with many other good and kind words'. There was, however,
one minor difficulty. The Earl had shown them no letter of
credence, and, much as they wanted to help, there was nothing
they could do until they were satisfied that Worcester spoke with
the full authority of the King. Might they therefore see his
letter of credence? The answer to this was that he had no letter,
and when he tried to persuade the Dean that he was in fact
speaking with Henry's authority he made no headway. Worcester told Wolsey: 'We have no credence to show to them in
our instructions, nor none ye told us by mouth. I am sure ye
forgot it for ye told me that it should be an article in our instructions.'[2] This incident is typical of the shadow boxing that
made it difficult for the Governor and his colleagues to carry out
decisions handed out to them from England.

On another occasion the Chapter demonstrated their skill in
getting what they wanted without giving up anything in return.
They wrote Wolsey a letter thanking him for arranging for the

---

[1] Cal. D VI, f. 301; *LP* ii, 2274.   [2] SP 1/11, f. 23; *LP* ii, 742.

King to confirm their former liberties; and they then went on to express their goodwill at great length. Only after much flowery prose, full of elegantly phrased gratitude, do they come to the point that really interested Wolsey, the fate of certain monies, which, presumably, he considered should have come to him. In fact, they were not part of his emoluments, but had been devoted to the upkeep of the Cathedral, as provided for by apostolic decree.[1]

In short, after the initial shock of the siege, and their decision to hand the city over to the English, both the civic authorities and the Dean and Chapter seem to have realized that they were in a much stronger position than had looked possible when the English cannon-balls were breaking up their walls and crashing into the streets. Indeed, so strong was their position that they may fairly be said to have played a cat-and-mouse game with the English government: except that in this case it was the mouse that teased and tormented the cat. The Earl of Worcester came to just this conclusion in 1515, although he used different animals in his simile—'they hover like a bird doeth for his prey'.[2] The roles of conqueror and conquered were reversed.

The King and Council were faced with the problem of how to notify and implement decisions made in England in such a way that they would be understood and accepted by the Tournaisiens. The method used was to recite the decision in letters patent drafted in French, so that they would be readily understood by the mass of the people, and to transmit them to the municipal authorities. They in turn exhibited them to the Governor, in the presence of the city's procurator and the King's procurator, when they were authenticated by the latter official. On the strength of this authentication the Governor then issued his letters patent (also in French), in which the King's letters were set out verbatim, authorizing the municipal authorities to have the decision enrolled in the city records. In the case of the Act of Parliament—the only Act which was

---

[1] Strype, pp. 19–20; *LP* ii, 1033.

[2] Cal. D VI, f. 198; *LP* ii, 856. Sir Richard Jerningham provided a long essay on the citizens' abuse of their privileges in January 1517 (SP 1/14, ff. 242–4; *LP* ii, 2858).

directly concerned with Tournai—the authentication was accomplished by a charter of *inspeximus*.[1]

Had the Tournaisiens welcomed integration with England, and showed that they were prepared to co-operate with the government, it seems likely that this embryonic system might have developed. The method chosen, which was probably not the result of deliberate planning, seems on the face of it to be clumsy; and had there been a substantial volume of continuing legislation in London affecting Tournai, perhaps a different procedure would have been adopted. The weakness in the arrangement described is that the citizens might have obtained concessions from the King in England which, when they were presented to the Governor in Tournai, would appear to him to be unacceptable; and he would then be in the unenviable position of having to choose between refusing to ratify the King's letters patent, or implementing a decision with which he did not agree. The fact that the King's procurator was in Tournai to signify the King's approval did not help much, since he would merely echo the original decision. Had the Governor been represented in England when the decisions were arrived at, there would have been no problem, as he could then have made his objections known; but in the handful of cases that have survived he was presented with an accomplished fact.

In the event, however, the pattern which appeared to be emerging in 1514 was not continued, partly because of the citizens' refusal to work amicably with the English authorities in Tournai or in London, and partly because it seems that the King, and in particular Wolsey, became disenchanted with the Tournaisiens, who could never be tied down to anything. The normal course in the latter part of the occupation was for instructions to be sent to the Governor in the hope that he would be able to have them carried out. On the whole he had

[1] See above, p. 134. In this the Act is given in French and is preceded by a passage in Latin: 'We have examined a certain act or ordinance by the authority of our parliament summoned and met on 24 January in the fifth year of our reign in our palace of Westminster passed with the assent of the lords spiritual and temporal and the commons of this same kingdom of ours in the same parliament by those who assisted at it and were gathered there. The clauses of the act apply as much to the citizens who are inhabitants within our city of Tournai, Tournaisis and the *bailliage*, which divine providence has brought within our dominion and power, as to our own subjects in our kingdom of England' (5 Henry VIII, c. 1; Hocquet (a), xli; *LP* i, 2699).

not much success; but it is unlikely that if more formal arrangements had been provided they would have been any more successful.

What light is thrown on the characters of the leading persons in the drama of occupied Tournai? Henry is revealed, at least in the campaign of 1513, as a man who valued his own foolish whims more than the manifest needs of his subjects. The campaign was designed to glorify him in the eyes of Europe. His destruction of Thérouanne, his victory in the Battle of the Spurs, in which the flower of French chivalry was routed, and his capture and occupation of Tournai confirmed him as a military genius, at least in his own estimation. It is clear, however, that Maximilian led him by the nose all through the 1513 campaign. The Emperor, playing second fiddle with great skill, got him to do everything he wanted, except hand over Tournai once it had been captured, which surely must have been his (the Emperor's) main objective. Otherwise, why did the expedition invest Tournai, when there were so many more sensible objectives from England's point of view? Henry was Maximilian's dupe in the 1513 campaign. Thereafter the Emperor disappears from the scene, so far as Tournai is concerned.

It is difficult to understand why Henry kept Tournai. Any of his subjects with the slightest knowledge of geography must have advised against retaining it, on the ground that it was untenable, or that it would be a shocking drain on England's resources. It is true that having got it, almost accidentally, Henry was faced with the problem of what to do with it. He could have sold it to Maximilian, only the Emperor had no money to spare. Or he could have sold it back to Louis XII at the earliest possible moment, which was when they made peace in 1514. Why keep a city which had some market value and was going to be costly to keep? Perhaps Henry was simply a child with a new toy, who could not bear to part with it; or he may have been like an angler who has landed a fish that he knows should be thrown back, but cannot bring himself to lose the evidence of his success.

The occupation itself throws a clearer light on Henry's interest in administration. He decided that the best way to deal with the city would be to play the part of a benevolent monarch, and to make life as easy as possible for his new subjects. He assumed that they would then be so grateful that they would do everything asked of them; and in this he was totally wrong. But having made this mistake, which he must have realized himself, he seems to have lost interest in the affairs of the city. When it appeared that the citizens were delighted to take advantage of all the latitude they were given, and to do nothing in return—in short, to have their cake and eat it—it was open to the King to adopt a really tough line with the city. He had his troops there, and the citizens could have been made to toe the line without much difficulty. Henry may have been inhibited by the fear that if too much pressure was brought to bear on the people it would precipitate a rising among them, but this was probably an error of judgement. The only rising by the citizens during the occupation stemmed from loyalty to France, and was perhaps made possible by the gentle line taken with the city up to that point. Except for the lower classes the people seem to have been docile, and they would probably have accepted without protest much sterner measures than Henry ever confronted them with.

Much of the foregoing is speculation; but it can be said that Henry made mistakes in capturing Tournai, in retaining it, and in failing to recognize quickly that if the city was to be properly governed a strong hand was needed. It is, however, also a matter for speculation as to how far England's attitude to Tournai, after the initial decision to keep the city, was determined by the King, and how far Wolsey was responsible. Certainly the King must have come into the discussion of major decisions, and there is plenty of evidence that he accepted responsibility for minor decisions which, it has been suggested above, might well have been left to the Governor;[1] but there is little doubt that Wolsey played the dominant rôle.

The strongest evidence of this lies in the innumerable letters from the Governor and council members in Tournai in which the writer is clearly addressing Wolsey as the supreme commander of Tournai, and, indeed, also as the man who is guiding the destinies of England. Sometimes a token letter is sent at the same time to Henry, on the ground that the sovereign was entitled to know what was going on; but whether the writers are seeking guidance on policy, or favours for themselves, their faith

---

[1] Chs. II and III above.

is pinned on Wolsey. He for his part makes it equally clear that for all practical purposes he has adopted the sovereign's rôle *vis-à-vis* the city. This does not mean that he did not discuss matters with Henry, or take decisions that he knew would be unpopular with him; but one can say with certainty that Tournai was governed by Henry and Wolsey in partnership, and that Wolsey was the senior partner.

That there was some interest in the respective rôles of King and Cardinal at the time is shown by a letter from the two Giustinianis to the Signory in 1519. They report that Sebastian had been received graciously by Francis, who had asked him about the qualities of the King of England. Did he favour peace or war; and which did Wolsey favour? Giustiniani said the King inclined towards peace with France, and so did Wolsey, who, indeed, boasted that he had made the present peace with France. This apparently amused the King, who said 'What, was it his doing, the surrender to me of Tournai?' He went on to express surprise that Henry should allow so much authority to Wolsey, and he blamed the Cardinal for assuming such vast responsibility, and so showing that he held the honour of the King in small account.[1]

It must be accepted that England gained virtually no political advantage from the occupation of Tournai. The ordinary Englishman may have been impressed by the evidence of his country's growing strength in Europe; but the monarchs whom Henry had set out to impress must have laughed up their sleeves at the way in which the Emperor had used him. It might, however, be possible to defend the occupation, if it could be shown that the sums which Henry received from the city, and from Francis, in payment for the surrender in 1519 showed a reasonable return on capital invested. It is not easy to identify all the costs Henry incurred in maintaining the garrison, buying building materials, and employing workmen, or to quantify them accurately; but a rough profit and loss account can be built up.

It is relatively easy to arrive at Henry's total receipts. Under the surrender treaty the citizens had to pay him a lump sum of 50,000 *écus d'or* or, say, £10,000;[2] the 6,000 *livres tournois* (say

[1] *VC* ii, 1271.
[2] Received by Sir Robert Dymock on 9 June 1514 (PRO 31/8/144, f. 251; *LP* i, 2984).

£650) which they normally paid to the French Crown each year; and an additional 4,000 *livres* (say £430) each year for ten years.[1] The last payment had still five years to run when the city was handed back, but Francis made himself responsible for meeting the outstanding balance. All these amounts are dwarfed by the 600,000 crowns he paid for the return of the city —about £120,000.[2]

The lack of detailed information about the size of the garrison all through the occupation makes it difficult to work out what it cost year by year. Some idea of the initial cost may be arrived at by taking the strength as 5,000, of whom 1,000 were cavalry, and applying the standard wages of 6d. a day for the infantry and 10d. for the cavalry. This puts the annual cost of the infantry at £36,500 and of the cavalry at £15,000—a total of £51,500. This is a rough and ready measure. It ignores the higher rates paid to captains, senior officers, and the yeomen of the guard (who were paid 8d. or 1s., compared with the ordinary private's sixpence), and any changes in the size of the establishment as things settled down during the first year. Sir Edward Poynings' own salary, for example, which was at the enormous rate of over £2,400 a year, was a significant part of the total cost; and when this and other special items are added it implies a total cost in the first year of round about £60,000— about £50,000 more than Henry received in tribute from the conquered city in the same year.

These figures must have been very much in the minds of the King and his advisers at the beginning of 1515, when they sent Mountjoy to replace Poynings, with instructions to reduce the size and cost of the garrison. At this time the treasurer's accounts[3] show that Sir Robert Dymock had been paying 'the captains and footmen' in 1514 at the rate of £35,000 a year, which confirms an establishment of 4,000. The same accounts show that actual payments to the infantry for the greater part of

---

[1] This was paid regularly, on 23 December 1513 and quarterly thereafter until 23 March 1517. For the six quarters 23 June 1517 to 23 September 1518 the money went to compensate those whose houses had been demolished to make way for the citadel. The payments made represent exactly half the ten-year liability; and they left 20,000 petty florins (or *livres tournois*) still due. This was equal to £2,222. 4s. 6d. (Cal. D VI, f. 96; Rymer, pp. 377–8.)

[2] The chronicler Hall refers (p. 564) to a payment of 400,000 crowns for the citadel, but I can find no record that this was ever paid.

[3] SP 1/12, ff. 164–70; *LP* ii, 1514.

1515 remained steady at about £1,610 for a four-weekly period, or at the rate of £20,000 a year. In the four weeks to 12 January 1516 the figure drops to £1,560, implying a further reduction of about three per cent.[1]

The next comprehensive and detailed figure for the cost of the garrison relates to the middle of 1516, when the annual total is put with commendable precision at £23,959. 17s. 6d. This is contained in the copy of 'The King's estate that Sir Edward Bensted paid the garrison by', which has already been referred to.[2] By far the greater part of the reduction (as compared with the figure for the first months of the occupation) is attributable to the smaller number of infantry. The cost of the separate establishments of the Governor, marshal, treasurer, porter, captain of the guard, and master of the ordnance remained virtually unchanged.

The establishment had been reduced to about 600 by the latter part of 1517, and it remained at that level for the rest of the occupation. If the original garrison of 5,000 cost about £60,000 a year, and it is assumed that the strength at mid year was reduced by about 1,000 every year, it is possible to work out a rough estimate of the total cost of the troops during the occupation, as follows:

Year ended September	Strength	Approximate Cost
1514	5000	£60,000
1515	4000	48,000
1516	3000	36,000
1517	2000	24,000
1518	600	8,000
4 months to January 1519	600	2,000
	Total	£178,000

These figures are no more than rough guesses, for the records which would make it possible to measure the cost accurately have not survived; but they are probably a conservative estimate of the cost of the troops—to which the cost of the King's works must be added to provide a figure for the over-all cost of the occupation.

[1] In November 1515 Mountjoy informed Wolsey that the pay of the infantry and cavalry amounted to £1,760 a month (Cal. E I, f. 76; LP ii, 1122).
[2] See p. 90 above.

19—E.O.T.

The cost of the King's works is more difficult to assess. There were three main headings: the wages of the artificers and labourers; the purchase of stone, brick, timber, and other materials, and tools for the workmen; and the cost of services, mainly the carriage of materials to the site, and the dewatering of the foundations, which was done by the use of pumps and horse-driven water-wheels. Many records of expenditure have survived, but they sometimes conflict and it is difficult to disentangle and reconcile them. In some cases the wage bills of the soldiers in the garrison and the artificers are lumped together; and there is no complete series of figures for the whole duration of the building work. Again, there is occasionally the problem of dating the documents. In these circumstances the best course is to sample the records and to attempt an estimate on the basis of that sample.

The wages paid to the workmen are recorded month by month from April 1516 to October 1518, which period includes the whole of the two years when building activity was at its height. Information about the numbers employed before April 1516 is scanty, but the construction of the citadel began in 1515 and there must have been a good deal of construction work in progress from the beginning of that year. The cost of the labour force varied with the seasons—another factor that makes it difficult to arrive at accurate estimates. In the spring and winter of 1516, for example, the wage bill came to only £700 a month, whereas at the height of the summer it was over £1,400. In the following year it varied from about £500 a month in the winter to over £1,500 in the summer. The total annual bills were about £12,000 in 1516, and £14,000 in 1517. The figure dropped in 1518 to about £2,000; and if the 1515 figure is put at, say, £5,000 it gives a total labour cost of £33,000.[1]

The cost of materials and tools in the year ended 28 March 1518 was just under £5,500. The two biggest items are lime (£1,700) and stone (£1,400), while bricks cost about £260. Other items in the account are ash poles for scaffolding, rope, handbarrows and wheelbarrows, timber, iron and steel, hammers and mattocks, anvils and bellows, nails, tubs and trays for carrying mortar, canvas, shovels and spades, materials for the pumps, including leather 'suckers' or plungers, a mere

[1] SP 1/15, ff. 45–52 b; SP 1/16, ff. 126–30; SP 1/18, ff. 83 b–86 b.

14*s.* worth of candles, and small sums spent on 'other necessaries'.[1] In the preceding year, to 28 March 1517, the cost of materials was almost exactly £5,000,[2] and it seems reasonable, therefore, to put the total cost of materials bought for the citadel during the four years in which it was being built at something less than £5,000 a year—say a total of £17,500 in the four years. This, added to the cost of labour—estimated at £33,000— brings the total to £50,500, a conservative figure, as it does not include all the sums paid for the carriage of stone, or the cost of building eight lime-kilns and their ancillary buildings.[3]

At the end of the occupation Henry could thus point to £120,000 as the realization value of Tournai, to which tribute of £15,000 can be added, making a total of £135,000. The city had cost him approximately £230,000—£178,000 for the garrison, plus £50,500 for the citadel. On the basis of these figures, which if anything err in the King's favour, he was nearly £100,000 out of pocket at the end of the day. After five and a half years of occupation he could do no more than show a loss that the English tax payer could ill afford. Had the immense effort that went into the building of the citadel been devoted instead to a similar enterprise in Calais (which could have been done for £178,000 less, as Calais was already provided with an adequate garrison), that English town could have been made well-nigh impregnable; and Henry's daughter Mary might have been saved the humiliation she suffered at the hands of the French when they captured Calais later in the century.[4]

It is difficult to build up an accurate picture of daily life in the garrison. The surviving records naturally concentrate on the difficulties the rank and file had to contend with, and on the whole what made existence tolerable for the officers and men is left to the imagination. There are, however, occasional references to the lighter side of life. The Queen's letter written from Greenwich 'to our trusty and well-beloved the provost and his brethren of my lord's city of Tournai', announcing the birth of the Princess Mary,[5] can hardly have had much interest for the

---

[1] *LP* ii, 4041.   [2] *LP* ii, 3073.   [3] E 101/504/4.
[4] The Crown's income varied greatly from year to year, but at this time it probably averaged about £200,000 a year. This provides a rough measure of the heavy cost of Tournai.
[5] *Arch.*, pp. 260–1; *LP* ii, 1556.

Tournaisiens to whom it was addressed, but it must have stirred
the loyal hearts of the English soldiers. Mountjoy was able to
report that 'upon the knowledge to us given of the Queen's good
speed, both with sermon, general procession, and Te Deum,
fires, with other rejoicing, we have given thanks and praising to
Almighty God therefor after the best manner that we could
devise.'[1]

There were religious festivals throughout the year, which
alleviated the monotony of the daily routine. The great annual
procession held in September (which had to be cancelled in
1513 because of the siege) attracted many from the surrounding
districts and was no doubt a memorable spectacle. Again, there
was occasional jousting, not as splendid as when the King and
his nobles took part, but still enough to provide some excite-
ment and stimulate conversation in the taverns. It seems likely
that the men's world was bounded by the walls of the city.
There was little incentive to venture further afield, especially
when walking was the only way to get about. Even those who
owned a horse and were therefore more mobile seldom ventured
out unless they had to. Sir Richard Whethill, for example, who
might have been expected to ride to the neighbouring towns
from time to time for a change of scene, told Wolsey 'I am here
like a prisoner for I have not been past once or twice three mile
without the city.'[2]

The most common pastimes were drinking, and playing the
many gambling games that worried the government in England
all through the sixteenth century, and which were just as popular with the English troops in Tournai as they were at home.
For the men a visit to the local tavern in the evening was probably the high point of their daily lives. Tavern brawls were not
uncommon. Wolsey's man, Dr. Richard Sampson, who seems
to have taken a special interest in Hansard the under-marshal
(another of Wolsey's men), has left an account of one.

A yeoman of the guard named Higgins had been drinking in
a tavern with other members of his company, when 'for fault of
good discipline' he struck the young barmaid in the face. Hansard happened to be passing at the time and, hearing the
woman's cries, gallantly went to the rescue, and 'with courteous
demeanour and words required Higgins to depart the house and

---

[1] SP 1/13, f. 39; *LP* ii, 1622.   [2] SP 1/12, f. 117; *LP* ii, 1437.

quietly with his servant as a prisoner to go to the walls'. The yeoman was obstinate, however, and the under-marshal had to send for tipstaves to provide an escort to take him to remain at the walls until the Governor decided what was to be done with him. When the tipstaves arrived, the prisoner 'in derision took off his cap with his left hand, thanking the marshal, and with his right hand privily drew his sword . . . wherewith the marshal turned, but this Higgins so suddenly struck him upon the nose a sore stripe that he could not avoid'. What befell the offending Higgins is not recorded, but perhaps allowance was made for the fact that he was in his cups. Moreover, Mountjoy disliked the under-marshal and may have been secretly grateful to the yeoman for damaging his nose. Sampson stressed that Hansard was in no way to blame for the incident. His only fault was that he was too lenient with the offender.[1]

One of the events in the Tournai calendar which must have been enjoyed by citizens and soldiers alike was the popinjay shooting held 'as the year goeth about the second day of March'. This event took place outside the city gates and was organized by the Brotherhood of St. George, whose members took it in turn to shoot with crossbows at the popinjay. Tradition demanded that the first bolt should be fired by someone standing in for the King. In 1515 Mountjoy appointed the *prévôt* to shoot for Henry, no doubt in the interest of maintaining good relations with the citizens. The *prévôt* protested that it was twenty years since he had fired a crossbow, but Mountjoy insisted, and to everyone's surprise he 'strake the popinjay, and so your Grace was king for that year of the popinjay'.

Next year he asked the porter, Sir John Tremayle, to shoot for the King. Tremayle took the affair very seriously, for it would have been too humiliating to fail as the King's proxy where the *prévôt* had succeeded. He put in some practice at the butts the day before the contest, without much success, which is hardly surprising as the crossbow was not an English weapon. However, all went well on the day. Miraculously the porter emulated the *prévôt*'s feat and made Henry the king of the popinjay for another year. Mountjoy told the King that if his proxy was successful three years running he would become emperor, 'whereunto belongeth many great royalties'. He

[1] SP 1/13, f. 208; *LP* ii, 1987.

added apologetically that he had not been present at the contest, partly because it was a Sunday and he had had to attend
mass, and partly because if he had left the city too many people
would have accompanied him—neither excuse carrying much
conviction. He also apologized for writing to Henry about such
trivial matters. He had done so because the French King's
proxy had not hit the popinjay in living memory. Tremayle's
success was 'much marvelled of and every man taketh it for a
good luck unto your Grace'.[1]

There was a considerable amount of strain in the relationship
between both the citizens and the soldiers on the one hand and
the municipal authorities and the Governor and council on the
other. This must have made life unpleasant at times. The city
fathers made it clear right from the start that they had no intention of co-operating in making Tournai an integral part of
Henry's dominions; and this inevitably put the three successive
Governors and their colleagues in an impossible position. They
were under constant pressure from the King and Wolsey to get
things done that could be accomplished only with the goodwill
of the city. This must have impaired their day-to-day relationships. Equally the common people, who at the start of the
occupation had 5,000 troops billeted on them, had little enthusiasm for the conqueror. It is true that they welcomed the huge
sums of money that found their way into the city through the
English soldiers, but there is little doubt that, on balance, most
of them would have preferred to do without the money and be
rid of the occupying forces.

Numbers of the English soldiers did marry local girls, no
doubt on the assumption that the occupation would last for
their lifetime; and they began to raise families, as many as four
children in some cases. This was the real beginning of integration, and no doubt, had the English remained in Tournai for a
generation, the process would have been greatly accelerated.
But six years was not enough to win over the population as a
whole, and when the garrison departed the married men had
the difficult choice of remaining behind with their wives, and
eventually becoming French, or taking their wives off to live in
a strange land. Four of them elected to remain, and the others

---

[1] Cal. E I, ff. 83–83 b; *LP* ii, 1621.

went off to England feeling that they had been let down by their King.[1]

Differences of opinion with the municipal authorities took on a variety of forms. In 1516 a row developed over the importation of duty-free wines by the royal officers. It was customary for them to be exempt from duty, but it was pointed out to Henry that, on the strength of letters patent obtained earlier from the French King, the municipal authorities were seeking to levy duty in spite of other letters patent exempting the royal officers. Henry agreed that their privilege should continue, particularly in view of their low salaries, and formally declared that they were exempt from duty on wines and other beverages kept in their cellars for the use of their families and servants, as was customary in the neighbouring countries. The royal officers—the *avocat*, *procureur*, and receiver, for example—were Tournaisiens, or at least natives of the Low Countries, and the municipal authorities' refusal to allow them to have duty-free wine may have been intended as a punishment for siding with the occupying force. The exemption provided by Henry seems not to have included the Governor and his council, but probably as the King's representatives they enjoyed the privilege automatically. The rank and file, however, had to pay the duty, much to their irritation.[2]

The garrison had to put up with hardships not unknown at home, but which were probably intensified because the men encountered them in a strange land. Their first winter in the occupied city was unusually cold. The river Scheldt, the waterway over which much of the city's commerce was carried, was frozen solid from 14 November 1513, only a few weeks after the occupation began, until 18 February 1514. The boats which brought in Tournai's foodstuffs and raw materials, and exported her finished goods, had to be replaced by carts and wagons.[3]

In 1514 there occurred one of the worst outbreaks of the plague in the history of the city. Strangely enough, there are only passing references to the epidemic in the correspondence between the garrison and England, and although there is no

---

[1] Cal. D VII, ff. 41 b, 57 b, 95; Hall, p. 596.

[2] C 76/197, m. 23; *LP* ii, 1719. The citizens were still arguing about exemption from the *maltôte* in the following year (SP 1/14, f. 241; *LP* ii, 2858).

[3] Cousin, p. 272.

doubt that it was extremely serious there is no record that any
of the men died from it, except a general statement by Cousin to
the effect that 'si fut en ladicte annee telle mortalité en la ville
de Tournay, qu'il y mourut bien trente mille personnes tant des
habitans de Tournay, que de la garnison Angloise'. This is
clearly an exaggeration, as if 30,000 people had died the whole
population would have been wiped out.[1] None of the senior
English officers was affected, but there was such panic among
the citizens at large that they left in large numbers—so large
that the right of *scarsage*, which allowed citizens to leave the
city, taking their goods and chattels with them, was suspended.
Although every precaution was taken that the authorities could
think of—for example, a merchant in the Rue de la Lornière
was forbidden to sell Oudenarde cheese, because it smelt so
powerfully that his neighbours thought it must be a source of
infection—the epidemic persisted for many months.[2]

Partly because of the unconcealed hostility in the city the
senior officers of the garrison were no more anxious to become
good Tournaisiens than the citizens were to become good
Englishmen. It has been shown above how the principal officers
tried to get home on one pretext or another.[3] Sir Richard
Whethill sent a *cri de cœur* to Wolsey in August 1516 which well
illustrates the restrained dissatisfaction common among the
council members. He was under the impression that there were
going to be changes among the senior posts in Tournai and
Calais, and he thought that he could do the King better service
in Calais. 'For that little that God hath sent me lieth there; and
there was I born, wherefore my mind is most there. And also the
King's subjects there would be glad I were among them, for
lightly our countrymen desireth most another, if they be kind
people. So that my mind is most there.' However, if the King
and Wolsey commanded him to remain in Tournai, he must
obey. His servant, who acted as clerk of his household, would be
able to prove to Wolsey that he spent all his salary as high
marshal and a good deal of his own money besides. He had no
doubt that if he continued to serve in Tournai he would eventually be able to cut his coat according to his cloth, but he

---

[1] Cousin, p. 272. Estimates of the city's population vary widely. Wolsey claimed
that it was 10,000, Whethill put it at 20,000. Edward Hall suggests 80,000.
Whethill was probably nearest the mark (Hall, p. 566; SP 1/15, f. 16; *LP* ii, 2972).

[2] Jopken, p. 9.   [3] See p. 42 above.

would never be able to save a penny, and no man liked working for nothing. If he was going to be posted away from Tournai, he wanted permission to leave twenty of his retainers behind, on the payroll of the garrison, as he could not afford to take them with him.

Having dealt with his personal problems, Whethill speaks of the hardships the captains and men were beginning to suffer. They all owed so much to the victuallers that their pay regularly disappeared on the very day they received it. There was never enough ready money available to keep the soldiers in funds, and therefore to provide enough working capital to enable the victuallers to keep adequate stocks of food. Everyone was living from hand to mouth. Even the tavern-keepers were refusing credit, as their fingers had been so badly burned. One of the real problems was the steady reduction in the size of the garrison. No one was prepared to give credit to the soldiers, for there was every likelihood that a man who ran up a big bill would be discharged before the next pay-day came round, and it was virtually impossible for the victuallers to prevent him from leaving with his debts unpaid.[1]

By far the best picture of the difficulties that faced the garrison is contained in the replies which were sent to Wolsey and the Council in May 1517, when the men were protesting against the introduction of payment six-monthly in arrear.[2] It seems that the Governor, who saw only too clearly the unhappy position of the troops, stage-managed their response to the King's proposal with great skill. The groups whose letters survive—the gentlemen (that is to say the captains), the vinteners (or corporals) of the yeomen of the guard, and 'the constables of Tournai being yeomen of the King's guard there'—all submitted reasoned arguments as to why the method of payment should not be changed. On the whole, they cover the same points, and, although it looks as if Jerningham may have indicated to them the line he thought was most likely to get a good hearing in London, their pleas have an unpleasant ring of truth.

All three groups attempt to expose the fallacy in the King's submission that conditions in Tournai are comparable with those in Calais; if they are not, his decision to institute half-yearly payment is inappropriate. In Calais 'the inhabitants and

[1] SP 1/13, ff. 281–281 b; *LP* ii, 2288.   [2] See p. 101 above.

householders be all of one nation of long continuance . . . glad to assist, help and trust each other as good and true subjects, whereas here they be the contrary'. In Tournai no one will give credit for 'meat and drink as well as for all other necessaries from payment to payment'. The position in Calais is very different. If anyone needs money he has only to go 'to the exchequer', where he will be given all his earnings to date. If he can provide a reasonable surety the treasurer will pay him the whole of his wages in advance. None of this applies in Tournai, despite the fact that the need there is much greater. Thus the gentlemen captains.

Their point is echoed by the vinteners. Calais is established 'of old time' and is inhabited all with English people. They are protected by an English pale to the south, and by the Channel and by England to the north; and they have English merchants who are prepared to victual them, if necessary on credit. Above all, in Tournai they have to pay the *maltôte*, whereas Calais is a free market. This tax amounts to as much as 40*s*. on a tun of wine and 1*s*. on a barrel of beer, and it is also charged on flesh and fish. The constables dutifully spell out the same point, using almost the same words, and conclude: 'it is to be considered that we be not among our special friends, as the King's garrisons of Calais and elsewhere, but we be among our friends by compulsion. And in such friends is no great trust and fidelity; but small faith or favour, without friendship or kindness.'

The second main theme is the decline in the value of English money in Tournai, a factor that does not apply in Calais. 'For 6*d*. now goeth not so far ne is not so good ne profitable as 5*d*. was wont to be.' The vinteners put it lower than the gentlemen, and claim that 6*d*. is not worth 6 groats in Flemish money, or, say, 4*d*. sterling. The constables, perhaps the least expert economists of the three groups, go one better still. They are paid in English money, but when they come to buy their victuals and other necessaries the penny sterling is worth no more than a Flemish penny, 'and thus in every three pence sterling there is one penny less'. A yeoman paid 12*d*. a day is getting no more than 8*d*. worth of purchasing power, 'which is great loss and damage to the garrison here'.

It is impossible to arrange credit on reasonable terms. Take the case of a member of the garrison who is a householder, and is forced to pledge something to provide the bare essentials for himself and his family. If he pledges goods worth 20*s*. he will raise no more than 7*s*. or 8*s*. 'And if he fail of the day of payment, incontinently he loses his gage or pledge of what value soever it be. In which their so doing is no manner of friendship.'

The constables—the lowest paid—are the most impassioned in their submission. Many are 10*s*. or 20*s*. in debt, both married and single men. It is not too difficult for the latter to survive the three months between payments, but it is very hard for married men with wife and 'two, three or four children apiece'. They are totally dependent on their wages, and while it is true that they can have bread and beer 'upon their scores and tallies', if they want flesh, fish, butter, eggs, or cheese they need to have ready money. If they have to borrow, they can do so only at a rate of interest which means in practice that 4*d*. worth of food costs 6*d*. or 7*d*.

The three groups conclude their appeals with well-drafted perorations. The 15 gentlemen captains—John Russell, who played a prominent part in the affairs of the garrison, heads the list of signatories—tell Wolsey that if he pleads their cause with the King he will do 'a great meritorious deed'. They remind him that most of them have no more than their wages to live on, that they have few friends in Tournai, and that because of their long absence from England they fear they have lost most of their friends there. The 10 vinteners seem to be mainly worried by the effect of the *maltôte*, for they wind up by claiming that if it is not removed from their purchases they will be driven to extreme poverty and have to leave Tournai; and no one will be prepared to take their place. The constables, 13 of whom sign the submission, beg Wolsey

not to take displeasure with your said poor men and daily orators for their rude writing unto your Grace, which lacketh as well learning as good counsel. But as they write to your Grace after their natural wits and as poverty and necessity constraineth them to write according to the truth, and further for the preservation of the said garrison and the welfare of the same.

Even if the suggestion that Sir Richard Jerningham (or perhaps a member of his council) sketched out the line that the men ought to take is well founded—and therefore that the

constables' statement that they wrote without 'good counsel'
and 'after their natural wits' was made with tongue in cheek—
the fact remains that there must have been more than a grain of
truth in the points made by the suppliants. Pay, which had been
no problem at the beginning of the occupation, had become
more and more difficult as the government in England struggled
to control the cost of the monster which the King had so easily
created in a moment of blind euphoristic egomania. In spite of
the steady reduction in the size of the garrison, the over-all cost
of remaining in Tournai mounted, because of the intensification
of the building programme. There was therefore never enough
money for the soldiers' pay and their standard of living suffered
accordingly.

The hard-headed, grasping, self-interested merchants of
Tournai were certainly not prepared to go out of their way to
make life easier for an occupying force which had been landed
on them through no fault of their own. If the English authorities
failed to keep their troops adequately paid, that was their
business. There was no reason why the local merchants should
try to do their job for them by extending credit, even if they
could afford it. If the garrison had been enabled to pay its way,
and become a valued customer of the city, the process of integration might have made some headway, even in a mere five
years; but there was no chance for the seed to take root when
the merchants, the backbone of the city, who respected successful management and despised failure, saw the garrison merely
as poor relations—and very distant relations at that—who were
a dangerous credit risk, and who might even have to be supported
out of charity. Again, if the original hope that two-way trade
would develop to the mutual benefit of Tournai and England
had materialized, the local merchants would have vied with
each other to share in the new business. It might seem to be
trading with the enemy in the eyes of the French Crown, but the
merchants' first loyalty was to their balance sheets. A new
trading relationship did not develop, however, and the unifying
influence of two-way trade was never felt.

The poverty of the soldiers could have been dealt with, had
the government put their minds to it; but there was little that
could be done about the feeling of isolation that permeated the
garrison and damaged morale. If there had been some sign that

the Tournaisiens were prepared to accept Englishmen into their community, life would have become more tolerable. No one likes to feel that he is an outcast. There was no such sign, however—inter-marriage excepted, and this of course may simply have made both parties outcasts in the eyes of both communities. After years of thinly veiled hostility, most Englishmen must have longed for the day when they could go home, just as the Tournaisiens longed for the day when they would again be master of their own destiny, under the distant and benevolent hand of Francis I. Indeed, life must have been more tolerable in the early months of the occupation, when there was always the danger of a revolt against English rule. The men, who were professional soldiers, then had something to occupy their minds; but in the later years, when it was clear that the city was simply waiting patiently to return to France, the monotony —relieved only by the occasional threat of French aggression, which never materialized—must have been well-nigh unbearable.

When, at last, in February 1519 the remnant of the garrison marched out, watched by a jubilant populace, their feelings cannot have been well disposed toward either the Tournaisiens celebrating their departure, or the English government which had placed them in this humiliating position. Five and a half years of hardship and misery, of exile in a hostile foreign territory, the expenditure of huge quantities of the King's treasure, had gone for nothing. The only tangible result was the splendid new citadel that had transformed a large part of the city. It was not completely finished, it is true, but it was the one positive product of the King's ill-considered decision in 1513; and, as the men marched from it for the last time, they must have pondered the wisdom of a government that spent five years creating something that was to be the wonder of Europe, at the cost of incalculable toil, and then presented it to the traditional enemy as a going concern.

Had the men been able to see into the future, as they headed in the direction of Lille, *en route* for Calais and home, they might have derived some comfort from the knowledge that the Tournaisiens' triumph was to be short-lived. Less than three years after Henry relinquished his hold on their city Charles V stepped in and took it for the Empire, which his grandfather Maximilian had probably intended to do in 1513; and the Tournaisiens found that they had exchanged one occupying power for another, rather less benevolent. This news, as it spread across England, may have given some slight satisfaction to the many hundreds of Englishmen who had spent five frustrating years grappling in vain with the chimera of occupied Tournai.

INDEX